Level 1

2 DISCS

PRACTICAL GRAMMAR

David Riley and John Hughes

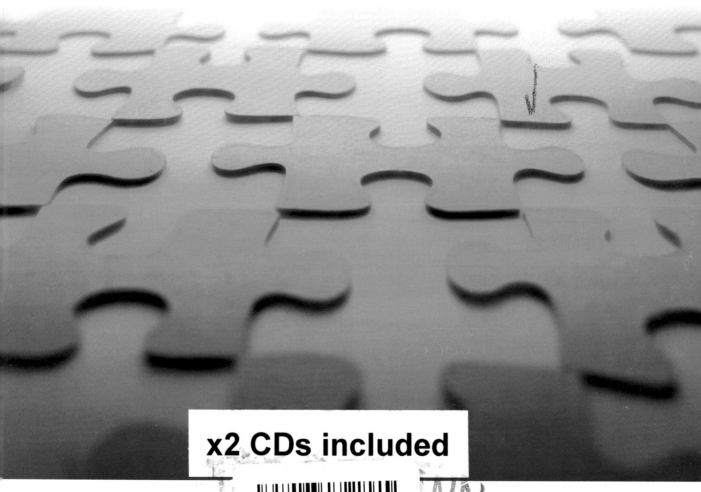

x2 CDs included

HEINLE
CENGAGE Learning

Australia • Brazil • Japan • Korea • Mexico • Sing

D1646800

WN

HEINLE
CENGAGE Learning™

Practical Grammar Level 1
David Riley and John Hughes

Publisher: Jason Mann

Senior Commissioning Editor: John Waterman

Development Editor: Shona Rodger

Product and Marketing Manager: Ruth McAleavey

Senior Content Project Editor: Natalie Griffith

Production Controller: Paul Herbert

Art Editor: Victoria Chappell

Art Director: Natasa Arsenidou

Cover Designer: Adam Renvoize

Text Designer: Rouli Manias, Ioanna Ioannidou

Compositor: Ioanna Ioannidou, Tania Diakaki

Audio: James Richardson

Dedication

David Riley was a well-known and highly respected ELT author, teacher and publisher. The original idea for the *Practical Grammar* series was his and he wrote many of the units in this book while suffering from cancer.
He didn't live to see the publication of this book but the memory of his inspiration and commitment to the project inspired everyone working on *Practical Grammar*.

This book is dedicated to David's wife, Pilar.

CENTRE	NEWARK
CHECKED	RIC
ZONE	PALE BLUE BLACK 428.24 RIL
LOAN PERIOD	1 WEEK

© 2010 Heinle, Cengage Learning

ALL RIGHTS RESERVED. No part of this work covered by the copyright herein may be reproduced, transmitted, stored or used in any form or by any means graphic, electronic or mechanical, including but not limited to photocopying, recording, scanning, digitising, taping, Web distribution, information networks, or information storage and retrieval systems, except as permitted under Section 107 or 108 of the 1976 United States Copyright Act, without the prior written permission of the publisher.

For permission to use material from this text or product, submit all requests online at **cengage.com/permissions**
Further permissions questions can be emailed to
permissionrequest@cengage.com

ISBN: 978-1-4240-1808-6 [with answers]
ISBN: 978-1-4240-1677-8 [without answers]

Heinle, Cengage Learning EMEA
Cheriton House
North Way
Andover
Hampshire
SP10 5BE
United Kingdom

Cengage Learning is a leading provider of customised learning solutions with office locations around the globe, including Singapore, the United Kingdom, Australia, Mexico, Brazil and Japan. Locate our local office at: **international.cengage.com/region**

Cengage Learning products are represented in Canada by Nelson Education, Ltd.

Visit Heinle online at **elt.heinle.com**
Visit our corporate website at **cengage.com**

Printed in Singapore
1 2 3 4 5 6 7 8 9 10 – 13 12 11 10 09

2002339
£15·00

Contents

Contents

Contents

Introduction

Welcome to *Practical Grammar* Level 1. This is the first in a series of grammar books for students of English. Level 1 introduces grammar to students at beginner to pre-intermediate level. It aims to:

- teach all the key grammar at elementary level.
- improve accuracy with grammar.
- help students use grammar in real-life situations, including conversations.

Organisation of the book

Practical Grammar Level 1 has 100 units, organised into blocks of five units. Each block is made up of four main units about an area of grammar and a fifth review unit. After every ten units, there is a progress test at the back of the book to check understanding. You'll also find extra useful information in the appendices (pages 232–237) and an index (pages 266–270) for quick reference. A key feature of the book is the CDs which you can use to listen to the conversations in the book and improve your pronunciation of grammar items.

Using *Practical Grammar* Level 1

Practical Grammar Level 1 is ideal for use as self study or in the classroom with a teacher. We present basic elementary grammar in the early units and then increase the difficulty in later units. Most students can begin at unit 1 and work through the rest of the units in order. Other students who are already familiar with some English grammar can choose different units and work on a specific area of grammar. (Use the contents or the index to do this.) If you want to use *Practical Grammar* Level 1 as a supplementary study book with your classroom course, you can also select particular units to match the lessons.

Grammar in real contexts

The rules of grammar are important but it's also important to see the grammar being used in a real-life situation. For this reason, each unit introduces the grammar through a short conversation or text. After the presentation of the grammar, there are exercises that practise the new language in authentic contexts with recordings on the CDs to hear the language in use.

Study at home (to the student)

This book helps you understand the basic grammar of English. Here are some ideas for using *Practical Grammar* Level 1:

- Study the grammar regularly. For example, do one unit every day. Read the introductory conversation or text and study the presentation of the grammar. Then complete the exercises and listen to the CDs.

- Complete the review unit and check you understand the grammar with the progress tests (pages 212–231).

- Study with a friend. Do the units together and read some of the conversations aloud.

- Repeat some of the units. If you find some of the grammar in a unit especially difficult, it's a good idea to repeat the unit.

- Remember that grammar isn't the only part of English. If you find new words in *Practical Grammar* Level 1, check them in your dictionary and write them down.

- Use the online component *MyPG*. The activities allow you to continue working with all the grammar in new contexts. There is a gradebook where you can build up a picture of your progress.

In the classroom (to the teacher)

Students can use *Practical Grammar* Level 1 for self study but you can also use it in class. It is aimed at students at beginner level, from elementary to pre-intermediate level.

If you are using a course book, *Practical Grammar* Level 1 will be a useful supplementary grammar book. The grammar becomes progressively harder over the 100 units and it reflects the order of the grammar often taught on courses.

Ask students to read the conversation or text at the beginning of the unit. If there is a conversation, you could ask two students to read it aloud to the class. Then read through the presentation of the grammar and deal with any questions the students might have.

As students work though the exercises, monitor their progress and help out with any questions they have. Students could also work in pairs or small groups for some exercises and compare their answers. In some units, the final exercise asks students to personalise the grammar and write their own sentences. Afterwards, ask some students to read theirs aloud or to compare with a partner.

If you have done the first four units of a section in class, you could set the review unit for homework. However, the review unit also includes help with pronunciation, vocabulary and listening linked to the grammar so sometimes you might want to work on these as a class.

The progress tests (pages 212–231) check students' progress after every ten units. You can use these in class to monitor how much students have learnt. If students have particular difficulties with certain parts of the test, you will be able to see if they need to work on any of the units again. Also note that for further practice you can use the online component *MyPG*. This component has a Content Management System, which allows you to set specific exercises to be completed in a set time. When students 'submit' the exercises, their scores appear in the gradebook allowing you to see how each student is progressing.

There are two CDs at the back of the book. They contain all the listening and pronunciation activities. Use them to help students hear the grammar in use and also for revision of the forms.

Overview of *Practical Grammar* Level 1

The units

Every unit is made up of two pages and has a similar format so it's easy to follow.

Title

The title tells you the main grammar area. Some units also have subtitles to give extra information.

Context

Practical Grammar teaches you how to use grammar in real situations. Each unit starts with a conversation or a short text to show the grammar in context. Read this first.

Presentation

The presentation explains the rules of the grammar and has information on the form, meaning and use of the grammar with example sentences. Use the presentation to help you complete the exercises.

Key vocabulary

When you use grammar, you also need words. Some units give you extra information about useful vocabulary in the unit.

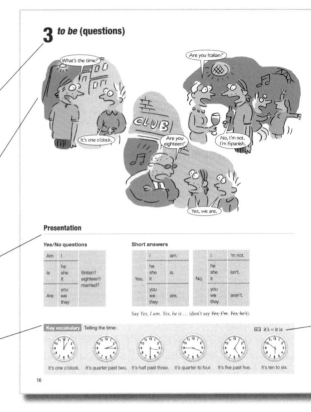

Review units

At the end of every block of four units, there is a review unit.

Grammar

This section gives extra practice of all the grammar in the four units. It's also a good way to check progress.

Pronunciation

It's important to know the rules of grammar but you also need to be able to say the grammatical forms correctly. *Practical Grammar* includes a pronunciation practice section with recordings.

Vocabulary

Practical Grammar teaches you the rules of grammar but it also contains lots of useful vocabulary in the units. The review units have exercises to help you remember the new words.

Listen again

A key feature of *Practical Grammar* is the listening practice. Listening is a great way to learn a new language. Here you listen again to one of the recordings from the four units and become more confident with the grammar in context.

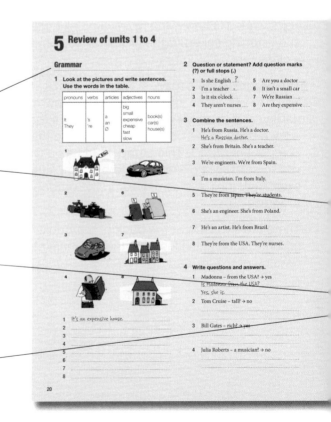

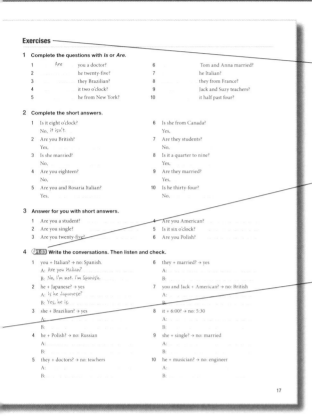

Exercises

Every unit gives lots of practice with the grammar. Always start with exercise 1 because it helps with learning the form of the grammar. Later exercises help you to understand its meaning.

Listening

A really useful feature in *Practical Grammar* is the recordings. Most units include a listening activity so you can listen to the completed exercise and hear the grammar in a real situation.

Tip

This gives you extra information about the grammar in real situations.

Progress tests

After every ten units, there is a progress test (see pages 212–231).

Appendices

These have more useful information on spelling and punctuation. There are also summaries of the key grammar areas, including verb forms (see pages 232–237).

Index

Use the index to find items of grammar quickly and help with terminology (see pages 266–270).

My PG

This online component provides extra practice of all the language covered in the book through a wide range of exercise types.

1 *am, is, are (to be)*

Hello. I'm Ernesto.
I'm from Brazil.
I'm twenty-three
and I'm single.

FRIENDS·NET

http://www.friends.net

Find friend

BACK   MORE   CONTACT   HOME

Presentation

Affirmative

I	am		I'm	
He She	is	from Brazil. eighteen. married.	He's She's	from Brazil. eighteen. married.
You We They	are		You're We're They're	

TIP Use *I'm, he's, you're* for speaking.

Key vocabulary Personal details: married, single (= not married)

Exercises

1 Match the sentences in the box to the pictures.

> **a** She's twenty-five.   **b** He's fifty.   **c** ~~She's two.~~   **d** They're sixteen.   **e** He's twelve.

1 _____c_____   2 _____   3 _____   4 _____   5 _____

2 Write sentences with the words in the box.

~~Brazil~~   Egypt   Italy   Japan   Russia   the USA

1 I'm from Brazil.

2 _____

3 _____

4 _____

5 _____

6 _____

3 Put the words in order. Use contractions.

1 are from Spain they   They're from Spain.
2 are married we   _____
3 am I from Russia   _____
4 is single he   _____
5 are twenty-one you   _____
6 am I single   _____
7 are from Japan they   _____
8 is from she the UK   _____
9 are from Poland we   _____
10 are China from you   _____

4 🎧 1.02 Write sentences. Then listen and check.

1 Andrea / Poland / 21 + single
   Hi. I'm Andrea. I'm from Poland. I'm twenty-one and I'm single.

2 Bruno / Germany / 32 + married

   _____

3 Marisol / Mexico / 18 + single

   _____

5 Complete sentences 1–4 for you and write sentences 5–8 for a friend. Use *He* and *She*.

1 I'm _____ . (name)   5 _____ . (name)
2 I'm from _____ . (country)   6 _____ . (country)
3 I'm _____ . (age)   7 _____ . (age)
4 I'm _____ . (married or single) 8 _____ . (married or single)

2 *to be* (negative)
a/an + occupation

She isn't Mexican.
She's from Argentina.

She isn't thirty-five.
She's thirty.

She isn't married. She's single.
She isn't a nurse. She's a doctor.

Presentation

Negative

I	am not			I'm not	
he she	is not	Mexican. from Mexico. thirty-five. married.		He isn't She isn't	Mexican. from Mexico. thirty-five. married.
you we they	are not			You aren't We aren't They aren't	

TIP These negative forms are also possible:
he's not, we're not …

a/an + occupation

Use *a/an* (indefinite article) with a person's occupation.

I'm You're He's She's	a doctor. an artist.
We're You're They're	doctors. artists.

* Use *a* before words that start with a consonant sound:
  a doctor, a teacher …

* Use *an* before words that start with a vowel sound:
  an artist, an engineer …

* Don't use *a/an* with plurals.
  Say *doctors* (don't say *a doctors*).

TIP Most plurals are formed by adding *-s* to the singular: *doctors, teachers, artists, engineers …*

See page 233: Spelling rules

Key vocabulary Occupations: artist, doctor, engineer, musician, nurse, student, teacher

Exercises

1 Complete the sentences with *a*, *an* or Ø (no article).

1 She's ___a___ doctor.
2 He's _____ artist.
3 They're _____ engineers.
4 I'm _____ teacher.
5 We're _____ doctors.
6 You're _____ musician.

7 She isn't _____ artist.
8 I'm not _____ student.
9 You aren't _____ teacher.
10 He isn't _____ engineer.
11 They aren't _____ nurses.
12 You aren't _____ artist.

2 Write negative sentences.

1 She's a doctor, not a nurse. *She isn't a nurse.*
2 I'm a student, not a teacher.
3 You're an engineer, not an artist.
4 They're Polish, not Russian.
5 We're musicians, not engineers.
6 She's Japanese, not Chinese.
7 He's single, not married.
8 I'm twenty, not twenty-one.
9 She's an artist, not a musician.
10 They're from Brazil, not Peru.
11 We're teachers, not students.
12 She's twenty-eight, not twenty-nine.

3 Correct the sentences. Use the words in the box.

| Australia France ~~India~~ Peru the USA |

1 The Taj Mahal is in Pakistan.
The Taj Mahal isn't in Pakistan. It's in India.

2 The Statue of Liberty is in Canada.

3 Machu Picchu is in Mexico.

4 The Eiffel Tower is in Italy.

5 The Sydney Opera House is in the UK.

3 *to be* (questions)

Presentation

Yes/No questions

Am	I	
Is	he she it	British? eighteen? married?
Are	you we they	

Short answers

Yes,	I	am.
	he she it	is.
	you we they	are.

No,	I	'm not.
	he she it	isn't.
	you we they	aren't.

Say *Yes, I am. Yes, he is* … (don't say ~~Yes, I'm. Yes, he's.~~)

Key vocabulary | Telling the time: **TIP** it's = it is

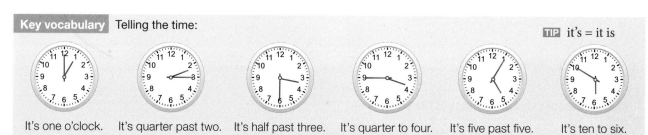

It's one o'clock. It's quarter past two. It's half past three. It's quarter to four. It's five past five. It's ten to six.

Exercises

1 Complete the questions with *Is* or *Are*.

1 _____Are_____ you a doctor?
2 _____ he twenty-five?
3 _____ they Brazilian?
4 _____ it two o'clock?
5 _____ he from New York?

6 _____ Tom and Anna married?
7 _____ he Italian?
8 _____ they from France?
9 _____ Jack and Suzy teachers?
10 _____ it half past four?

2 Complete the short answers.

1 Is it eight o'clock?
No, _it isn't._

2 Are you British?
Yes, _____

3 Is she married?
No, _____

4 Are you eighteen?
No, _____

5 Are you and Rosaria Italian?
Yes, _____

6 Is she from Canada?
Yes, _____

7 Are they students?
No, _____

8 Is it quarter to nine?
Yes, _____

9 Are they married?
Yes, _____

10 Is he thirty-four?
No, _____

3 Answer for you with short answers.

1 Are you a student? _____
2 Are you single? _____
3 Are you twenty-five? _____

4 Are you American? _____
5 Is it six o'clock? _____
6 Are you Polish? _____

4 🔊1.03 Write the conversations. Then listen and check.

1 you + Italian? → no: Spanish.
A: _Are you Italian?_
B: _No, I'm not. I'm Spanish._

2 he + Japanese? → yes
A: _Is he Japanese?_
B: _Yes, he is._

3 she + Brazilian? → yes
A: _____
B: _____

4 he + Polish? → no: Russian
A: _____
B: _____

5 they + doctors? → no: teachers
A: _____
B: _____

6 they + married? → yes
A: _____
B: _____

7 you and Jack + American? → no: British
A: _____
B: _____

8 it + six o'clock? → no: half past five
A: _____
B: _____

9 she + single? → no: married
A: _____
B: _____

10 he + musician? → no: engineer
A: _____
B: _____

4 *am, is, are* + adjective
a/an or no article

Presentation

Singular

I'm You're She's He's	hungry. young.
It's	expensive. an expensive car.

Plural

We're You're They're	hungry. young. young students.
They're	expensive. expensive cars.

a/an or no article

Use *a/an* (indefinite article) with adjective + singular noun: *It's an expensive car.*

Don't use *a/an* with plural nouns: *They're expensive cars.*

> **TIP** Say *an expensive car, a young student* … (don't say ~~a car expensive, a student young~~ …)
> Say *expensive cars, young students* … (don't say ~~expensives cars, youngs students~~ …)

Key vocabulary Adjectives: angry, beautiful, thirsty, hungry, tired, cheap/expensive, slow/fast, happy/unhappy, cold/hot, poor/rich, short/tall, small/big, old/young

Exercises

1 Write affirmative sentences.

1 Charles isn't tall.   He's short.

2 Elizabeth isn't young.

3 The USA isn't small.

4 Michael isn't short.

5 David and Victoria aren't poor.

6 iPods aren't big.

7 I'm not old.

8 We aren't rich.

2 🔊 **1.04** **Complete the sentences with *a, an* or Ø (no article). Then listen and check.**

1 It's ____a____ cheap car.
2 They're _____ fast cars.
3 She's _____ young teacher.
4 He's _____ rich.
5 It's _____ beautiful.
6 It's _____ beautiful book.

7 We're _____ poor students.
8 I'm _____ poor student.
9 They're _____ Italian teachers.
10 It's _____ expensive house.
11 She's _____ young engineer.
12 You're _____ American.

3 **Write sentences. Use the adjectives in the box.**

cold   hot   ~~hungry~~   thirsty   tired

1 I'm hungry.
2 _____
3 _____
4 _____
5 _____

4 **Correct the sentences.**

1 John's happy.   John isn't happy. He's unhappy.
2 Sue's angry.   _____
3 Lee's unhappy.   _____

19

5 Review of units 1 to 4

Grammar

1 Look at the pictures and write sentences. Use the words in the table.

pronouns	verbs	articles	adjectives	nouns
It They	's 're	a an Ø	big small expensive cheap fast slow	book(s) car(s) house(s)

1  5

2  6

3  7

4  8

1 It's an expensive house.
2 ....
3 ....
4 ....
5 ....
6 ....
7 ....
8 ....

2 Is it a question or a statement? Add a question mark (?) or a full stop (.)

1 Is she English ?   5 Are you a doctor
2 I'm a teacher .   6 It isn't a small car
3 Is it six o'clock   7 We're Russian
4 They aren't nurses   8 Are they expensive

3 Combine the sentences.

1 He's from Russia. He's a doctor.
   He's a Russian doctor.

2 She's from Britain. She's a teacher.
   ....

3 We're engineers. We're from Spain.
   ....

4 I'm a musician. I'm from Italy.
   ....

5 They're from Japan. They're students.
   ....

6 She's an engineer. She's from Poland.
   ....

7 He's an artist. He's from Brazil.
   ....

8 They're from the USA. They're nurses.
   ....

4 Write questions and answers.

1 Madonna – from the USA? → yes
   Is Madonna from the USA?
   Yes, she is.

2 Tom Cruise – tall? → no
   ....
   ....

3 Bill Gates – rich? → yes
   ....
   ....

4 Julia Roberts – a musician? → no
   ....
   ....

5 the Rolling Stones – American? → no

6 Ferraris – expensive? → yes

5 Write negative sentences. Use contractions.

1 Tom Cruise – tall
Tom Cruise isn't tall.

2 Bill Gates – poor

3 The Rolling Stones – American

4 Madonna – from Italy

5 Ferraris – cheap

6 Julia Roberts – a musician

Pronunciation: contractions

6 🔊1.05 **Listen and tick what you hear.**

1	He is not	He isn't ✓
2	I am	I'm
3	She is	She's
4	They are	They're
5	We are not	We aren't
6	It is not	It isn't
7	You are	You're

Vocabulary

7 Match to make six occupations.

1	art	ent	artist
2	doct	er	
3	engin	ian	
4	music	ist	
5	teach	or	
6	stud	eer	

8 Write the times.

1 It's quarter to eight.

2

3

4

5

6

9 Write the opposite adjectives.

1	tall	sh ort
2	rich	p
3	old	y
4	big	sm
5	fast	sl
6	expensive	ch
7	married	s
8	hot	c

Listen again

10 🔊1.06 **Listen. Are the sentences true (T) or false (F)?**

1	Andrea is Polish.	T
2	Andrea is married.	
3	Bruno is thirty.	
4	Bruno is married.	
5	Marisol is Mexican.	
6	Marisol is nineteen.	

6 Where is/are ...?
Prepositions of place (in, on, next to, under)

Man: Where's the phone?
Woman: It's on the chair.
Man: Oh, thanks. Where are the car keys?
Woman: I don't know. Are they on the table?
Man: No, they aren't.

Presentation

Yes/No questions		
Is it	on	the chair?
Are they		the table?

Where questions		
Where	's	the phone?
	are	the car keys?

Affirmative + preposition		
It's	on	the chair.
They're		the table.

TIP Use *the* (definite article) with both singular and plural nouns: *the phone, the keys.*

Prepositions of place

in   on   next to   under

Key vocabulary Everyday objects: bag, book, camera, chair, keys, phone, pen, table, wallet

Exercises

1 Read the answers and look at the picture. Write the questions. Use *Where's the ...?* or *Where are the ...?*

1 Where's the phone?   It's on the table.
2 _____ It's next to the chair.
3 _____ They're under the chair.
4 _____ It's next to the phone.
5 _____ They're on the chair.
6 _____ It's under the chair.
7 _____ It's under the table.
8 _____ They're in the bag.

2 Look at the picture in exercise 1 again. Correct the prepositions in the sentences. Two are correct.

1 Two pens are ~~in~~ the chair. _____on_____

2 The keys and the wallet are under the chair. _____

3 The books are under the bag. _____

4 The bag is next to the table. _____

5 The camera is next to the phone. _____

6 The phone is under the table. _____

3 🔊**1.07** Complete the sentences. Use *It's* or *They're* and *in, on, next to* or *under*. Then listen and check.

1 _____It's under_____ the chair.

2 _____They're in_____ in the bag.

3 _____ the book.

4 _____ the camera.

5 _____ the table.

6 _____ the bag.

7 _____ the chair.

8 _____ the wallet.

9 _____ the phone.

10 _____ the bag.

23

7 There is/are ...
Prepositions of place *(in the corner, in the middle, in front of, behind)*

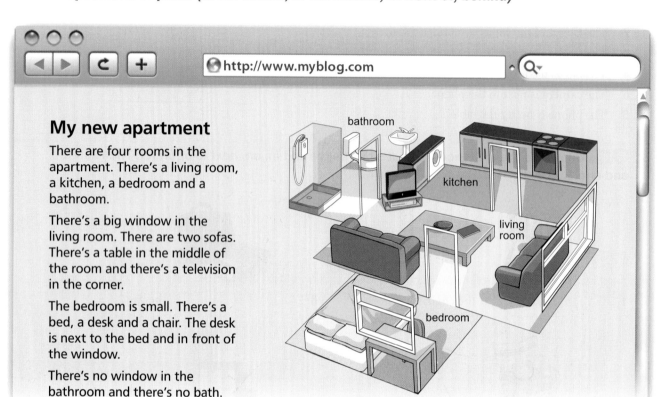

My new apartment

There are four rooms in the apartment. There's a living room, a kitchen, a bedroom and a bathroom.

There's a big window in the living room. There are two sofas. There's a table in the middle of the room and there's a television in the corner.

The bedroom is small. There's a bed, a desk and a chair. The desk is next to the bed and in front of the window.

There's no window in the bathroom and there's no bath. There's a shower.

Presentation

Affirmative

There's	a one	sofa.
There are	two three four	sofas.

TIP there's = there + is

Negative

There isn't	a	sofa.
There aren't	two	sofas.

TIP there isn't = there is not
there aren't = there are not
There's no sofa. = There isn't a sofa.

Prepositions of place

in the corner / in the corner of the room

in the middle / in the middle of the room

in front of the window

behind the door

Key vocabulary Rooms and furniture: living room, kitchen, bedroom, bathroom, bath, bed, chair, desk, door, shower, sofa, table, television, window

Exercises

1 Complete the sentences with *There's* or *There are.*

1   There's a table in the kitchen.
2   _____ four chairs in the corner.
3   _____ no television in the bedroom.
4   _____ a table next to the sofa.
5   _____ a sofa between the windows.
6   _____ two bathrooms.

2 Match the sentences to the apartments.

1   The bedroom's big. B
2   The bedroom's small. ☐
3   The chair's behind the door in the bathroom. ☐
4   The television's in front of the sofa. ☐
5   There are four chairs and a table in the middle of room. ☐
6   There are three windows in the living room. ☐
7   There's a bath and there's a shower. ☐
8   There's a chair next to the bed. ☐
9   There's a big bed in the middle of the room. ☐
10 There's a big sofa. ☐
11 There's a big window in the living room. ☐
12 There's a shower – there's no bath. ☐
13 There's a table and four chairs in the corner. ☐
14 There's no sofa. ☐

A

B

3 🔊 1.08 Look at the picture and write sentences. Use the words in brackets. Then listen and check.

1   (two windows)
    There are two windows in the room.

2   (a big sofa)
    There's a big sofa in the middle of the room.

3   (two chairs)
    _____

4   (desk)
    _____

5   (computer)
    _____

6   (television)
    _____

8 Is there ...?

Prepositions of place *(opposite, in front of, between, behind)*

Woman:	Is there a cash machine near here?
Man:	Yes, there is. It's in Marlowe Street, opposite the supermarket.
Woman:	Thank you.
Man:	You're welcome.

Guest:	Excuse me.
Receptionist:	Yes?
Guest:	Is there a restaurant in the hotel?
Receptionist:	Yes, there is. It's on the first floor.
Guest:	Is there a lift?
Receptionist:	No, there isn't. Sorry.

Presentation

Yes/No questions

Is there a	cash machine restaurant	near here? in the hotel?

Short answers

Yes, there is.	No, there isn't.

Prepositions of place

in (Marlow Street), on the (third) floor

opposite

in front of

between

behind

Key vocabulary Places in town: café, cash machine, cinema, gym, hotel, office, restaurant, swimming pool, supermarket, taxi rank

In a hotel: reception, lift, the ground/first/second/third floor

Exercises

1 Put the conversations in order.

Conversation 1

- [ ] Yes?
- [ ] Yes, there is. It's behind the supermarket.
- [ ] Thank you.
- [ ] Is there a taxi rank near here?
- [1] Excuse me.
- [ ] You're welcome.

Conversation 2

- [ ] Yes?
- [ ] Thank you.
- [ ] No, there isn't. But there's a swimming pool on the third floor.
- [ ] Excuse me.
- [ ] You're welcome.
- [ ] Is there a gym in the hotel?

2 Look at the hotel lift and the questions. Write the answers.

1 Is there a restaurant in the hotel? *Yes, there is. It's on the first floor.*
2 Is there a gym? *No, there isn't.*
3 Is there a swimming pool?

4 Is there a café?

5 Is there a cash machine?

6 Where's reception?

3 (1.09) Read the answers and look at the map. Write the questions. Then listen and check.

1 *Is there a cinema near here?*
   Yes, there is. It's in Gill Street, next to the café.
2 ....
   Yes, there is. It's next to the cinema.
3 ....
   Yes, there is. It's in Burton Street, behind the café.
4 ....
   Yes, there is. It's in Long Street.
5 ....
   Yes, there is. It's opposite the cinema.
6 ....
   Yes, there is. It's between the supermarket and the restaurant.

4 Answer these questions about your town.

1 Is there a cinema? Where is it?
   Yes, there is. It's in Union Street opposite the pizza restaurant.

2 Is there a cash machine? Where is it?

3 Is there a supermarket? Where is it?

4 Is there a swimming pool? Where is it?

5 Is there a taxi rank? Where is it?

6 Is there an Italian restaurant? Where is it?

9 There is/are + some/any
Countable and uncountable nouns

Woman:	There's some coffee.
Man:	Good. Is there any sugar?
Woman:	Yes, there is.
Man:	Are there any biscuits?
Woman:	No, there aren't. And there isn't any milk.

Presentation

Affirmative + *a/an/some*

	a	biscuit. banana.
There's	an	apple. egg.
	some	bread. butter. coffee. milk. sugar.
There are	some	apples. bananas. biscuits. eggs. oranges.

Negative + *any*

There isn't	any	bread. butter.
There aren't	any	apples. bananas.

Yes/No questions + *any*

Is there	any	coffee? sugar?
Are there	any	biscuits? eggs?

Short answers

Yes,	there is. there are.	No,	there isn't. there aren't.

Countable and uncountable nouns: *some* and *any*

Some nouns are countable: *one egg, two eggs, three eggs …*

Some nouns are uncountable: *bread, milk, sugar …*

Use *some* in affirmative statements …

- with plural countable nouns: *There are some eggs.*
- with uncountable nouns: *There is some bread.*

Use *any* with countable and uncountable nouns …

- in negative statements: *There aren't any eggs. There isn't any bread.*
- in questions: *Are there any eggs? Is there any bread?*

Key vocabulary Food and drink: apples, bananas, biscuits, bread, butter, coffee, eggs, milk, oranges, sugar

Exercises

1 🔊 **1.10** **Look at the picture. Complete the text with the words in the box. Then listen and check.**

apples   banana   biscuits   bread   butter   coffee   eggs   ~~milk~~   sugar

There's some ¹ _milk_ and some ² _____ in the fridge and there are some ³ _____ . There are some ⁴ _____ under the table. There's some ⁵ _____ on the table and there's a ⁶ _____ . There's some ⁷ _____ on the shelf. There isn't any ⁸ _____ and there aren't any ⁹ _____ .

2 **Look at the picture in exercise 1 again. Match the answers to the questions.**

1 Is there any milk? `e`
2 Are there any apples? ☐
3 Is there any bread? ☐
4 Is there any sugar? ☐
5 Are there any biscuits? ☐
6 Are there any eggs? ☐
7 Is there any butter? ☐

a No, there isn't.
b Yes, there are. They're in the fridge.
c Yes, there is. It's on the shelf.
d Yes, there is. It's on the table.
e ~~Yes, there is. It's in the fridge.~~
f No, there aren't.
g Yes, there are. They're under the table.

3 **Look at the picture. Complete the sentences with _a, an, some_ or _any_.**

1 There isn't _any_ bread.
2 There's _____ orange.
3 There aren't _____ biscuits.
4 There are _____ eggs.
5 There's _____ banana.
6 There isn't _____ butter.
7 There's _____ coffee.

4 **Look at the picture in exercise 3 again. Write questions and answers.**

1 coffee   _Is there any coffee? Yes, there is._
2 biscuits _____
3 sugar   _____
4 eggs   _____

29

10 Review of units 6 to 9

Grammar

1 Look at the plan. Complete the description with *There's a*, *There isn't a* or *There are*.

[1] __There are__ two windows in the living room. [2] _____ sofa.
[3] _____ four chairs and a table in the middle of the room. The television's in the corner.

The bedroom's big. [4] _____ bed, a desk and a chair. The bed's in the middle of the room. The desk and the chair are in the corner.

[5] _____ shower.
[6] _____ bath in the bathroom.

2 Complete the table with the words in the box.

> ~~apples~~ bananas biscuits butter
> bread coffee eggs milk sugar

	food	drink
countable	apples	
uncountable		

3 Tick (✓) the possible words.

1 There isn't any …
   a milk. ✓   **b** biscuits.   **c** bread. ✓
2 There are some …
   a biscuits.   **b** coffee.   **c** sugar.
3 There's a …
   a bread.   **b** banana.   **c** apple.
4 There isn't any …
   a coffee.   **b** apples.   **c** sugar.
5 There aren't any …
   a bananas.   **b** sugar.   **c** eggs.
6 There isn't an …
   a apple.   **b** egg.   **c** coffee.
7 Are there any …
   a eggs?   **b** bread?   **c** coffee?
8 Is there any …
   a milk?   **b** biscuits?   **c** bananas?
9 There are some …
   a coffee.   **b** bananas.   **c** eggs.
10 There's a …
   a apple.   **b** bread.   **c** biscuit.

4 **Complete the conversation with the words in the box.**

're are aren't in on some any

A: Where ¹_____ the car keys? Are there
²_____ keys in the kitchen?

B: No, there ³_____ but there are
⁴_____ keys in the living room. They're
⁵_____ the desk ⁶_____ the corner.

A: Are you sure?

B: Oh, sorry. Here they are. They ⁷_____ in
my bag.

Pronunciation: *is/are*

5 **🔊1.11 Listen and tick what you hear.**

1	There isn't …		There aren't …	
2	Where's …?	✓	Where are …?	
3	Is there …?		Are there …?	
4	There's …		There are …	
5	There isn't …		There aren't …	
6	Where's …?		Where are …?	
7	Is there …?		Are there …?	
8	There's …		There are …	

6 **Write the words for things in the home.**

1 d~sk _____ *desk*

2 s~f~ _____

3 b~d _____

4 t~l~v~s~~n _____

5 t~bl~ _____

6 sh~w~r _____

7 b~th _____

8 d~~r _____

9 w~nd~w _____

10 ch~~r _____

Vocabulary

7 **Look at the picture. Are the sentences true (T) or false (F)?**

1 The phone's under the chair. _____ F

2 The bag's on the chair. _____

3 The keys are next to the wallet. _____

4 There are some books in the bag. _____

5 The pens are on the camera. _____

6 The wallet's under the chair. _____

7 The phone's next to the camera. _____

8 The keys are next to the camera. _____

9 The bag is under the table. _____

10 The camera is on the table. _____

8 **Circle the word that is different.**

1 apples bananas (biscuits) oranges

2 sugar coffee milk tea

3 café shower supermarket restaurant

4 door hotel office gym

5 camera keys wallet table

6 kitchen bedroom window bathroom

7 sofa chair table reception

Listen again

9 **🔊1.12 Listen. Are the sentences true (T) or false (F)?**

1 There's some coffee in the fridge. _____

2 There aren't any eggs. _____

3 There's a banana on the table. _____

4 There's some sugar. _____

5 There are some biscuits. _____

11 *have got*

New Message

To:	Jim D
Subject:	new car
From:	Nina Trufanow

Attached: car06.jpg

Hi Jim
We've got a new car!
Nina & Phil

Presentation

Use *have got* and *has got* to talk about …

- possessions: *We've got a new car.*
- appearance: *She's got blonde hair.*
- people in your life: *He's got two children.*
- illnesses: *I've got a headache.*

Affirmative

I you we they	have got	I've got You've got We've got They've got	two children. a new car. dark hair. a cold.
he she	has got	He's got She's got	

Negative

I You We They	haven't got	any children. a new car. dark hair. a cold.
He She	hasn't got	

Yes/No questions

Have	you we they	got	any children? a new car? dark hair?
Has	he she		a cold?

Short answers

Yes,	I / you / we / they	have.
	he / she	has.

No,	I / you / we / they	haven't.
	he / she	hasn't.

TIP Say *I'm 21. I'm 1 metre 79. I'm hot. I'm cold.* (don't say ~~I have 21 years. I have 1 metre 79. I have hot. I have cold.~~)
I'm cold. (a feeling) ≠ *I've got a cold.* (an illness)

Key vocabulary Appearance: blue/brown eyes, blonde/brown/dark hair, a nice smile, a tattoo
Illness: a cold, the flu, a headache, paracetamol

Exercises

1 Write the contractions.

1 I have got   *I've got*

2 She has got

3 We have not got

4 He has got

5 They have got

6 He has not got

2 Write sentences.

1 Joe / a nice house   *Joe's got a nice house.*

2 Annika and Ray / not / a car

3 you / a bike?

4 Catherine / a sister?

5 we / not / any children

6 I / not / a cold. I / the flu

3 🔊**1.13 Complete the conversations. Then listen and check.**

Conversation 1

A: ¹   *Have*   Mark and Anna ²   *got*   any children?

B: Yes, ³   a son and a daughter.

Conversation 2

C: What's the matter?

D: ⁴   a headache. ⁵   you ⁶   a paracetamol?

C: No, ⁷   . Sorry.

Conversation 3

E: ⁸   Lizzie ⁹   a car?

F: Yes, ¹⁰   an Audi TT.

E: Really? ¹¹   a boyfriend?

4 Complete the text with *is* or *has got*.

Penelope Cruz ¹   *is*   an actress. She ²
1m 68. She ³   dark hair and brown eyes. She
⁴   a nice smile. She ⁵   from Spain.
She ⁶   a brother, Eduardo, and a sister, Monica.

5 🔊**1.14 Write about Johnny Depp. Then listen and check.**

1 an actor

2 1m 79

3 brown hair, brown eyes

4 thirteen tattoos

5 from the USA

6 a brother and two sisters

12 Possessive adjectives

Gates 15-22

Woman: Have you got your ticket?
Man: Yes, I have.
Woman: And your credit card?
Man: Yes, of course.
Woman: And your mobile?
Man: Yes, yes, I've got my mobile and I've got my keys and …
Woman: What about your passport?
Man: Oh, no!

Presentation

Use possessive adjectives to talk about objects, people and places.

Subject pronouns	Possesive adjectives	
I	my	I've got my ticket.
you	your	Have you got your passport?
he	his	His parents are Italian.
she	her	Her father's from Argentina.
it	its	Venice is famous for its canals.
we	our	Our camera's a Nikon.
they	their	Their daughter's a doctor.

A possessive adjective has got one form for singular and plural: *his brother, his parents.*

Key vocabulary **Everyday objects:** credit card, glasses, laptop, mobile (= mobile phone), passport, ticket
Adjectives: awful, brilliant, fantastic, great, terrible
People in your life: mother, father, parents, son, daughter, children, husband, wife, brother, sister

Exercises

1 Write sentences.

1 my keys ✓   I've got my keys.
2 your laptop ✗   You haven't got your laptop.
3 our passports ✓
4 his glasses ✗
5 her camera ✓
6 our credit cards ✗
7 my mobile ✓
8 their tickets ✓

2 Write sentences.

1 I've got a Nikon camera. It's fantastic!   *My camera's fantastic!*
2 She's got a new motorbike. It's great!
3 He's got a Dell laptop. It's brilliant!
4 We've got an old car. It's terrible!
5 They've got an old television. It's awful!

3 ⏺1.15 Complete the text with *his, her, their* or *its*. Then listen and check.

Ana's Argentinian but ¹_____ husband, Jacob, isn't from Argentina. ²_____ father's
Nigerian and ³_____ mother's Scottish. Ana's got a sister and a brother. ⁴_____ sister's a
teacher and ⁵_____ brother's a doctor. He's married. ⁶_____ wife's Italian. They've got
two children: a son and a daughter. ⁷_____ daughter's ten and ⁸_____ son's six. They've
also got a dog. ⁹_____ name is Rex.

4 Choose the correct words.

1 Jane hasn't got *she / her* passport.
2 *We / Our* new motorbike is fantastic.
3 *She / Her* is a doctor.
4 *I / My* haven't got a fast car.
5 Where are *you / your* glasses?
6 *He / His* father is from the USA.

7 What's *it's / its* name?
8 *They / Their* son has got an apartment opposite the park.
9 Have you got *I / my* phone?
10 *We / Our* have got a house near here.
11 *He / His* mobile is on the table.
12 *I / My* mother is from Madrid.

5 Complete the sentences about a friend. Use the words in brackets.

1 My friend *has got two sisters. Their names are Clare and Penny.* (brothers/sisters)
  My friend _____ (brothers/sisters)
2 He/She _____ (married/single)
3 He/She _____ (children/dog)
4 He/She _____ (car/bike)

13 *this, that, these, those* (demonstrative pronouns)
The pronoun *one*

Presentation

Singular

this	that	Which one?
this one	that one	The red one.

This	one
That	
Which	one?

Plural

these	those	Which ones?
these ones	those ones	The blue ones.

These	ones
Those	
Which	ones?

Key vocabulary Clothes and accessories: coat, hat, shirt, shoes, trainers, trousers, sunglasses, watch
Colours: black, white, red, yellow, blue

Exercises

1 Look at the pictures and complete the questions. Use *this, that, these* or *those*.

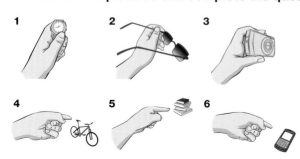

1 Is this _____ your watch?
2 Are these _____ your sunglasses?
3 _____ your camera?
4 _____ your bike?
5 _____ your books?
6 _____ your phone?

36

2 Look at the pictures and write sentences. Use the words in the table.

This That	coat hat shirt	is	big. small. old.
These Those	shoes trainers trousers	are	

1 These trainers are old.
2 ....
3 ....
4 ....
5 ....
6 ....

3 Look at the pictures and complete the conversations.

1

A: That's my phone. ....
B: Which one? ....
A: The black one. ....

2

A: That's ....
B: Which .... ?
A: The ....

3

A: Those ....
B: Which .... ?
A: The ....

4 🎧1.16 Complete the conversation with *one, that* or *which*. Then listen and check.

A: Who's ¹................................... girl?
B: ²......................... ³......................... ?
A: The ⁴........................... in the red shoes.
B: ⁵........................... 's Sue. She's my girlfriend.

14 Possessive 's and possessive pronouns
whose

Woman: You've got it!
Man: What?
Woman: My laptop.
Man: This isn't your laptop.
Woman: Whose is it?
Man: It's Karen's.
Woman: Well, where's mine?
Man: Oh, Tim's got yours.
Woman: And who's Tim?
Man: He's my brother. But he's on holiday.

Presentation

Possessive 's	Possessive adjective	Possessive pronoun
	It's my laptop.	It's mine.
	They're your sunglasses.	They're yours.
It's Karen's mobile. It's my sister's mobile.	It's her mobile.	It's hers.
It's my brother's T shirt. It's Tim's T-shirt.	It's his T-shirt.	It's his.
	It's our camera.	It's ours.
It's my parents' camera.	It's their camera.	It's theirs.

Possessive 's

- Add 's to a singular noun: *My sister's husband.*
- Add ' to a plural noun: *My sisters' husbands.*

Possessive pronouns

A possessive pronoun has got one form for singular and plural.

It's my book. It's mine.

They're my books. They're mine.

You can use a noun + possessive 's in the same way: *Whose mobile is this? It's David's. / It's my brother's.*

Whose

Whose laptop is this? It's mine.

Whose sunglasses are these? They're mine.

Exercises

1 **⊙1.17** Write questions with *whose* and the answers. Then listen and check.

Harry

Lisa

Tim

1 mobile

2 books

3 sunglasses

4 camera

5 laptop

6 trainers

1 A: Whose mobile is this?
   B: I think it's Harry's.

2 A: Whose books are these?
   B: I think they're Lisa's.

3 A: ....
   B: ....

4 A: ....
   B: ....

5 A: ....
   B: ....

6 A: ....
   B: ....

2 Write sentences with possessive pronouns.

1 That's Harry's mobile.
  It's his.

2 Those are Tim's trainers.

3 These are Lisa's books.

4 This is Lisa's laptop.

5 These are Harry's sunglasses.

6 That's Tim's camera.

3 Rewrite the sentences. Use possessive pronouns.

1 This is my laptop and that's your laptop.   This is mine and that is yours.
2 Those are their books and these are our books. ....
3 This is her camera and that's your camera. ....
4 This is my laptop and that's his laptop. ....

4 What is the *'s* in the underlined words? Write *is*, *has* or *P* (for possessive *'s*).

1 Is this <u>Lisa's</u> mobile? ___P___
  No, <u>she's</u> got a Nokia. ___has___

2 <u>That's</u> a nice camera. ....
  Yes, <u>it's</u> a Nikon. ....

3 Have you got <u>Harry's</u> laptop? ....
  No, this is <u>Tim's</u>. ....

4 I think <u>Tim's</u> got my book. Where is he? ....
  <u>He's</u> on holiday. ....

5 This <u>one's</u> mine. ....
  No, <u>that's</u> yours. ....

6 Where is <u>Tim's</u> camera? ....
  <u>It's</u> in his bag. ....

39

15 Review of units 11 to 14

Grammar

1 Choose the correct forms.

1 I's got blue eyes. / (I've got blue eyes.)
2 She hasn't got a motorbike. / She haven't got a motorbike.
3 Has you got a cold? / Have you got a cold?
4 Yes, I has. / Yes, I have.
5 No, he hasn't. / No, he haven't.
6 We's got two children. / We've got two children.
7 He's got a new laptop. / He've got a new laptop.
8 Have she got dark hair? / Has she got dark hair?

2 Correct the sentences. Use the possessive *'s*.

1 Venus is ~~Serena~~ sister.   Serena's
2 Sofia father is Francis.
3 Bob daughter is Peaches.
4 The Clintons daughter is Chelsea.
5 Barbara is George mother.
6 Jane brother is Peter.
7 Richard is Judy husband.
8 Charles is Elizabeth son.

3 Complete the sentences with a possessive adjective.

1 I've got ____my____ keys.
2 London is noisy but _____ parks are quiet.
3 Maria has got _____ guitar lesson tonight.
4 Mark and Julia are in the house. This is _____ car.
5 A: Is this _____ mobile phone?
   B: No, it isn't. My phone is in my bag.
6 This is Ben's dog. _____ name is Loki.
7 We've got two sons. _____ son's names are Matt and Sam.
8 Jane hasn't got _____ glasses.

4 Rewrite the sentences. Use *It's* or *They're* and the words in the box.

hers   his   mine   ours   theirs   yours

1 Those are David's keys.
   They're his.
2 That's Melanie's camera.
   It's hers.
3 This is my car.
   _____
4 These are Jack's sunglasses.
   _____
5 That's Tom and Katie's house.
   _____
6 This is Poppy's laptop.
   _____
7 Those are your trainers.
   _____
8 These are our credit cards.
   _____

5 Look at the picture. Write questions and answers.

1 Which one is Mike's?
   The black one.
2 Which ones are Ellen's?
   The yellow ones.
3 _____
   _____
4 _____
   _____

Pronunciation: /s/ or /z/

6 🔊 **1.18** Listen to the final *s* in these words.

/s/	/z/
books	keys
shirts	trousers

Then listen and tick /s/ or /z/.

		/s/	/z/	
1	hotels	/s/	/z/	✔
2	T-shirts	/s/	/z/	
3	apples	/s/	/z/	
4	laptops	/s/	/z/	
5	coats	/s/	/z/	
6	eyes	/s/	/z/	

Vocabulary

7 **Complete the table with the words in the box.**

> ~~boyfriend~~ brother daughter
> father ~~girlfriend~~ husband
> mother sister son wife

♂	♀
boyfriend	girlfriend

8 **Match to make six everyday objects.**

1	pass	era	passport	
2	credit	glasses		
3	sun	ch		
4	lap	port		
5	cam	card		
6	wat	top		

9 **Are the sentences true (T) or false (F)?**

1	John's got a red T-shirt.	T
2	His trousers are black.	
3	Penny's got a yellow coat.	
4	Her trousers are blue.	
5	She's got blue eyes.	
6	He's got blue eyes.	
7	They've got blonde hair.	
8	Their shoes are white.	

Listen again

10 🔊 **1.19** **Listen and complete the table with their possessions.**

Harry	mobile
Lisa	
Tim	

16 Present simple 1
Conjunctions: *and/but*

Man:	Where are you from?
Woman:	I'm from Spain but I live in London. I work in a bank.
Man:	Have you got any brothers and sisters?
Woman:	I've got one brother, Alberto. He works in a hospital and he lives in Madrid.

Presentation

Use the present simple to talk about …

- routines: *I walk to work every day.*

- permanent situations: *She lives in New York.*

Affirmative

I You We They	live work	in London.
He She	lives works	

Third person (*he/she/it*) *s*: key spelling rules

- Most verbs: *live → lives, start → starts, work → works …*

- Verbs ending with *-s, -sh* or *-ch*: *finish → finishes, watch → watches …*

- Verbs ending with consonant + *-y*: *study → studies …*

- Irregular verbs: *have → has, do → does …*

See page 233: Spelling rules

Conjunctions: *and/but*

- Use *and* for extra information: *He works in a hospital and he lives in Madrid.*

- Use *but* to show difference: *I'm from Spain but I live in London.*

> **Key vocabulary** **Verbs:** finish, have, live, start, study, walk, watch (television), work
> **Have:** have lunch, have a break
> **Occupations:** banker, chef, doctor, nurse, teacher, waiter

Exercises

1 **Write sentences about where they live.**

1	I / Spain / but / London	*I'm from Spain but I live in London.*
2	Alberto / Spain / and / Madrid	*Alberto's from Spain and he lives in Madrid.*
3	Tessa / Greece / and / Athens	
4	Jim and I / the UK / but / Tokyo	
5	Yang and Li / China / but / Paris	
6	Dan / Australia / and / Melbourne	

2 **Write sentences about where they work. Use the words in the box.**

| bank   hospital   school   restaurant |

1 Alberto's a doctor.   *He works in a hospital.*
2 Nina's a banker.   *She works in a bank.*
3 Tessa's a teacher.
4 Dan's a waiter.
5 Yuko and Tomi are nurses.
6 Juana and I are chefs.

3 **🔊 1.20 Choose the correct verbs. Then listen and check.**

My wife [1] *work /* (*works*) in a bank and I [2] *work / works* in a hospital. I [3] *start / starts* work
at nine o'clock every day. My wife [4] *start / starts* at eight but she [5] *have / has* a break at half
past ten. We both [6] *have / has* lunch at half past twelve. She [7] *finish / finishes* work at five
o'clock and I [8] *finish / finishes* at half past five. In the evening she [9] *study / studies* English
and I [10] *watch / watches* television.

4 **Complete the description of Sophie and Emma's routines.**

	Sophie	Emma	Larry	Dan
start	10:00	09:30	16:30	17:00
break	15:00	15:00	19:30	19:30
finish	16:30	16:00	23:30	24:00

Sophie and Emma are chefs. Sophie [1] *starts*
work at ten o'clock and Emma [2] _____
at half past nine. They [3] _____ a break at
three o'clock. Sophie [4] _____ work at half
past four and Emma [5] _____ at four o'clock.

5 **Look at the timetable in exercise 4 again. Write a description
of Larry and Dan's routines.**

Larry starts

6 **Write a description of your routine.**

17 Present simple 2 (negative and questions)
Subject and object pronouns

Dad: Mum loves sushi! Do you like it?
Daughter: No, I don't. I hate it. It's horrible.
Dad: Do you like Chinese food?
Daughter: Yes, I do but I prefer pizza.

Girl: Do you like horror films?
Boy: No, I don't. Why?
Girl: *Evil Twin* is on. Karena Lars is in it.
Boy: Oh, I like her.

Presentation

Affirmative and negative

I You We They	like don't like	sushi. pizza. horror films. him.
He She	likes doesn't like	her.

TIP don't = do + not
    doesn't = does + not

Yes/No questions

Do	I you we they	like	sushi? pizza? horror films? him?
Does	he she		her?

Short answers

Yes,	I / you / we / they	do.
	he / she	does.

No,	I / you / we / they	don't.
	he / she	doesn't.

Subject and object pronouns

Subject pronouns	I	you	he	she	it	we	they
Object pronouns	me	you	him	her	it	us	them

Key vocabulary People in your life: brother, girlfriend, parents, children, father (dad), mother (mum), friend
Likes and preferences: love, like, prefer, don't like, hate

Exercises

1 Match the questions to the answers.

1 Do you like Matt Damon? [c]
2 Do you like pasta? [ ]
3 Do you like Avril Lavigne? [ ]
4 Do you like hip-hop? [ ]
5 Do you like Oasis? [ ]

a No, I don't. I hate rock music.
b Yes, I do. She's fantastic.
c ~~Yes, I do. He's great.~~
d Yes, I do but I prefer jazz.
e Yes, I do. I love Italian food.

2 Read the conversations and name the person.

	Nancy	Luke	Fran	Matt
hip-hop	☺	☹☹	☺☺	☹
jazz	☺☺	☺	☹	☹☹
rock	☹	☺☺	☺	☺☺

1 A: Does she like rock?
  B: Yes, she does but she prefers hip-hop.
     Fran

2 A: Does she like hip-hop?
  B: Yes, she does but she prefers jazz.

3 A: Does he like hip-hop?
  B: No, he doesn't and he hates jazz.

4 A: Does he like hip-hop?
  B: No, he hates it. He likes rock.

3 ⏵1.21 Complete the conversations with *do, does, don't, doesn't, like* or *likes*. Then listen and check.

1 A: _____Do_____ you _____like_____ pasta?
  B: No, I _____ .

2 A: _____ your boyfriend _____ Chinese food?
  B: No, he _____ but he _____ Japanese food.

3 A: _____ your parents _____ sushi?
  B: My mother _____ it but my father _____ .

4 Choose the correct words.

1 Sharon likes Omah but he doesn't like (her)/ she.
2 I like Sharon but I don't think she likes I / me.
3 My brother's girlfriend is awful – I hate her / she.
4 Jared's parents are nice. I like them / they.
5 Tom's a good friend. We like him and he likes we / us.
6 Mike doesn't like Rene and she hates he / him.

5 ⏵1.22 Write sentences with object pronouns. Then listen and check.

1 I don't like hip-hop.   _I don't like it._
2 I like the Rolling Stones.   _____
3 I don't like Madonna.   _____
4 I love rock.   _____
5 I like Tom but I prefer Sally.   _____

18 Adverbs of frequency

Woman:	My husband and I love the opera.
Man:	Really? How often do you go?
Woman:	Every month. What about you?
Man:	Me? I never go to the opera. I prefer football.
Woman:	Then why are you here?
Man:	Oh, I've got a free ticket. Do you ever watch football?
Woman:	No, I don't.

Presentation

Use adverbs of frequency to talk about how often you do something.

Adverbs of frequency: one-word adverbs

100%	always
	often
	sometimes
	not often
0%	never

- One-word adverbs go before the main verb*.

He	often sometimes never	goes to the opera. watches football.

*but one-word adverbs go after the verb *to be*:
She is often late for work.

- With *not often*, use *don't* and *doesn't*.

I	don't	often	go to the opera.
She	doesn't		watch football.

Adverbs of frequency: phrases

When the adverb is a phrase, it goes at the end of the sentence.

	once a twice a three times a	day. week. month. year.
He goes to the opera	every	day. week. month. year.

Questions

Do you ever	go to the opera?
How often do you	watch football?

- Use a time reference with *always*: *I always go to the cinema at the weekend.*

Key vocabulary Sport and leisure: (play/watch) football, tennis, golf, basketball; (go to the) cinema, theatre, opera
Days of the week: Sunday, Monday, Tuesday, Wednesday, Thursday, Friday, Saturday

Exercises

1 Look at the table. Write sentences.

	Opera	Cinema	Theatre
Lucy	never	often	once a year
John	every month	twice a week	not often
Chris and Sally	three times a year	every Tuesday	sometimes

1 Lucy / opera
2 John / opera
3 Lucy / cinema
4 Chris and Sally / cinema
5 John / cinema
6 Chris and Sally / theatre
7 Lucy / theatre
8 John / theatre

Lucy never goes to the opera.
John goes to the opera every month.

2 Put ∧ in the sentences for the words in brackets.

1 I play football twice ∧week. (a)

2 They always go to the cinema Saturdays. (on)

3 Jenny goes to the opera once year. (a)

4 I play basketball three a month. (times)

5 Li often go to the cinema. (doesn't)

6 Anita goes to the cinema weekend. (every)

7 I watch football once a. (week)

8 I go to the theatre a year. (twice)

3 Put the words in order.

1 go I never opera the to
2 a football once plays Steve week
3 always Donna golf on plays Sundays
4 go sometimes the theatre they to
5 Carlo doesn't tennis often play
6 basketball every I play Thursday

I never go to the opera.

4 ⏺1.23 Complete the conversation with the words in the box. Then listen and check.

do ~~ever~~ every love how to twice

A: Do you ¹ _____ever_____ go ² _____ the cinema?
B: Yes, I ³ _____ . I go ⁴ _____ weekend. ⁵ _____ often do you go to the cinema?
A: Oh, I ⁶ _____ the cinema. I go ⁷ _____ a week.

5 Complete the sentences so that they are true for you.

1 I always _____
2 I sometimes _____
3 I never _____

19 *Wh-* questions

Host: For $100,000 ... When do Americans celebrate Independence Day? Is it on May 1, June 14 or July 4?
Contestant: I think it's July 4.
Host: That's correct. Now, for $175,000 ... What are the colours of the Jamaican flag? Are they black, gold and green, red, green and gold or red, green and black?
Contestant: I think it's black, gold and green.
Host: That's correct. Well done. Now, for $250,000 ... Where do tigers live? Is it in Africa, in Asia or in Europe?
Contestant: Er ... is it Africa?

Presentation

Verb *to be*

What	is	the capital of Ecuador?
	are	the colours of the Jamaican flag?

Other verbs

Where	do	tigers you they	live?
	does	he she it	

Question words

Where do you live?

When is your birthday?

What is your name?

Which one do you like?

Why do you like the blue one?

Who do you live with?

How do you spell your name?

What time do you start work?

How long is this river?

How high is Mount Everest?

How many do you want?

How often do you go to the cinema?

Exercises

1 Choose the correct words.

1 Where *do* / *does* you live?

2 What *is* / *are* the capital of Sweden?

3 What time *do* / *does* she start work?

4 What *is* / *are* your name?

5 Who *do* / *does* they live with?

6 How many *do* / *does* he want?

7 How long *is* / *are* this film?

8 Which one *do* / *does* your brother like?

9 When *is* / *are* his birthday?

10 What *do* / *does* his sister do?

2 Complete the quiz with question words. Then do the quiz and check your answers below.

Quiz

1. _____ does the President of the USA live?
   A in the White House   **B** in the Green House   **C** in the White Palace
2. _____ do penguins live?
   A in the Arctic   **B** in the Antarctic   **C** in the UK
3. _____ high is Mount Everest?
   A 7,532 metres   **B** 8,848 metres   **C** 9,321 metres
4. _____ does your brain stop growing?
   A at 13 years old   **B** at 15 years old   **C** at 18 years old
5. _____ of these is a hexagon?
   A ⬠   **B** ⬡   **C** ⬡
6. _____ is the capital of Ecuador?
   A La Paz   **B** Lima   **C** Quito
7. _____ long do elephants live?
   A 35 years   **B** 70 years   **C** 100 years
8. _____ is Luke Skywalker's father?
   A Darth Vader   **B** Chewbacca   **C** Yoda
9. _____ do bats sleep?
   A at night   **B** in the day   **C** at the weekend
10. _____ does 'aloha' mean in Hawaiian?
    A hello   **B** goodbye   **C** hello or goodbye

Answers: 1A 2B 3B 4A 5C 6C 7B 8A 9B 10C

3 Match the questions to the answers.

1 How long do you sleep at night? `g`
2 What do you do in the evening? ☐
3 What do you have for breakfast? ☐
4 What time do you have lunch? ☐
5 Where do you have lunch? ☐
6 Where do you live? ☐
7 Where do you work? ☐

a In London.
b Half past twelve.
c I watch television.
d In a bank.
e In a restaurant.
f Toast and coffee.
g ~~Eight hours.~~

4 🔊1.24 Write questions about Yuko. Then listen and check.

1 What time does she have _____ breakfast? At eight o'clock.
2 _____ study? In the morning.
3 _____ for lunch? A sandwich.
4 _____ afternoon? She plays golf.
5 _____ dinner? In a restaurant.
6 _____ television in the evening? For two hours.

20 Review of units 16 to 19

Grammar

1 Look at Bill's sentences. Then write about Chantal using the words in brackets.

Bill

Chantal

1 I live in London. (Paris)
   She lives in Paris.

2 I work in a school. (a bank)

3 I start work at nine o'clock. (eight)

4 I finish work at half past four. (six)

5 I have sandwiches for lunch. (sushi)

6 I study French. (English)

7 I play football. (tennis)

8 I watch television every day. (never)

9 I never go to the opera. (once a month)

10 I love rock music. (hate)

11 I sleep ten hours every night. (six)

12 I don't often eat in restaurants. (often)

2 Write Chantal's answers to the questions.

1 Do you live in Paris?
   Yes, I do.

2 Does Bill live in Paris?
   No, he doesn't.

3 Do you like rock music?

4 Does Bill like rock music?

5 Do you ever eat in restaurants?

6 Do you like sushi?

7 Does Bill work in a school?

8 Do you watch television?

9 Does Bill go to the opera?

10 Does Bill play football?

3 Complete the sentences with *do, does, don't* or *doesn't*.

1 _____Does_____ your uncle like jazz?

2 Bill _____ live in Paris – he lives in London.

3 I like Japanese food but I _____ like sushi.

4 Where _____ you live?

5 What time _____ Chantal start work?

6 I _____ go to the theatre. I prefer the cinema.

7 _____ Marc play tennis?

8 How often _____ he play tennis?

9 How long _____ you have for lunch?

10 _____ you like football?

11 What _____ you have for breakfast?

12 Anne _____ eat pasta.

4 Put the words in order.

1 but like hip-hop I I prefer rock
I like hip-hop but I prefer rock.

2 always cinema go Monday on the to we

3 doesn't often she television watch

4 don't I jazz like

5 a bank my in in sister Paris works

6 at half Jim starts nine past work

7 play I a once tennis week

8 do ever go the theatre to you ?

5 Choose the correct pronouns.

1 (I)/ Me like she / her but she / her doesn't like I / me.

2 We / Us don't like he / him and he / him doesn't like we / us.

3 They / Them like I / me and I / me like they / them.

6 Write the question words.

1 _When_ is Martin's birthday?
2 _____ are you from?
3 _____ time do you get up?
4 _____ one does she prefer?
5 _____ is that man over there?

Pronunciation: /s/, /z/ or /ɪz/

7 ⏸1.25 Listen to the final s in these verbs.

/s/ works /z/ lives /ɪz/ finishes

Listen and tick /s/, /z/ or /ɪz/.

		/s/	/z/	/ɪz/
1	plays	/s/	/z/ ✓	/ɪz/
2	watches	/s/	/z/	/ɪz/
3	does	/s/	/z/	/ɪz/
4	eats	/s/	/z/	/ɪz/
5	studies	/s/	/z/	/ɪz/

Vocabulary

8 Complete with go, play or have.

1 _play_ football
2 _____ to the theatre
3 _____ a break
4 _____ lunch
5 _____ golf
6 _____ to the cinema
7 _____ dinner
8 _____ to the opera
9 _____ breakfast

9 Match to make five words for people in your life.

1 bro — ents   _brother_
2 girl   er   _____
3 par — ther   _____
4 moth   dren   _____
5 chil   friend   _____

10 Complete the table with the words in the box.

banker chef doctor
nurse teacher waiter

bank	hospital	restaurant	school
1 banker	2	4	6
	3	5	

Listen again

11 ⏸1.26 Listen and write the questions.

1 What time does she have breakfast?
2 _____
3 _____
4 _____
5 _____
6 _____

21 *can* (ability)
Adverbs of manner

Presentation

Use *can* to describe ability.

Affirmative and negative

I / You / He / She / It / We / They	can	play ...
	can't (cannot)	

Questions

Can	I / you / he / she / it / we / they	play ...?

Short answers

Yes, I can.	No, I can't.

Can is a modal verb. This means no third person *s*.

Say *He can play the guitar.* (don't say ~~He cans play the guitar.~~)

Adverbs of manner

- Use adverbs of manner to talk about how we do something:

  *He can play the guitar really **well**.*

  *She can't run very **fast**.*

- Put the adverb of manner at the end of the sentence.

  Say *He can play the saxophone really well. He can play really well.*

  (don't say ~~He can play really well the saxophone.~~)

Exercises

1   Match the questions to the answers.

1   Can you speak Chinese?   `c`
2   Can you run fast?   ☐
3   I can play the guitar. Can you play a musical instrument?   ☐
4   I can't play the guitar. Can you?   ☐
5   Can you play golf?   ☐

a   Yes, I can play the saxophone.
b   No, but I can swim fast.
c   ~~Yes, I can. But not very well.~~
d   No, but I can play tennis.
e   No, I can't, but my friend can play really well.

2 Complete the conversations with *can* or *can't*.

Conversation 1

A: I ¹ _____can_____ swim ten kilometres. ² _____ you?

B: No, I ³ _____ swim but I ⁴ _____ run fast.

Conversation 2

C: ⁵ _____ you play the piano?

D: No, I ⁶ _____ but I can sing very well.

C: Great. ⁷ _____ you sing this song?

Conversation 3

E: My mother and father are from Barcelona. They ⁸ _____ speak Catalan.

F: ⁹ _____ you and your brothers speak Catalan?

E: No, we ¹⁰ _____ speak it very well. We always speak Spanish.

Conversation 4

G: ¹¹ _____ you play tennis?

H: Yes, I ¹² _____ but not very well. ¹³ _____ you?

G: No, I ¹⁴ _____ . I'm terrible but my sister ¹⁵ _____ play really well.

3 Choose the correct forms.

1 (Can)/ *Can't* you play the piano?

2 Can you *speak / play* Arabic?

3 No, I *can / can't*.

4 She can't swim *very well / not very well*.

5 Yes, I *can / can't*.

6 Can you play the guitar *well / not very well* ?

7 I *can / can't* run fast but I can swim well.

4 🔊1.27 Write the conversations. Then listen and check.

1 you + speak Spanish? → no: speak Chinese

A: Can you speak Spanish?

B: No, I can't. I can speak Chinese.

2 they + play the piano? → yes + very well

A: _____

B: _____

3 she + run fast? → yes

A: _____

B: _____

4 you + play tennis? → yes: also + play golf

A: _____

B: _____

5 he + speak three languages? →
no + but + speak two languages

A: _____

B: _____

5 Complete the sentences so that they are true for you.

1 I can play _____ but I can't play _____ .

2 I can speak _____ but I can't speak _____ .

22 *can* (offers and requests)

Presentation

Use *Can I ...?* and *Can you ...?* for offers and requests.

Offers

Can I help (you)?
Can I get you a drink?

Requests

Can I have a drink, please?
Can you help me, please?

Responding to offers and requests

A: Can I help you? B: Yes, please. / Thanks very much.

A: Can you help me, please? B: Sure. / Certainly. / Of course. / No, sorry.

TIP Notice *you* and *me* in offers and requests.
Offer: *Can I + verb + **you** ...?*
Request: *Can you + verb + **me** ...?*

Key vocabulary **Verbs:** ask, borrow, buy, close, have, help, get, lend, open, speak (to), use, wait

Exercises

1 Complete the questions with *Can I* or *Can you*. Are they requests or offers? Write *R* or *O*.

1   Can I   I help you?   ☐ O
2   _____ help me, please?   ☐
3   _____ ask you a question?   ☐
4   _____ have a drink?   ☐
5   _____ get me a drink?   ☐

6   _____ get you a drink?   ☐
7   _____ buy you lunch?   ☐
8   _____ use your phone?   ☐
9   _____ lend me your phone?   ☐
10 _____ borrow your phone?   ☐

2 (●1.28) **Write requests or offers. Add possessive adjectives where necessary. Then listen and check.**

1   I / borrow / car?   Can I borrow your car?
2   you / speak / to her?
3   I / open / the window?
4   I / buy / you / lunch?
5   you / get / me / a drink?
6   I / carry / bag?
7   you / help / me?
8   you / lend / me / phone?
9   I / use / laptop?
10 you / answer / the phone?

3 **Put the conversations in order.**

Conversation 1
☐ Yes, can I speak to Maria Turner, please?
☐ Yes, thanks very much.
☐ 1 Hello. Can I help you?
☐ I'm afraid not. She isn't here today. Can I get her secretary?

Conversation 2
☐ Can I get you some water?
☐ 1 Hello, Max. How are you?
☐ Sure.
☐ Thanks very much. And can you open the window?
☐ Fine, but it's very hot today!

Conversation 3
☐ I don't have any money. Can you buy me lunch today?
☐ Well, can I borrow some money?
☐ Sorry, I can't go for lunch today. I don't have time.
☐ Certainly. How much do you need?
☐ 1 Can I ask you a question?
☐ Sure.

Conversation 4
☐ Yes. Press this button.
☐ Sure. Here it is.
☐ 1 Excuse me. Can I use your phone, please?
☐ Thanks. Sorry, it doesn't work. Can you help me?

4 **Look at the offers and requests. Choose the best responses.**

1   Can you answer the phone for me?   **a** Sure.   **b** Yes, I can. Do you want me to?
2   Can I show you how to use this machine?   **a** Thanks very much.   **b** Yes, you can.
3   Can we have a break?   **a** Yes, thanks.   **b** Certainly.
4   Can you help me, please?   **a** Of course.   **b** Thanks.
5   Can I have a glass of water, please?   **a** No, you can't.   **b** Certainly.
6   Can your daughter play the piano?   **a** Yes, she can.   **b** Certainly.
7   Can I help you lift this?   **a** Yes, you can.   **b** Yes, thanks.
8   I can't play chess. Can you?   **a** No, I can't.   **b** No, thanks.

23 *would like* + noun (requests and offers)

Waiter:	Good evening.
Man:	Hello. We'd like a table for two, please.
Waiter:	Certainly. Would you like a table near the window?
Woman:	Yes, please.

Man:	Would you like some wine?
Woman:	No, thanks. I'd like some water, please.
Man:	Would you like a dessert?
Woman:	No, thanks. I'd like a cup of coffee.

Presentation

Use *would like* + *noun* for polite requests and offers.

Requests

I'd like	a table for two.
We'd like	a cup of coffee.
	some water.

Offers

Would you like	a table near the window?
	a dessert?
	some water?

Responses

Certainly. / Sure.

Responses

Yes, please.	No, thanks.

TIP I'd = I would
We'd = We would

TIP Don't say ~~No, I wouldn't~~. It isn't polite.

Key vocabulary In a restaurant: waiter, table, the menu, the bill, order (food)
Food and drink: cheese, (a cup of) coffee, dessert, green salad, ice cream, soup, water, wine

Exercises

1   🔊1.29 **Complete the conversations with the words in the box. Then listen and check.**

Certainly   I'd   like   please   thanks   we'd like   Would   ~~Would you like~~

Conversation 1

Waiter:	Good evening. My name's Mario and I'm your waiter.
Customer:	Hello.
Waiter:	¹ _Would you like_ the wine menu?
Customer:	Yes, ² _____. And ³ _____ some water, please.
Waiter:	⁴ _____.

56

Conversation 2

Customer: Excuse me, we'd like to order now.

Waiter: Sure.

Customer: ⁵_____ like some soup and he'd like a green salad.

Waiter: Certainly. ⁶_____ you like some wine?

Customer: No, ⁷_____ . But I'd ⁸_____ a cup of tea, please.

2   Put the words in order.

1   like please soup I'd some   I'd like some soup, please.

2   you like would the menu?   _____

3   like I'd coffee some   _____

4   you some would bread like?   _____

5   we'd please like some water   _____

6   I'd bill like please the   _____

3   🔊 1.30 Write offers and responses for each picture. Then listen and check.

1   A: Would you like a cup of coffee?
    B: No, thanks. I'd like the bill, please.

4   A: _____
    B: _____

2   A: _____
    B: _____

5   A: _____
    B: _____

3   A: _____
    B: _____

6   A: _____
    B: _____

24 Imperative

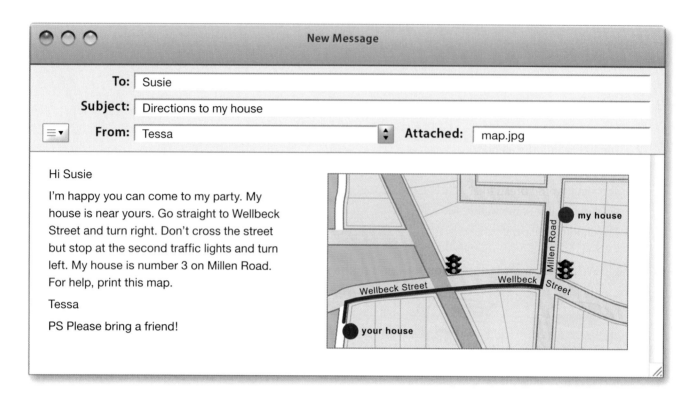

New Message

To: Susie

Subject: Directions to my house

From: Tessa   **Attached:** map.jpg

Hi Susie

I'm happy you can come to my party. My house is near yours. Go straight to Wellbeck Street and turn right. Don't cross the street but stop at the second traffic lights and turn left. My house is number 3 on Millen Road. For help, print this map.

Tessa

PS Please bring a friend!

Presentation

Use the imperative for …

- giving directions: *Go straight to …, Turn left at the traffic lights.*
- orders: *Stop! Go! Be quiet!*
- instructions: *Print (this map). Send an email.*
- requests and offers (informal): *Bring a friend. Come in. Take a seat. Have a drink.*

TIP You can use the imperative for requests and offers to friends. You can add *Please*: *Please bring a friend. Please come in.*

Affirmative

Turn left.
Go straight.

Negative

Don't turn left.
Don't stop.

TIP Say *Stop!* (don't say *You stop!*)

Key vocabulary Directions: turn left/right, go straight, cross (the road)
Places in town: road, sign, street, supermarket, traffic lights, map

Exercises

1 🔊**1.31** Look at the map. Complete the directions with the words in the box. Then listen and check.

> don't go go stop turn turn

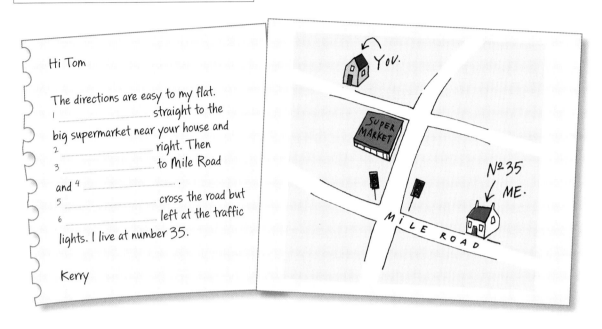

Hi Tom

The directions are easy to my flat.
1 _____ straight to the
big supermarket near your house and
2 _____ right. Then
3 _____ to Mile Road
and 4 _____ .
5 _____ cross the road but
6 _____ left at the traffic
lights. I live at number 35.

Kerry

2 Match the orders to the signs.

> **a** Don't smoke. **b** ~~Stop.~~ **c** Go. **d** Don't turn right. **e** Don't walk. **f** Don't take photographs.

1 __b__ 2 ____ 3 ____ 4 ____ 5 ____ 6 ____

3 Match 1–10 to a–j.

1	Come in!	[c]
2	Where's the supermarket?	
3	It's expensive.	
4	The traffic light is red.	
5	This exercise is difficult.	
6	It's hot in here.	
7	I'm thirsty.	
8	There's a map with the email.	
9	It's late.	
10	I haven't got a pen.	

a Go to bed!
b Please open the window.
c ~~Take a seat.~~
d Turn left and it's in front of you.
e Stop.
f Lend me yours, please.
g Don't buy it.
h Have some water.
i Print it.
j Please help me.

25 Review of units 21 to 24

Grammar

1 Complete the requests and offers with *you* or *me*.

1 Can I help _____you_____ ?
2 Would _____ like a table for two?
3 Can I get _____ a drink?
4 Get _____ a drink, please.
5 Can _____ lend _____ your mobile phone?
6 Excuse _____ . Can I speak to Laura?
7 Can you help _____ ?
8 Can I buy _____ lunch?
9 Would _____ like the bill now?
10 Can I ask _____ a question?

2 Correct the mistakes.

1 He cans play the piano.
   He can play the piano.
2 I don't can sing well.
   _____
3 Do you would like the menu?
   _____
4 Does he can play tennis?
   _____
5 Stops at the traffic lights!
   _____
6 She can fast run.
   _____
7 I like some water, please.
   _____
8 The light is red. Stops!
   _____
9 Come in. Take a seat. You have a drink!
   _____
10 Turn right! Don't to turn left!
   _____

3 Choose the correct responses.

1 I'd like a menu, please.
   a Of course. ✓   b Yes, I'd like.
2 Would you like some water?
   a No, thanks.   b No, I would.
3 Can you speak English?
   a Yes, I speak.   b Yes, I can.
4 Can I borrow your car?
   a Yes, I can.   b No, sorry.
5 Can you help me?
   a Certainly.   b Excuse me.
6 Can you play the saxophone?
   a Well.   b No, not very well.
7 Would you like some soup?
   a Yes, I'd like.   b Yes, please.
8 Can you help?
   a Sure.   b Yes, please.
9 We'd like this table, please.
   a No, thanks.   b Certainly.
10 Can I get you a drink?
   a Thanks very much.   b Yes, I can.

4 Write *R* (request), *O* (offer), *D* (direction) or *Or* (order).

1 Can I borrow your map?   R
2 Would you like lunch?   ....
3 Be quiet!   ....
4 Turn left at the supermarket.   ....
5 Stop!   ....
6 Can you stop?   ....
7 Can I get you a drink?   ....
8 Don't cross at the traffic lights.   ....
9 Go now!   ....
10 Please bring some wine.   ....

5 **Find three sentences.**

1 I can you help me please bring a friend

I can.

Can you help me, please?

Please bring a friend.

2 can you give me a drink please go

3 no I can't play the piano please

4 can you lend me your phone me at ten o'clock

5 yes I would not like a dessert thank you very much

Pronunciation: strong and weak forms of *can*

6 1.32 **Listen to the pronunciation of *can* and *can't* in these sentences.**

/kæn/ /kɑːnt/ /kən/

Can you sing? I can't play the piano. I can sing.
Yes, I can.

Now listen to five sentences and tick the pronunciation you hear.

1 /kæn/ /kɑːnt/ ✓ /kən/
2 /kæn/ /kɑːnt/ /kən/
3 /kæn/ /kɑːnt/ /kən/
4 /kæn/ /kɑːnt/ /kən/
5 /kæn/ /kɑːnt/ /kən/

Vocabulary

7 **Circle the word that is different.**

1 guitar piano saxophone sing
2 well badly beautiful slowly
3 please ask borrow lend
4 waiter map menu bill
5 cheese coffee dessert green salad
6 road sign right traffic lights

8 **Choose the correct verbs.**

1 Can you *sing / speak* Chinese?
2 How well can you *run / play* tennis?
3 Can I *lend / borrow* your car?
4 *Open / Close* the window! It's very cold.
5 Can I *get / have* you a tea or coffee?
6 Can I *ask / speak* to the manager, please?
7 We *like / 'd like* some water, please.
8 *Turn / Cross* left at the supermarket.
9 *Turn / Go* straight to the end of the street.
10 *Go / Cross* the road at the traffic lights.

Listen again

9 1.33 **Listen and tick (✓) what they would like.**

Menu

soup
bread and cheese
green salad
ice cream

Drinks

water
wine
tea
coffee

26 Comparatives

Presentation

Use the comparative form to compare two things.

Adjective	Comparative
young	young**er**
fast	fast**er**
beautiful	**more** beautiful
expensive	**less** expensive

Regular adjectives

Add *-er* to short adjectives: *younger, faster …*

Use *more/less* with long adjectives: *more beautiful, less expensive …*

Irregular adjectives

Some adjectives are irregular.

Adjective	Comparative
good	better
bad	worse

than

You often use *than* after the comparative adjective: *My car is faster than your car.*

Key spelling rules

- Double the last consonant + *-er* for some one-syllable adjectives: *hot → hotter, big → bigger …*
- Change *y* to *i*: *happy → happier, angry → angrier …*

See page 233: Spelling rules

Key vocabulary Adjectives: young/old, fast/slow, cheap/expensive, big/small, good/bad, hot/cold, long/short, tall/short, boring/interesting, dangerous, safe, beautiful, happy (*short* is the opposite of *long* and *tall*)

Exercises

1 Complete the sentences with the comparative form of the adjectives in brackets.

1 Your car is _____faster_____ (fast) than mine.
2 My brother is _____ (old) than me.
3 I can buy a laptop – they're _____ (cheap) now.
4 A bicycle is _____ (expensive) than a car.
5 South Africa is _____ (hot) than Iceland.
6 I speak good English, but hers is _____ (good).
7 He's _____ (happy) because it's the holiday.
8 You are _____ (beautiful) than ever!
9 It's _____ (safe) to travel by train than by car.

2 Look at the pictures and write comparative sentences.

1 motorbike / fast / bicycle
A motorbike is faster than a bicycle.

2 she / tall / him

3 red bike / expensive / blue bike

4 her book / interesting / his book

3 Read the sentences. Then write two sentences to compare the information.

1 Karen's twenty-nine. Tom's thirty.
Karen's younger than Tom. Tom's older than Karen.

2 The Mississippi River is 3,733 kilometres. The Amazon River is 6,712 kilometres.

3 My flat is 1,000 m². Your house is 1,500 m².

4 Today, the temperature in Rome is 21°C. London is 5°C.

27 Superlatives

Animal quiz

Can you answer these questions about animals?

1 Which is the heaviest animal in the world?
   A Blue Whale   **B** Elephant   **C** Giraffe

2 Which is the fastest animal on land?
   A Snake   **B** Cheetah   **C** Crocodile

3 Which is the slowest animal on land?
   A Elephant   **B** Tortoise   **C** Crocodile

4 Which is the loudest animal in the world?
   A Blue Whale   **B** Elephant   **C** Crocodile

5 Which animal has the longest life?
   A Elephant   **B** Giraffe   **C** Tortoise

6 Which animal is the most dangerous?
   A Crocodile   **B** Blue Whale   **C** Tortoise

heavy / heavier / heaviest

Answers: 1A 2B 3B 4A 5C 6A

Presentation

Use the superlative form to compare three or more things.

Adjective	Superlative
fast	fast**est**
heavy	heav**iest**
loud	loud**est**
dangerous	**most** dangerous

the

You use *the* before the superlative:
Blue whales are the heaviest animals.

Regular adjectives

Add -*est* to short adjectives: *fastest, heaviest …*

Use *most/least* with long adjectives: *most dangerous, least expensive …*

Irregular adjectives

Adjective	Superlative
good	best
bad	worst

Key vocabulary Animals: blue whale, cheetah, crocodile, elephant, giraffe, snake, tortoise

Exercises

1 Complete the sentences with the superlative form of the adjectives in brackets.

1 Mr Bao from Mongolia is the _____tallest_____ (tall) man in the world.

2 The _____ (short) woman in the world is 79 centimetres tall.

3 The blue whale is the _____ (big) animal in the world.

4 I think snakes are the _____ (dangerous) animals.

5 The River Nile in Egypt is the _____ (long) river in the world.

6 Damascus in Syria is the _____ (old) city in the world.

7 Luxembourg is the _____ (safe) city in Europe.

8 Moscow is the _____ (expensive) city in the world.

9 Mount Everest is the _____ (high) mountain in the world.

10 I'm sure elephants are the _____ (heavy) animals on land.

2 ⓕ1.34 Write a comparative and superlative sentence with the adjectives. Then listen and check.

1 Animal: tortoise / snake / cheetah (slow)

A snake _is slower than a cheetah._

The tortoise _is the slowest animal._

2 Country: Ethiopia / Italy / Norway (hot)

Italy _____

Ethiopia _____

3 Ocean: the Pacific Ocean / the Indian Ocean / the Mediterranean Sea (big)

The Indian Ocean _____

The Pacific Ocean _____

4 Country: Switzerland / India / Russia (small)

India _____

Switzerland _____

5 Transport: aeroplane / car / bicycle (fast)

A car _____

The aeroplane _____

3 Correct the sentences.

1 I'm the worsest at English in my class.
I'm the worst at English in my class.

2 I think Brazil is best football team in the world.

_____

3 Snakes are the more dangerous animals in my country.

_____

4 I don't think he's a gooder actor than De Niro.

_____

5 Your bags are heavy but my bag is the most heavy.

_____

65

28 Adverbs

Presentation

Use adverbs to talk about how people do something:

They play beautifully.

Do they play any songs quietly?

Regular adverbs

Add *-ly* to an adjective to make an adverb.

Adjective	Adverb
beautiful	beautiful**ly**
loud	loud**ly**
quietly	quiet**ly**
quick	quick**ly**
bad	bad**ly**

See page 233: Spelling rules

Irregular adverbs

Some adjectives and adverbs are irregular. Do not add *-ly*.

Adjective	Adverb
good	well
fast	fast
late	late
early	early
hard	hard

Position of adverbs

The adverb often comes:

- after the object of the sentence: *He plays **the saxophone well**.*
- after the verb if there is no object: *He can **play well**.* (don't say ~~He plays well the saxophone.~~)

TIP You can add *really* or *very* to some adverbs: *He plays the drums **really** loudly. She sings **very** well.*

Exercises

1 **Complete the sentences with the adverb form of the adjectives.**

1 Your sister sings ___beautifully___ (beautiful).

2 Why do you play your music _____ (loud)?

3 Please work _____ (quiet).

4 We're late! You need to walk _____ (quick).

5 Play this part of the music _____ (slow).

6 That's amazing. You play the guitar really _____ (good).

7 He speaks really _____ (fast).

8 Jane and Steve are _____ married (happy).

9 I play tennis really _____ (bad).

10 The party will end really _____ (late).

11 My mother and father work really _____ (hard).

12 I left work _____ (early).

2 🔊1.35 **Choose the correct words. Then listen and check.**

1 I play the guitar very *bad* / *badly.*

2 Her hair is *beautiful* / *beautifully.*

3 I can't hear you. Speak *loud* / *loudly* for me, please.

4 Close the door *quiet* / *quietly.* Natasha is sleeping.

5 Your dog runs *quick* / *quickly.*

6 Let's take the train. The bus is very *slow* / *slowly* at this time.

7 I'm *happy* / *happily* today. I passed my tests!

8 That music is very *loud* / *loudly*!

9 You dance really *good* / *well.*

10 Our children play *happy* / *happily* in the garden.

11 She's a *quiet* / *quietly* girl.

12 Eat your food *slow* / *slowly.* There's no hurry.

3 **Correct the adverbs.**

1 I can swim very ~~fastly.~~ *fast*

2 You played that song beautifuly.

3 I want to leave work earlily.

4 Walk quietily. There's an exam next door.

5 I speak English very goodly.

6 Do you work happyly?

4 **Complete these sentences so that they are true for you.**

1 I _____ beautifully.

2 My friend _____ quickly.

3 My teacher _____ well.

4 I speak English _____ .

5 I _____ well but I _____ badly.

29 Comparative adverbs

Who is the best employee? Who works harder? Pierre or Paolo?

Pierre starts work earlier than Paolo ...

... but Paolo goes home later than Pierre ...

... and Paolo works more quickly than Pierre ...

... but Pierre speaks better English than Paolo.

Presentation

Use comparative adverbs to compare how people do something:

Pierre starts work earlier than Paolo.

Paolo goes home later than Pierre.

With adverbs ending in *-ly*, you usually say *more + -ly*.

With some adverbs (*loud, quick, slow*) you can also add *-er*. This is more informal.

Adverb	Comparative adverb
late	later
early	earlier
hard	harder
fast	faster
loudly	more loudly / louder
quietly	more quietly
quickly	more quickly / quicker
slowly	more slowly / slower
well	better
badly	worse

Exercises

1 Complete the sentences with comparative adverbs.

1 I get up _____later_____ (late) than you.

2 He starts work _____ (early) these days.

3 I can't sing _____ (well) than Pavarotti.

4 This computer works _____ (fast) than the old one.

5 Can you drive _____ (slow), please?

6 They work _____ (hard) than my parents.

7 Pierre swims _____ (well) than Paolo.

8 Can you speak _____ (quiet), please?

9 I think girls can shout _____ (loud) than boys!

2 Read the two sentences. Compare them in two ways.

I get up at 6 a.m. You get up at 7 a.m.

1 You get up later than me.

2 I get up earlier than you.

Michael runs 1 kilometre in 7 minutes 30 seconds. Martin runs 1 kilometre in 6 minutes.

3 Michael _____

4 Martin _____

Victoria plays the piano very well. Julia plays it badly.

5 Victoria _____

6 Julia _____

3 Put the words in the order.

a speak you slowly more can? _____

b you more can speak loudly? _____

c our meeting earlier starts _____

d starts later on Tuesdays work he _____

4 ⊙1.36 Complete the telephone conversation with sentences a–d from exercise 3. Then listen and check.

A: Good morning. Can I help you?

B: Hello. Can I speak to Pierre?

A: Sorry, I can't hear you. [1] _____ ?

B: I'd like to speak to Pierre, please.

A: Sorry, he isn't here. [2] _____ . Can I take a message?

B: Yes, please. My name is Agathe. Can you tell him [3] _____ tomorrow?

A: Sorry. [4] _____ ?

B: Sure. Our meeting starts at twelve o'clock, not two o'clock tomorrow.

A: OK. Thanks.

30 Review of units 26 to 29

Grammar

1 Complete the adverts with the correct form of the words in the box.

> expensive ~~fast~~ good
> hard hot well quiet

Is your car slow?

Would you like a ¹ _faster_ car than your old one? Is your old car expensive?
Would you like a ² _____ car?
OF COURSE YOU WOULD! DRIVE A XT007 TODAY.
For the ³ _____ experience on the road!

Translators WANTED

Do you work ⁴ _____ than other people?
Can you speak Chinese ⁵ _____ ?
We need translators for our new business in Beijing.

‘ My dream holiday has a sun as ⁶ _____ as this and there are no people so it's as ⁷ _____ as this. But it isn't as expensive as this. ’

No problem. Just call:
0800 777 7000
and book a cheap dream holiday today!

2 Correct the mistake in each sentence.

1 Can you play golf better ᐱ^{than} your dad?

2 The weather today is ^{hotter} ~~hoter~~ than yesterday.

3 Blue whales are biggest animals in the world.

4 He's the hapiest student in my class.

5 I run fast than you.

6 Is he worser at English than you?

7 A tortoise goes slowly than a snake.

8 This ice cream is the bestest in the world.

9 This café is expensive than that café.

10 This TV show is funier than the other one.

3 Complete the adjectives and adverbs.

1 My brother is young ^{er} than my sister.

2 Is this the heavi _____ animal in the world?

3 Your children play very quiet _____ .

4 Can you speak more loud _____ ?

5 Paolo gets home late _____ than Pierre.

6 You sing really bad _____ !

7 Can you get up earl _____ tomorrow?

8 Walk more quick _____ , please.

4 Put the words in order.

1 bigger London than Edinburgh

_____

2 the this film other than longer isn't one

_____

3 study hard they exams their very for

_____

Pronunciation: sentence stress

5 🔊**1.37** **Listen and underline the stressed words.**

1 <u>Whales</u> are <u>bigger</u> than <u>elephants</u>.
2 Mike's bigger than Martin.
3 English is easier than Maths.
4 Your car isn't faster than mine.
5 Tom is taller than his brother.
6 This is the most expensive car.

6 **Circle the word that is different.**

1 Animals on land: cheetah   giraffe   (blue whale)
2 Places to eat and drink:
café   restaurant   supermarket
3 Places to buy things: shop   library   supermarket
4 Transport: office   bus   underground
5 When you get up: late   early   loudly
6 How you sing: slowly   well   badly
7 How you run: quickly   early   slowly

Vocabulary

7 **Write opposite adjectives in the crossword.**

Across	Down
3 bad	1 cold
6 long	2 old
7 boring	4 safe
9 fast	5 expensive
10 quiet	8 big

8 **Write the adjectives in exercise 7 in the comparative and superlative form.**

Across

3 bad – worse – worst
  good – better – best
6
7
9
10

Down

1
2
4
5
8

Listen again

9 🔊**1.38** **Listen and complete the message.**

MESSAGE

To: 1 ....
From: Agathe

The meeting starts
2 ....
tomorrow. It starts
at 12 p.m. not
3 .... p.m.

31 Present continuous

Presentation

Use the present continuous *(to be + -ing)* to talk about actions right now.

Affirmative and negative

I	'm 'm not	
He She	's isn't	having a shower.
You We They	're aren't	

Key spelling rules

- Most verbs: *read → reading, sleep → sleeping ...*
- Verbs ending consonant + *-e*: *have → having, come → coming ...*

See page 233: Spelling rules

Yes/No questions

Are	you they	
Is	he she	having a shower?

Short answers

	I	am.
Yes,	he / she / it	is.
	you / we / they	are.

	I	'm not.
No,	he / she / it	isn't.
	you / we / they	aren't.

Wh- questions

What Where	are	you they	eating?
	is	he she	

Key vocabulary Verbs: come, cook, have (a shower), play (chess), read, sleep, watch (television/a film)

Exercises

1 **Look at the pictures and write sentences. Use the present continuous.**

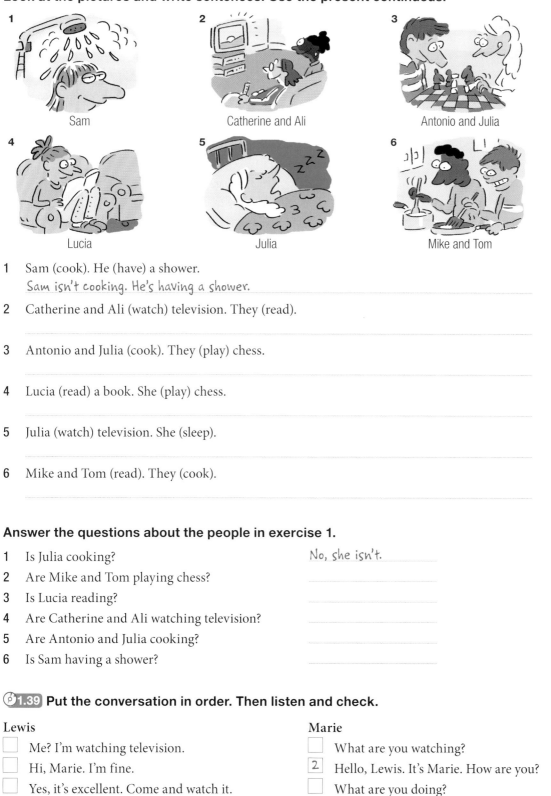

1 Sam
2 Catherine and Ali
3 Antonio and Julia
4 Lucia
5 Julia
6 Mike and Tom

1 Sam (cook). He (have) a shower.
   Sam isn't cooking. He's having a shower.

2 Catherine and Ali (watch) television. They (read).

3 Antonio and Julia (cook). They (play) chess.

4 Lucia (read) a book. She (play) chess.

5 Julia (watch) television. She (sleep).

6 Mike and Tom (read). They (cook).

2 **Answer the questions about the people in exercise 1.**

1 Is Julia cooking?   No, she isn't.
2 Are Mike and Tom playing chess?
3 Is Lucia reading?
4 Are Catherine and Ali watching television?
5 Are Antonio and Julia cooking?
6 Is Sam having a shower?

3 ⏺**1.39** **Put the conversation in order. Then listen and check.**

Lewis

☐ Me? I'm watching television.
☐ Hi, Marie. I'm fine.
☐ Yes, it's excellent. Come and watch it.
[1] Hello?
☐ I'm watching a film.

Marie

☐ What are you watching?
[2] Hello, Lewis. It's Marie. How are you?
☐ What are you doing?
☐ OK. See you in five minutes.
☐ Is it any good?

32 Present simple and present continuous
State verbs

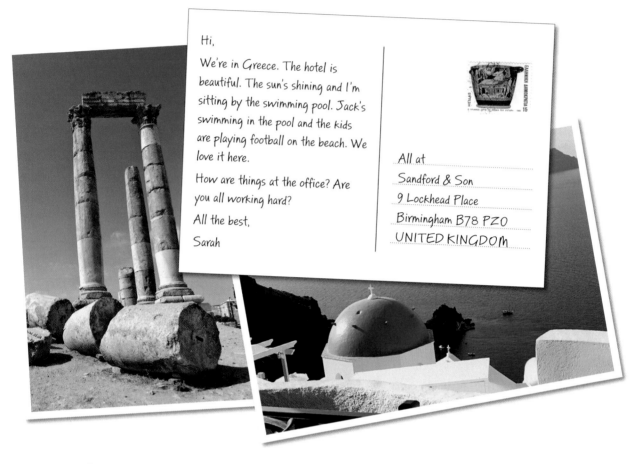

Hi,

We're in Greece. The hotel is beautiful. The sun's shining and I'm sitting by the swimming pool. Jack's swimming in the pool and the kids are playing football on the beach. We love it here.

How are things at the office? Are you all working hard?

All the best,

Sarah

All at
Sandford & Son
9 Lockhead Place
Birmingham B78 PZO
UNITED KINGDOM

Presentation

Present simple

Use the present simple to talk about …

- situations that do not change:
  Sarah lives in Birmingham.

- routines:
  She travels to work by bus.

Present continuous

Use the present continuous to talk about …

- temporary situations:
  She's staying in a hotel in Greece.

- actions now:
  Right now she isn't working. She's on holiday.

State verbs

You don't normally use these verbs in the continuous form: *be, like, love, hate, want.*

Present continuous: key spelling rules

- Verbs ending consonant + vowel + consonant: *sit → sitting, swim → swimming …*
- Verbs ending consonant + vowel + -y: *stay → staying, play → playing …*

See Unit 31 and page 233: Spelling rules

Key vocabulary Verbs: boil, cycle, do (your homework), drive, eat, freeze, hate, learn, like, live, love, make (friends), play, sit, smoke, start, stay, study, swim, take (the train), turn off, want, watch (TV), work (hard), write (to somebody)

Exercises

1 **Look at the pictures and complete the sentences. Use the present simple or present continuous of the verbs.**

1 Helen _____works_____ (work) in the hospital from Monday to Friday.

2 She _____ (not work) at the moment. It's Saturday and she _____ (read) a book in the garden.

3 She usually _____ (cycle) to work.

4 Today she _____ (not cycle) to work because it _____ (rain). She _____ (drive) her car to the hospital.

2 **Choose the correct forms.**

1 Tigers *live* / *are living* in India.

2 Usually I *drive* / *'m driving* to the office, but this week I *take* / *'m taking* the train.

3 Oh, no! It *rains* / *'s raining* again.

4 No, thank you. I *don't smoke* / *'m not smoking*.

5 A: *Do you like* / *Are you liking* opera?
  B: Yes, I *do.* / *am.*

6 A: What *do you do* / *are you doing*?
  B: I *write* / *'m writing* to my parents.

7 A: Is the tea ready?
  B: Almost. The water *boils* / *'s boiling*.

8 Water *freezes* / *'s freezing* at 0°C.

9 We *always go* / *'re always going* to the cinema at the weekend.

10 It *rains* / *'s raining* a lot in Scotland.

11 I *speak* / *'m speaking* German but not very well.

12 Ssh! I *watch* / *'m watching* a film.

13 I *have* / *'m having* lunch with my grandparents every Sunday.

14 Ari can't come out. She *does* / *'s doing* her homework.

15 Turn off the TV. Nobody *watches* / *'s watching* it.

16 *Do you want* / *Are you wanting* tea or coffee?

3 **⏺1.40 Marcia is studying Italian in Rome. Complete her email to her parents. Use the present simple or present continuous of the verbs. Then listen and check.**

○ ○ ○   New Message

Hi,
Rome is fantastic. I ¹ _____'m having_____ (have) a great time and I ² _____ (learn) a lot of Italian. School ³ _____ (start) at 09:30 every day. We ⁴ _____ (study) for four hours, then we ⁵ _____ (have) lunch. The classes ⁶ _____ (be) excellent. I ⁷ _____ (have) lunch right now. I ⁸ _____ (sit) in a beautiful café in Piazza di Spagna. I ⁹ _____ (eat) pasta and I ¹⁰ _____ (do) my homework. The other students ¹¹ _____ (be) very nice – I ¹² _____ (make) a lot of new friends.
See you soon,
Marcia

---

33 Present continuous (for future arrangements)

Man: Are you free on Saturday morning?
Woman: No, I'm not. I'm seeing Anne.
Man: What are you doing in the afternoon?
Woman: I'm playing tennis in the park but I'm not doing anything in the evening.

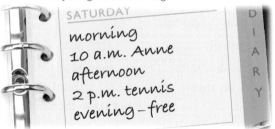

SATURDAY
morning
10 a.m. Anne
afternoon
2 p.m. tennis
evening - free

DIARY

Presentation

You can use the present continuous to talk about personal plans and future arrangements.
You often mention the time and/or place.

Key vocabulary Time references: in the morning/afternoon/evening, all day, at the weekend, next week

Exercises

1 🔊**1.41** **Put the conversation in order. Then listen and check.**

☐ *On the Beach 2*. It starts at eight o'clock.
☐ I'm not doing anything. Why?
☐ We're going to the cinema. Would you like to come?
☐ 1 What are you doing on Friday?
☐ Yes, please. What film are you seeing?

2 **Write sentences about their plans for next week. Use the present continuous.**

1   I / see Anne / Monday morning
    I'm seeing Anne on Monday morning.

2   I / go to the cinema / Tuesday evening

3   Louise / not have lunch with Rita / Sunday

4   Max / go to the beach / Friday morning

5   Where / you have dinner / Wednesday evening?

6   Who / they meet / Monday morning?

3 Imagine this is your diary. Match the questions to the answers.

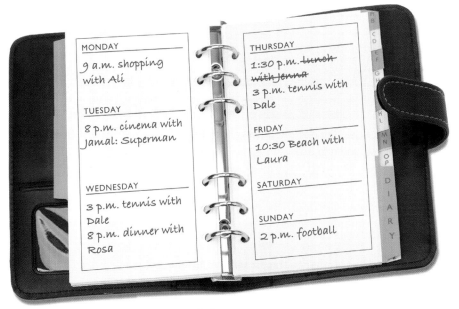

MONDAY
9 a.m. shopping with Ali

TUESDAY
8 p.m. cinema with Jamal: Superman

WEDNESDAY
3 p.m. tennis with Dale
8 p.m. dinner with Rosa

THURSDAY
1:30 p.m. ~~lunch with Jenna~~
3 p.m. tennis with Dale

FRIDAY
10:30 Beach with Laura

SATURDAY

SUNDAY
2 p.m. football

1 Are you free on Monday morning? **g**
2 Who are you going to the beach with? ☐
3 Are you playing football at the weekend? ☐
4 Are you seeing Rosa next week? ☐
5 What are you doing on Saturday? ☐
6 What are you doing on Tuesday evening? ☐
7 What film are you seeing? ☐
8 Are you free on Wednesday morning? ☐
9 When are you going to the beach? ☐
10 When are you seeing Jenna? ☐

a Yes, I am, but I'm playing tennis in the afternoon.
b Jamal and I are going to the cinema. Would you like to come?
c *Superman.*
d Yes, I am. We're playing on Sunday afternoon.
e On Friday.
f Laura.
g ~~No, I'm not. I'm going shopping with~~ Ali.
h I'm not seeing Jenna this week.
i Yes, I am. I'm having dinner with her on Wednesday.
j I'm not doing anything all day.

4 Look at the diary again. Complete the questions for these answers.

1 What .... *are you doing on* .... Wednesday afternoon?
   I'm playing tennis with Dale.
2 Who .... Wednesday evening?
   Rosa.
3 When .... ?
   On Sunday.
4 What .... ?
   Nothing.
5 Where .... Friday?
   To the beach.
6 When .... with Ali?
   On Monday morning.

34 *going to*

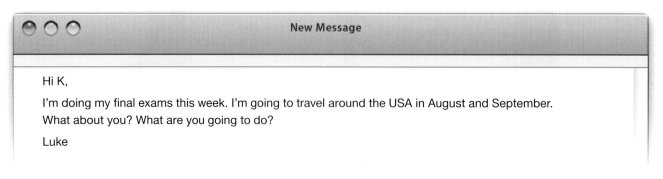

New Message

Hi K,

I'm doing my final exams this week. I'm going to travel around the USA in August and September.
What about you? What are you going to do?

Luke

Presentation

Use *going to* for future intentions. It is similar to the present continuous.

Affirmative and negative

I	'm 'm not		
He She	's isn't	going to	travel around the USA.
You We They	're aren't		

Yes/No questions

Are	you	going to	travel around the USA?

Short answers

Yes, I am.	No, I'm not.

Wh- questions

What	are you	going to	do?

> **Key vocabulary** Education: university, primary school, college, exam

Exercises

1 What are they going to do in the summer? Answer the questions.

Mike   Julia

George and Morry   Nicola

1 What's Mike going to do?   He's going to travel around the USA.
2 What's Julia going to do?
3 What are George and Morry going to do?
4 What's Nicola going to do?

2 **Answer the questions.**

1 Is Mike going to travel around the USA?   Yes, he is.

2 Are George and Morry going to have a holiday?

3 Is Mike going to learn to drive?

4 Is Julia going to work in a laboratory?

5 Are George and Morry going to travel around the USA?

3 **Complete the conversation with** *going to* **and the verbs in brackets.**

Richard: ¹ _____ (we book) a taxi tonight?

Sally: No. It's OK. Michelle ² _____ (drive) us there.

Richard: But she ³ _____ (not know) anyone at the party.

Sally: I know. She isn't coming to the party. She ⁴ _____ (meet) a friend in
          town so she ⁵ _____ (take) us.

Richard: Oh, I see.

4 🎧 **1.42** **Complete the conversation with** *going to* **and the verbs in the box. Then listen and check.**

~~do~~	do	stay	travel	teach	work

Jeff: What ¹ _____ are you going to do _____ in the summer, Teresa?

Teresa: Alec and I ² _____ English in Africa.

Jeff: How long ³ _____ there?

Teresa: Six weeks. We ⁴ _____ in a primary school in Sudan.
         What ⁵ _____ , Jeff?

Jeff: I ⁶ _____ around Europe.

5 **Put the words in order.**

1 are do going in the summer to what you ?   What are you going to do in the summer?

2 a I'm going have holiday not to

3 a in going I'm laboratory to work

4 are going study to what you ?

5 Physics going I'm study to

6 are study what to after you going university ?

6 **There is one word missing in each sentence. Write it in.**

1 I ∧'m going to buy a new jacket.

2 We're going leave at three o'clock.

3 Maggie is to get a job in the college.

4 They're going to home after school.

5 He going to meet us there?

6 When are you going have lunch?

7 I think it going to snow tonight.

8 Are Jemima and Hugo to work in an office?

79

35 Review of units 31 to 34

Grammar

1 **What are they doing? Look at the pictures and write sentences.**

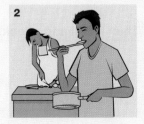

1 He's playing tennis.
2 ....
3 ....
4 ....
5 ....
6 ....

2 **Write the sentences in exercise 1 in the negative form.**

1 He isn't playing tennis.
2 ....
3 ....
4 ....
5 ....
6 ....

3 **Write sentences about your plans. Use the present continuous of *go, have* or *play*.**

Monday	¹ tennis, Jules
Tuesday	² cinema, Mazda
Wednesday	³ beach, my mum
Thursday	⁴ library, Sarah
Friday	⁵ dinner, Joe
Saturday	⁶ shopping, Nicky
Sunday	⁷ lunch, my family

1 On Monday I'm playing tennis with Jules.
2 ....
3 ....
4 ....
5 ....
6 ....
7 ....

4 **Look at the diary again. Complete the questions.**

1 What .... are you doing on Monday .... ?
   I'm playing tennis.
2 Who .... ?
   Jules.
3 What .... ?
   I'm going to the beach.
4 Where .... ?
   We're going to the library.
5 When .... ?
   I'm seeing him on Friday.
6 Who .... ?
   Nicky.
7 What .... ?
   I'm having lunch with my family.

5 What are they going to do? Write sentences.

1 2 3

4 5 6

1 I / read my emails
  I'm going to read my emails.

2 I / phone my mum

3 He / have a piano lesson

4 She / study in the library

5 We / play tennis

6 They / go shopping

Pronunciation: contractions

6 🔊1.43 **Listen to six sentences. How many words do you hear? Contracted forms (*I'm, aren't, isn't*) count as one word.**

1	*3*	4	
2		5	
3		6	

Vocabulary

7 Complete with *have* or *play*.

1 *play* the piano
2 _____ tennis with somebody
3 _____ lunch with somebody
4 _____ a shower
5 _____ basketball
6 _____ dinner with somebody
7 _____ the guitar
8 _____ chess
9 _____ a great time

8 Complete the conversation with the phrases in the box.

> Are you free on Saturday evening?
> Can I call you back? Is it any good?
> It's excellent.

Clive: Hi. John. ¹ _____

John: I'm not sure. Why?

Clive: We're going to the cinema. We're going to see *Brain Dead 2*.

John: ² _____

Clive: ³ _____

John: I think I'm free. ⁴ _____

Clive: Sure.

9 Match 1–6 to a–f to complete her plans.

1 First of all, she's going to study [c]
2 Then she's going to live in [ ]
3 In Paris she's going to work [ ]
4 She's going to stay with [ ]
5 After that, she's going to travel [ ]
6 Then she's going to come [ ]

a a French family.   d home.
b around Australia.   e in a bank.
c ~~French for six months.~~   f Paris for a year.

Listen again

10 🔊1.44 **Listen and complete the conversation.**

A: What ¹ _____ Friday?

B: I ² _____ anything. Why?

A: We ³ _____ cinema. Would you like to come?

B: Yes, please. What ⁴ _____ seeing?

A: *On the Beach 2*. It ⁵ _____ o'clock.

was/were

○ ○ ○   **New Message**

Hi Rona

Sorry, I wasn't at home on Saturday but I was busy. It was my sister's birthday so my family were at her house. It was a great party! How was your weekend? Can we meet tomorrow?

Best wishes

Sam

Presentation

Use *was/were* to talk about the past.

Present	Past
am/is	was
are	were

Affirmative

I / He / She / It	was	busy.
You / We / They	were	

Negative

I / He / She / It	wasn't	at home on Saturday.
You / We / They	weren't	

Yes/No questions

Was	I / he / she / it	at the party?
Were	you / we / they	

Short answers

Yes,	I / he / she / it	was.
	you / we / they	were.

No,	I / he / she / it	wasn't.
	you / we / they	weren't.

> **Key vocabulary** Time references: yesterday, last night, on Saturday, last year, in 1999
> Special days: birthday, party, wedding, anniversary

Exercises

1 Read the email. Choose the correct forms.

○ ○ ○   **New Message**

Hello Sam
I ¹(was) / were busy on Sunday. It ² *was / were* my parents' 25th wedding anniversary. My brothers and sisters ³ *was / were* all at their house for the party. It ⁴ *was / were* great fun!
How ⁵ *was / were* your sister's birthday? ⁶ *Was / Were* there many people at her party?
Can you meet me at five tomorrow?
Rona

2 **Read about George's parents and Yukio's twin brothers. Are sentences 1–8 true (T) or false (F)?**

My father and mother were born in 1957. He was from the USA but they were at Oxford University in England and their wedding was in England. Last year was their 25th wedding anniversary.

My brothers were born on 25th October, 1989. They were both at school at the same time but they weren't at the same university. Last week they were both twenty-one years old. There was a big party at our house for them.

1 George's parents were born in the same year. ....

2 They were from the USA. ....

3 His mother was at Oxford University. ....

4 Their wedding was last year. ....

5 Yukio's brothers were born on the same day. ....

6 They weren't at the same school. ....

7 Their twenty-first birthday was last week. ....

8 It wasn't a big party. ....

3 **1.45** **Complete the conversations with *was, were, wasn't* or *weren't*. Then listen and check.**

Conversation 1

A: Hello, Nancy. How [1].............. your weekend?

B: Great! Mike and I [2].............. in New York.

A: That's amazing!

B: It [3].............. my birthday.

A: Happy Birthday!

Conversation 2

C: [4].............. James here this morning?

D: No, he [5].............. .

C: Where [6].............. he?

D: I think he [7].............. in a meeting with Sue and Rona. They [8].............. in Sue's office.

C: No, they [9].............. because I was with Sue in her office all morning!

Conversation 3

E: How [10].............. your sister's wedding?

F: Really good!

E: [11].............. it big?

F: No, there [12].............. many people, just family and good friends.

37 *There was/were*

When I was a child ...

Now

When I was a child, there was a park and a river with a bridge across it. I think there was a café on the left and there were some trees and houses behind it. And twenty years ago there weren't these shops and the road in front wasn't busy with all these cars.

Presentation

Affirmative and negative

There	was wasn't	a	park.
	were	some	houses.
	weren't	any	

Yes/No questions

Was	there	a	park?
Were		any	houses?

Short answers

Yes, there was/were.	No, there wasn't/weren't.

Key vocabulary **Places in town:** park, shop, café, road, cinema, pedestrian crossing, playground, bridge, skyscraper
Location: in front, behind, on the left/right, near here, next to, in the middle, across

Exercises

1 Complete the sentences with *there was, there were, there wasn't* or *there weren't*.

1 _____There was_____ a cinema next to the post office.

2 When I was a boy, _____ three houses here. Now it's an office block.

3 A: Was there a busy road here?

B: No, _____ . It was quiet.

4 _____ a shop but there was a café.

5 A: Were there houses or skyscrapers?

B: When I was here two years ago, I think _____ some skyscrapers.

6 A: Were there any trees next to the pond?

B: No, _____ .

2 Look at the pictures and answer the questions.

Two years ago   Now

1 Was there a road here?   Yes, there was.

2 Was there a market in the square?   No, there wasn't. There were cars.

3 Was there a café next to the bank?

4 Were there any shops on the left?

5 Were there two restaurants on the right?

6 Was there a pedestrian crossing?

7 Was there an Indian restaurant?

3 Match 1–8 to a–h.

1	Was there a café	b	a	there was a playground in the park.
2	When I was a student, there		b	~~on the left?~~
3	Last year there were		c	there wasn't.
4	Two years ago, I		d	think there was a bank next to the cinema.
5	When I was child,		e	wasn't a library here.
6	Were there		f	two restaurants on the right.
7	Was		g	there a car park here?
8	Was there a shop on the corner? No,		h	two bridges across the river?

38 *could* (past ability)

Ludwig van Beethoven

(1770–1827) **Composer**

Beethoven was born in Germany. When he was a child, he could play the organ very well. Later in life he couldn't hear but he could write music.

Presentation

Use the modal verb *could* to describe ability in the past.

He could play the organ very well.
He couldn't hear his music.
Could he play the organ?

TIP You often use *How well/far …?* with *could*:
How well could he play the guitar? Very well.
How far could he run? About twenty kilometres.

Key vocabulary Occupations: composer, boxer, writer, scientist, painter, singer

Exercises

1 Complete the texts with *could* or *couldn't*.

Muhammad Ali

(1942–) **Boxer**

When he was at school, Muhammad Ali ¹ _____couldn't_____ read very well but he ² _____ move very fast!

Helen Keller

(1880–1968) **Writer**

When she was a child, she ³ _____ see or hear but when she was an adult she ⁴ _____ speak and write books.

Albert Einstein

(1879–1955) Scientist

When he was a child, he ⁵_____ speak well but he was the best student in the class.

Pablo Picasso

(1881–1973) Painter

His father was an art teacher but when Picasso was thirteen he ⁶_____ paint better than his father. He was born in Spain but he ⁷_____ also speak French.

Edith Piaf

(1915–1963) Singer

Between the ages of three and seven, Edith ⁸_____ see and from eight to fourteen she ⁹_____ hear. But when she was an adult she ¹⁰_____ sing and was famous around the world.

2 🎧1.46 **Complete the conversations with the sentences in the box. Then listen and check.**

> How well could you play the piano   How far could you run?   ~~Could you speak Chinese~~
> I couldn't play tennis   Could your father speak Chinese?   What could he play?

Conversation 1

A: ¹ Could you speak Chinese _____ when you were a child?

B: Yes, I could. My mother was Chinese and my father was English.

A: ² _____

B: No, he couldn't, but my mother could speak English.

Conversation 2

C: ³ _____ when you were a child?

D: Not very well, but I could play the violin. My father was a music teacher.

C: ⁴ _____

D: The piano, the violin and the saxophone, but he couldn't play the guitar.

Conversation 3

E: Do you run nowadays?

F: No, but when I was at school I could run a long way.

E: ⁵ _____

F: A half marathon. But I couldn't swim very well. Could you?

E: Yes, I could, but ⁶ _____

39 *Could …?* and *Would you like …?* (polite requests and offers)

Man: Hello, could I speak to Shelby, please?
Woman: Sorry, Shelby isn't here. Would you like to leave a message?
Man: Thanks, could you tell her I called?
Woman: Sure. Could I have your name, please?
Man: Yes, it's Hanif.
Woman: Could you spell that?
Man: H-A-N-I-F.

Presentation

Use *Could I/you* + verb …? for polite requests and *Would you like* + *to* -infinitive …? for polite offers.

> Could I have your name please?

> Could you spell that?

> Would you like to leave a message?

You can also use *Can …?* for requests but *Could …?* is more polite and formal.

TIP Don't say ~~Could I to have your name? Would you like leave a message?~~

Responses to requests and offers: *Sure. / Yes … / Thanks very much. / Certainly. / Thanks, but …*

TIP Don't say ~~No, I wouldn't. No, you couldn't.~~ It isn't polite.

Key vocabulary Verbs: call, borrow, email, give, help, leave, lend, order, see, speak (to), take, tell (me/her), watch

Exercises

1 **1.47** Complete the conversations with *could* or *would*. Then listen and check.

Conversation 1

A: Hello. [1]____Could____ I speak to Mr Gates, please?

B: I'm sorry, he's out. [2]_____ you like to leave a message?

A: Thanks. [3]_____ he email the photographs to me?

B: Sure. [4]_____ I have your name, please?

A: Yes, it's Carrie Aitken. [5]_____ you give him my email address?

B: Of course.

A: It's carrie@morris.com.

Conversation 2

C: Good afternoon. ⁶_____ you like to order?

D: Yes, please.⁷_____ I have a pizza, please?

C: Certainly. ⁸_____ you like anything to drink?

D: I'd like some water and ⁹_____ I see the wine menu, please?

C: Of course.

Conversation 3

E: What's this DVD?

F: It's a film about a family in America. They buy a house with ghosts in! ¹⁰_____ you like to borrow it?

E: Yes, it sounds great. What about this one with Tom Cruise? ¹¹_____ I watch it, too?

F: Sure, but ¹²_____ I have them back by Friday?

Conversation 4

G: ¹³_____ you look at my car, please?

H: Yes, sure. The engine doesn't sound good. ¹⁴_____ you leave it here until tomorrow?

G: OK. See you later.

H: One moment! ¹⁵_____ you like to give me the keys?

G: Sorry, I nearly forgot!

2 Put the pronouns in the box into the sentences.

> him + you   them   we   me

1   Could ⌃ leave a message?
       |

2   Would like to buy something, madam?

3   Could you give your number again, please? I can't find it.

4   Harry is out. Would you like to call you later?

5   I'd like some soup and she'd like a salad. And could see the wine menu, please?

6   You can borrow the films but could I have back by the weekend?

3 Write requests and offers.

1   would / like me / help you   *Would you like me to help you?*

2   could / leave / message

3   could / lend / me / DVD

4   would / like / speak / Marc

5   could / borrow / pen

6   could / spell / name

7   would / like / something / drink

8   would / like / borrow / car

9   could / lend / mobile phone

10   would / like / see / menu

40 Review of units 36 to 39

Grammar

1 Complete the sentences with the words in the box.

could   couldn't   ~~was~~   wasn't   were   weren't

Frida Kahlo

Edgar Degas

Yo Yo Ma

Bruce Lee

Celine Dion

The Wright brothers

1 Frida Kahlo _____was_____ born in Mexico.

2 At the age of four, Yo Yo Ma _____ play the cello.

3 There _____ fourteen children in Celine Dion's family.

4 For the last twenty years of artist Edgar Degas' life, he _____ see.

5 Bruce Lee's parents were from Hong Kong but he _____ born there.

6 The Wright brothers _____ graduates from high school or university.

2 Complete these sentences so that they are true for you.

1 I was born in _____ .

2 I could read at the age of _____ .

3 There were _____ children in my mother's family.

4 When I was a child I couldn't _____ but I can now!

3 Put the conversation in order.

☐ Yes, it's 0770 768 3322.

☐ Yes, please. Could you tell him Nigella called?

☐ 1 Hello. Could I speak to Raymond, please?

☐ So that's Nigella on 0770 768 3322.

☐ Sure. Could I have your number?

☐ That's right. Thanks. Bye.

☐ I'm sorry, he's out. Would you like to leave a message?

4 Correct the sentences.

1 They ~~wasn't~~ at the party.
They weren't at the party.

2 Sorry, I can't come yesterday.

3 I were born in Brazil.

4 There was houses on the left.

5 Would you like a sit here?

6 Could I to order some ice cream?

7 Was they born in Italy?

8 Could you say him I called?

9 Could I lend your car?

Pronunciation: strong and weak forms of *was*

5 (1.48) **Listen to the pronunciation of *was* and *wasn't* in these sentences.**

/wəz/
He was here yesterday.

/wɒz/   /wɒz/
Was he here yesterday? Yes, he was.

/wɒznt/
She wasn't at home.

Now listen to five sentences and tick the pronunciation you hear.

1	/wəz/	/wɒz/ ✓	/wɒznt/
2	/wəz/	/wɒz/	/wɒznt/
3	/wəz/	/wɒz/	/wɒznt/
4	/wəz/	/wɒz/	/wɒznt/
5	/wəz/	/wɒz/	/wɒznt/

6 **Read about a town and write the places on the map.**

There was a supermarket on the left of the restaurant. The bus station was next to the supermarket. The bank was between the bus station and the cinema. The café was on the right of the cinema and on the left of the post office. There was a train station between the restaurant and the post office.

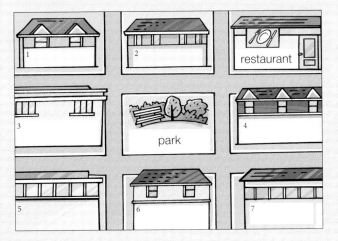

Vocabulary

7 **Circle the word that is different.**

1 sister (boxer) father grandmother
2 cinema café skyscraper car
3 singer piano violin saxophone
4 composer bridge writer painter
5 today birthday wedding anniversary

8 **Complete the questions, requests and offers with the verbs in the box.**

buy	have	leave	lend
order	run	speak	spell

1 Would you like to ___order___ dinner?

2 Would you like to _____ a message?

3 A: Could I _____ your name, please?

   B: Yes, it's Sarah Hunt.

4 A: Could you _____ your name?

   B: Yes, it's S-O-P-H-I-E.

5 A: Could you _____ me this book?

   B: OK, but can I have it back by Friday?

6 A: Could I _____ to Rona, please?

7 A: How far can he _____?

   B: About 20 kilometres.

8 A: Would you like to _____ anything?

   B: Yes, please. I'd like two kilos of apples.

Listen again

9 (1.49) **Listen. Are the sentences true (T) or false (F)?**

1 Nancy was in New York at the weekend.   T

2 It was her wedding anniversary.   _____

3 James wasn't here in the morning.   _____

4 Sue and Rona were with James.   _____

5 It was a big wedding.   _____

6 There weren't any family or friends.   _____

41 Past simple (regular verbs)

Curriculum Vitae

JAMES LAKE

1980:	Born
1998–1999:	Round-the-world gap year
1999–2005:	Medical College
2006–2007:	Volunteer doctor in Africa
2007–Present:	Work in hospital

> I was born in 1980. When I finished school, I travelled around the world and visited China, Australia and parts of South America. In 1999, I started college and studied medicine for six years. After I graduated from college, I worked in Africa for a year and then I started my job at the hospital in 2007.

Presentation

Use the past simple to talk about finished actions and events.

Regular verbs

Add *-ed* to regular verbs to form the past simple: *started, finished*.

I / You / He / She / It / We / They	started finished	college in 1999.

TIP Verbs have one form in the past simple.

Past simple (regular verbs): key spelling rules

- Two syllable verbs ending with *-y: study → studied* (not *studyed*)
- Verbs ending with *-e: live → lived*
- Many verbs ending in vowel + consonant (not *-w, -x* or *-y*) double the consonant: *travel → travelled, stop → stopped* (not *traveled, stoped*)

See page 234: Spelling rules

Pronunciation

With verbs ending with a /t/ or /d/ sound (e.g. *start, need, graduate)*, *-ed* adds an extra syllable: *start* = one syllable, *started* = two syllables (start / ed).

Key vocabulary Regular verbs: finish, graduate, join, live, qualify, start, stop, study, travel, visit, walk, work
Time references: in 1999, last night/month/year, two years ago, for three years, yesterday, this morning, on Monday, then

Exercises

1 Read the CV. Are sentences 1–6 true (T) or false (F)?

C V

1982: Born
1987–2000: School
2001–2005: University
2005–present: Accountancy firm

1 He started work in 2006. ....
2 He finished school in 2000. ....
3 He studied at university for two years. ....
4 He started school in 1987. ....
5 He was born in 1982. ....
6 He joined an accountancy firm in 2005. ....

2 Which are correct? Correct the spelling mistakes.

1 studyed   *studied*
2 tried   ✓
3 visitted   ....
4 played   ....

5 graduated   ....
6 stoped   ....
7 traveled   ....
8 qualifyed   ....

3 Complete the sentences with the past simple of the verbs.

1 I ____*started*____ (start) this job four years ago.
2 They .... (finish) work at nine o'clock last night.
3 Richard .... (graduate) from Oxford University last month.
4 We .... (visit) the Taj Mahal in India last year.
5 I .... (work) for Microsoft for three years.
6 She .... (travel) home by taxi.
7 They .... (walk) home yesterday.
8 Sally .... (stop) work at lunchtime yesterday.
9 My family .... (live) in Canada for two years.
10 We .... (study) English for two hours this morning.

4 🔊 1.50 Read about Nicole and complete the text. Then listen and check.

1999	Finish school
1999	Start university
2003	Graduate with Spanish degree
2003–4	Travel around South America with friend
2004–5	Study for teaching certificate / Qualify in 2005
2005	Join private language school

I [1] .... school in 1999 and I [2] .... university in the same year. After I [3] .... from university with a degree in Spanish, I [4] .... around South America with a friend for nearly a year. After that I [5] .... for a certificate in teaching and [6] .... in 2005. Finally I [7] .... a private language school where I still teach Spanish today.

42 Past simple (irregular verbs)

Hi Safi

We're having a great time. We got to the hotel on Saturday and went straight to the beach. We sat there all day and swam in the sea. On Sunday we took a taxi to the local market and bought some delicious bread and cheese. We ate our lunch in the park outside the palace. Then we did some sightseeing in the afternoon. We're back on the beach today!

Love

Anna

Presentation

Irregular verbs

Some verbs are irregular. They do not add *-ed: go → went* (not ~~goed~~), *make → made* (not ~~maked~~).

See page 235: Irregular verbs

> **Key vocabulary** Collocations (verb + noun): do homework, go sightseeing / do some sightseeing, get up, go shopping / do some shopping, make lunch, take a taxi

Exercises

1 Match the past simple form.

~~ate~~ bought did gave got had made sat saw swam took went

1	eat	ate	5	get		9	buy	
2	sit		6	go		10	take	
3	do		7	have		11	give	
4	swim		8	make		12	see	

2 Complete the sentences with the past simple of the verbs.

1 We _____ate_____ (eat) fish at a restaurant last night.
2 I _____ (go) to Spain on holiday last summer.
3 She _____ (buy) a new suit for work at the weekend.
4 I _____ (have) a bicycle when I was a child.
5 They _____ (do) their homework last night.
6 We _____ (swim) in the pool in the park on Sunday.
7 You _____ (take) a taxi to the station last week.
8 She _____ (make) lunch for us yesterday.
9 He _____ (get) up late this morning.
10 I _____ (sit) in the sun all afternoon.
11 We _____ (give) her a camera for her birthday.
12 They _____ (see) some horses on the beach this morning.

3 ⓐ1.51 Complete the conversation with the past simple of the verbs in the box. Then listen and check.

| buy   do   eat   ~~get up~~   go   have   sit   swim   take |

A: How was your holiday?
B: Great! We ¹ _____got up_____ late every day and ² _____ in the hotel pool before breakfast.
A: How was the food at the hotel?
B: Not bad, but we usually ³ _____ in one of the local restaurants. We ⁴ _____ some delicious fish dishes.
A: So, were you near the coast?
B: Yes, we were. We ⁵ _____ the hotel bus down to the sea and ⁶ _____ on the beach in the afternoon.
A: Were there many places to visit?
B: Mark ⁷ _____ sightseeing but I wasn't interested. I ⁸ _____ some shopping on the last day. Look! I ⁹ _____ this beautiful bracelet at a local market.

4 Regular or irregular verbs? Correct the mistakes.

1 maked _____made_____
2 took ✓
3 visited _____
4 goed _____
5 studied _____
6 buyed _____
7 walked _____
8 eated _____
9 sitted _____
10 swimmed _____
11 haved _____
12 took _____
13 travelled _____
14 joinned _____
15 tryed _____
16 stopped _____
17 finished _____
18 gived _____

43 *did/didn't* (negative and questions)

A: Did you leave home when you were eighteen?
B: Yes, I did. Did you?
A: No, I didn't. I was twenty-four. That's normal in my country.

C: Did you go to university?
D: No, I didn't. I started work after school and then I met my first husband.
C: Did you have any children?
D: No, we didn't and we got divorced a year later. Then I got married to Roger. We celebrated our twentieth anniversary yesterday.
C: Congratulations!

Presentation

Use ***didn't*** for negative sentences in the past simple.

Use ***Did ...?*** for questions in the past simple.

Use ***did*** or ***didn't*** for short answers.

Negative

I / You / He / She / We / They	didn't	go	to university.

TIP Say *They didn't get married.* (don't say ~~They didn't got married.~~)

Questions

Did	I / you / he / she / we / they	go	to university?

TIP Say *Did you work there?* (don't say ~~Did you worked there?~~)

Short answers

Yes, I / you / he / she / we / they did.	No, I / you / he / she / we / they didn't.

Key vocabulary **Life events:** leave school, start work, leave home, get married/divorced, have children, celebrate an anniversary/a birthday
People in your life: partner (≠ husband/wife)

Exercises

1 Write a past simple sentence for each picture 1–8. Use the phrases in the box.

> get divorced get married ~~leave school~~
> meet new partner not get married again ~~not go to university~~
> not have any children start work in an office

1 She left school in 1995.
2 She didn't go to university.
3 _____
4 _____
5 _____
6 _____
7 _____
8 _____

2 Complete the questions and answers with *did* or *didn't*.

1 A: _____Did_____ you study English at school?
   B: No, I _____ .
2 A: _____ you get married?
   B: Yes, I _____ . I got married to Bill.
3 A: _____ you have children?
   B: Yes, we had two. Susie is eight and Stella is five.
4 A: _____ Bill leave home before university?
   B: No, he _____ . He left home after university.

3 🔊1.52 Write the questions for these answers. Then listen and check.

1 A: Did _____you get married_____ ?
   B: Yes, I did. I got married in 1981.
2 A: Did _____ at university?
   B: No, I didn't. I met Bill after university.
3 A: Did _____ any children?
   B: Yes, I had a girl. Michelle is three.
4 A: Did _____ last night?
   B: No, I didn't. I'm doing my homework now.
5 A: Did _____ to the airport?
   B: No, I took a taxi. It's faster than the bus.
6 A: Did _____ to Spain on holiday?
   B: No, we didn't. We went to France.
7 A: Did _____ late this morning?
   B: No, I didn't. I got up early.

1995

1998

44 Past simple questions
Object and subject questions

Igor: I'd like to do a language course in England next summer.

Saskia: Good idea! I did a course in Brighton last summer.

Igor: Where did you study?

Saskia: I studied at the Seafront School of English.

Igor: Who organised your accommodation?

Saskia: Someone at the language school. I stayed with an English family. They were really nice.

Igor: How were the meals?

Saskia: Not bad actually. Breakfast was delicious.

Presentation

Use past simple questions to ask about finished events in the past:

Where did you study?

Who organised your accommodation?

How were the meals?

Object questions

You often ask questions in the past simple with *did*. You want information about the object of a sentence.

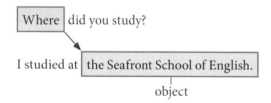

Subject questions

You can also ask questions about the subject of the sentence. Do not use *did* with a subject question.

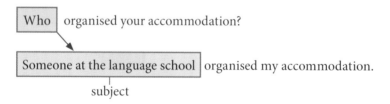

TIP Remember not to use *did* with *was/were* questions (see Unit 36).
Say *How were the meals?* (don't say *How did the meals be?*)

Exercises

1 **Put the words in order to make questions.**

1   stay did where you   *Where did you stay?*

2   stayed there who

3   did what you do yesterday

4   made sandwich who your

5   how many to the party went people

6   plans what changed your

7   did TV programme the what time start

2 **Match the responses a–g to the questions 1–7 in exercise 1.**

a   I didn't go because the weather was bad.   ☐

b   Gordon and Ann.   ☐

c   Eight o'clock.   ☐

d   I played tennis with Rafa.   ☐

e   At the Belvedere Hotel. | 1 |

f   About thirty people.   ☐

g   My mother made it.   ☐

3 **Are questions 1–7 in exercise 1 subject or object questions? Write *S* or *O*.**

1 | O | 2 ☐   3 ☐   4 ☐   5 ☐   6 ☐   7 ☐

4 **🎧 1.53 Write questions for these answers. Then listen and check.**

1   A: When *did she leave home?*

B: She left home in 2006.

2   A: What

B: They studied Biology at university.

3   A: Who

B: Martin and Rachel studied Biology at university.

4   A: When

B: I started my job five years ago.

5   A: What

B: The weather changed my plans. It was raining.

6   A: Where

B: I met Sheila in Australia.

7   A: Why

B: I didn't like my boss so I left my job.

8   A: Who

B: My mother lived in this house.

9   A: How long

B: We travelled in Patagonia for six months.

45 Review of units 41 to 44

Grammar

1 Write the sentences in the past simple.

1 I eat breakfast at seven o'clock.
   I ate breakfast at seven o'clock.

2 They go on Tuesday.

3 We don't have time for lunch.

4 Who lives here?

5 Do you know her?

6 Why do you walk to work?

7 Sorry, I'm not at home.

8 How far do you swim?

2 Correct the mistakes.

1 Did you liked Spain?
   Did you like Spain?

2 When do you lived there?

3 Who did wrote that book?

4 I studied in Bologna for a year.

5 We didn't went to the cinema last night.

6 Why you leave university early?

7 Did you visited the Eiffel Tower?

8 She maked a delicious pasta dish.

9 When you get divorced?

3 Complete the timeline with the phrases in the box.

> in 1990   last month
> last week   last year   this morning
> two weeks ago   yesterday

- two minutes ago
- 1 ....
- 2 ....
- 3 ....
- 4 ....
- 5 ....
- 6 ....
- 7 ....

4 Write the past simple of the verbs.

1 do   did
2 leave
3 get
4 celebrate
5 go
6 take
7 make
8 graduate
9 stop
10 travel

5 Complete the sentences with the past simple verbs from exercise 4.

1 Suzy and Jane _____ shopping for new shoes yesterday.

2 Karen _____ school in 2008.

3 Tom and Natalie _____ their twentieth wedding anniversary last month.

4 David _____ his homework and then he watched a DVD.

5 Petra _____ around Europe for six months last year.

6 Mel _____ smoking three weeks ago.

7 Julia _____ from university with a degree in Physics last June.

8 I _____ a taxi to the restaurant because it was raining.

9 Matt and Kathy _____ married last summer.

10 Jenny _____ dinner but she didn't eat anything.

6 Number the events in order.

a We joined the same company after university. ☐

b I left school in 1998. ☐

c I met my husband in my final year at university. ☐

d We had our first child last year. ☐

e I started university straight after. ☐

f I was born three years later. ☐

g My parents met in 1977. ☐ 1

h They got married three years later. ☐

Pronunciation: syllables

7 🔊1.54 Listen to these verbs. How many syllables are there?

1 started _____ 2
2 finished _____
3 studied _____
4 joined _____
5 visited _____
6 worked _____
7 played _____
8 stopped _____
9 travelled _____
10 lived _____
11 walked _____
12 graduated _____

Listen again

8 🔊1.55 Listen and choose the correct answers.

1 Did they get up late every day?
   a Yes, they did. ✓
   b No, they didn't.
   c Yes, they got.

2 Did they swim in the pool after breakfast?
   a Yes, they did.
   b No, they didn't.
   c No, they swam.

3 Was the fish good at the local restaurants?
   a Yes, it was.
   b No, it wasn't.
   c Yes, they were.

4 Were they near the coast?
   a Yes, they were.
   b No, it wasn't.
   c No, they weren't.

5 Did they walk to the beach?
   a Yes, they walked.
   b No, they didn't.
   c No, they did take the bus.

6 Did she do some sightseeing?
   a Yes, Mark did.
   b Yes, she did.
   c No, she didn't.

7 When did she go shopping?
   a Yes, she did.
   b On the last day.
   c No, she didn't.

8 What did she buy?
   a Yes, she did.
   b Yes, she bought.
   c A bracelet.

46 must/mustn't

Bella: Bye, Dad.
Dad: Bye, Bella. And don't forget – you must be home by ten-thirty.
Bella: What? Ten-thirty? You're joking!
Dad: No, I'm not. You mustn't be late. Bye, Bella.
Bella: But …

Presentation

Use *must* and *mustn't* to talk about obligation and prohibition.

Affirmative and negative

I / You / He / She / It / We / They	must / mustn't	be home at ten.

Must and *mustn't* are modal verbs. This means:

- No third person *s*
  Say *He must go.* (don't say ~~He musts go.~~)

- No auxiliary *do*
  Say *I mustn't go.* (don't say ~~I don't must go.~~)

- No past tense
  (don't say ~~I musted go.~~)

- No *to* before the verb
  Say *They must go.* (don't say ~~They must to go.~~)

Exercises

1 Read the sentences. Who is speaking: your boss, your doctor, your parents or a police officer?

1 You must be home by eleven.   *parents*
2 You must eat more vegetables.   ....
3 You mustn't smoke in the office.   ....
4 You must take more exercise.   ....
5 You mustn't use your mobile when you're driving.   ....
6 You must study for your exam.   ....
7 You must visit your grandmother on Sunday.   ....
8 You must finish those emails by five o'clock.   ....

2 **Read the imperatives. Write sentences with *must* or *mustn't*.**

1   Don't use your mobile here!   *You mustn't use your mobile here.*
2   Eat more fruit!
3   Don't drink the water here!
4   Park on the left!
5   Visit your grandparents!
6   Don't take photographs here!
7   Don't talk in class!
8   Turn your mobile off!
9   Phone me when you arrive!
10 Don't phone after ten o'clock!

3 **🎧1.56 Complete the conversations with *must* or *mustn't*. Then listen and check.**

Conversation 1

A: What did the doctor say?
B: He says I [1] *must* eat more fruit and vegetables, I [2] _____ smoke, I [3] _____ drink more water and I [4] _____ drink wine.
A: You're joking!

Conversation 2

C: What did the teacher say?
D: He says we [5] _____ do more homework, we [6] _____ talk in class and we [7] _____ study for the exam!
C: Oh, no!

Conversation 3

E: What did your boss say?
F: He says I [8] _____ be late, I [9] _____ park in his parking place and I [10] _____ finish all those emails.
E: Oh.

Conversation 4

G: What did the police officer say?
H: He says I [11] _____ drive faster than 50 kilometres an hour in the town centre and I [12] _____ obey the traffic lights. Oh, and I [13] _____ pay £250 because I drove through that red light.
G: Oh, no!

4 **Correct the mistake in each sentence.**

1   Rachel musts leave at six.   *Rachel must leave at six.*
2   You don't must do that!
3   We must to drive on the left in the UK.
4   She doesn't must be late for her interview.
5   I musts get up at six every day.
6   They must to ask their parents.

47 *have to, have got to, don't have to, must and mustn't*

RULES FOR WAITERS
*Work starts at five. You mustn't be late.
*You have to wash your hands before you start work.
*You don't have to wear a uniform. Black trousers and a white shirt are fine.
*You must be polite to customers at all times!

Presentation

Use *have to*, *must* and *mustn't* to talk about obligation.

Use *don't have to* to say that there is no obligation to do something.

- *don't have to* doesn't mean the same as *mustn't*

  You don't have to do it. = It isn't necessary.

  You mustn't do it = Don't do it!

- *have got to* means the same as *have to*

  You've got to wash your hands. = *You have to wash your hands.* (*have got to* is informal.)

TIP There isn't much difference between *have to* and *must*. You can use *must* to talk about personal obligations:
I must lose some weight.

Have to is more impersonal:
Police officers have to wear a uniform.

Affirmative and negative

I You We They	have to don't have to	wear a uniform.
He She	has to doesn't have to	

Yes/No questions

Do	I / you / we / they	have to	wear a uniform?
Does	he / she		

Short answers

Yes,	I / you / we / they	do.
	he / she	does.

No,	I / you / we / they	don't.
	he / she	doesn't.

Key vocabulary **Work:** clean the kitchen, clear the table, cook the food, job, job description, rules, serve the customers, tidy the clothes, wear a uniform
Clothes: shirt, trousers, uniform

Exercises

1 Choose the correct forms.

1 Shop assistants _must_ / _mustn't_ be polite to customers.

2 Teachers _have to_ / _don't have to_ wear a uniform.

3 Nurses _must_ / _don't have to_ wash their hands.

4 Engineers _have to_ / _don't have to_ get a special qualification.

5 Taxi drivers in the UK _don't have to_ / _mustn't_ drive on the right.

6 Police officers _have to_ / _mustn't_ wear a uniform.

7 Waiters _have to_ / _don't have to_ cook the food.

8 Journalists _have to_ / _don't have to_ ask questions.

2 🎧1.57 Complete the conversations about jobs with _do, does, have to, has to_ or _mustn't_. Then listen and check. What are the jobs in conversations 1 and 2?

Conversation 1

A: What time do you start work?

B: I ^{1} ___have to___ be there at nine o'clock. I ^{2}_____ be late.

A: ^{3}_____ you ^{4}_____ wear a uniform?

B: Yes, I ^{5}_____ .

A: What jobs ^{6}_____ you ^{7}_____ do?

B: I ^{8}_____ clean the restaurant and serve the customers.

Conversation 2

C: Does Emily like her new job?

D: Yes, because she doesn't ^{9}_____ get up early! The shop doesn't open until ten.

C: ^{10}_____ she ^{11}_____ serve the customers?

D: Yes, she ^{12}_____ . And she ^{13}_____ tidy the clothes.

C: Can she smoke?

D: No, she ^{14}_____ smoke in the shop so she ^{15}_____ smoke on the street.

3 Look at the rules and the job descriptions. Write sentences about Paolo and Macy. Use _has to, doesn't have to_ or _mustn't_.

1 food   Paolo _has to cook the food._

           Macy _doesn't have to cook the food._

2 smoke   Paolo and Macy _____

3 tables   Paolo _____

           Macy _____

4 uniform   Paolo and Macy _____

5 late   Paolo and Macy _____

6 customers   Paolo _____

           Macy _____

RULES
- Work starts at nine – don't be late
- No smoking
- Wear a uniform

JOB DESCRIPTIONS
Paolo: Cook the food

Macy: Clear the tables, serve the customers

48 *should/shouldn't*

Presentation

Use *should* for strong advice.

Affirmative and negative

| I / You / He / She / It / We / They | should | buy that dress. |
| | shouldn't | |

Yes/No questions

Should I buy that dress?

Short answers

Yes, you should.   No, you shouldn't.

Wh- questions

What should I do?

Should is a modal verb. This means:

- No third person *s*
  Say *He should do it.* (don't say ~~He shoulds do it.~~)
- No auxiliary *do*
  Say *You shouldn't do it.* (don't say ~~You don't should do it.~~)
- No past tense
  (don't say ~~You shoulded do it.~~)
- No *to* before the verb
  Say *You should do it.* (don't say ~~You should to do it.~~)

Key vocabulary Adjectives: awful, beautiful, great, horrible, terrible, terrific, ugly

Exercises

1 Comment on the advice. Use *That's true / not true* and *shouldn't*.

1 You should smoke.   That's not true. You shouldn't smoke.
2 You should take exercise.   That's true.
3 You should eat healthy food.
4 You should drink a lot of coffee.
5 You should work twelve hours a day.
6 You shouldn't go on holiday.

2 **Give advice. Use *should / shouldn't buy* and *it* or *them*.**

www.**shopnet**.com

| buy it | buy it | buy it | buy it | buy it | buy it |

1   That jacket's terrific.   You should buy it.

2   Those trousers are awful.

3   These shoes are great.

4   That shirt is horrible.

5   This dress is beautiful.

6   Those ties are ugly.

3 **🔊1.58** **Complete the conversation with *should* or *shouldn't*. Then listen and check.**

Joe: You work too hard. You ¹_____should_____ work less.

Mark: Yes, but …

Joe: You ²_____ go on holiday.

Mark: Yes, but …

Joe: And you ³_____ drink all that coffee.

Mark: Yes, but …

Joe: And you smoke? You ⁴_____ stop now.

Mark: Yes, but …

Joe: And you look terrible! You ⁵_____ take more exercise.

Mark: Yes, but …

Joe: And doughnuts! You ⁶_____ eat healthier food.

Mark: Yes, but …

Joe: Yes, but what?

Mark: Oh, nothing.

4 **Correct the mistake in each sentence.**

1   I think you should to buy those shoes.

2   They don't should pay that much money!

3   Rita shoulds ask me first.

4   Do we should leave now or later?

5   Gerald should to do more exercise.

6   What shoulds he do about the problem?

49 *had to / didn't have to* (past obligation)

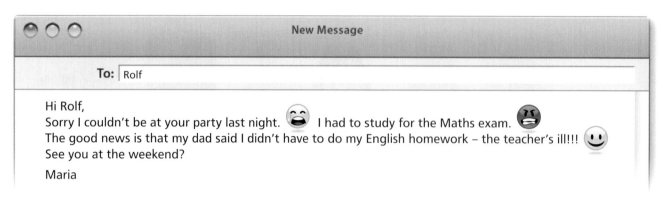

New Message

To: Rolf

Hi Rolf,
Sorry I couldn't be at your party last night. 😫 I had to study for the Maths exam. 😣
The good news is that my dad said I didn't have to do my English homework – the teacher's ill!!! 🙂
See you at the weekend?

Maria

Presentation

Had to is the past of *have to*.

Affirmative and negative

I / You / He / She / It / We / They	had to	study for the Maths exam.
	didn't have to	

Yes/No questions

Did you have to study for the Maths exam?

Short answers

Yes, I did.	No, I didn't.

TIP Say *I didn't have to do it.* (don't say ~~I hadn't to do it.~~)
Say *Did you have to do it?* (don't say ~~Had you to do it?~~)

Key vocabulary Education: do homework, English, French, Geography, Maths, Music, Science, study for an exam

Exercises

1 **Tony and Lisa were at school five years ago. What did they have to study? Use *had to* or *didn't have to*.**

	Tony	Lisa
Maths	x=4y-3	
French	(Bonjour)	
Geography		
Science		

1   Tony + Lisa / Maths
    They had to study Maths.

2   Lisa / French

3   Tony / French

4   Tony + Lisa / Geography

5   Tony + Lisa / Science

2 **Last year, Simon was a soldier. Match the sentences to the pictures.**

1   He had to be fit. `e`
2   He had to call the officers 'sir'. ☐
3   He had to clean the floor. ☐

4   He had to get up early. ☐
5   He had to type letters. ☐
6   He had to wear a uniform. ☐

YES, SIR!

a

b

c

d

e

f

3 🔊**1.59** **Simon is talking to David, a friend, about being a soldier. Complete the conversation with *did, didn't, have to* or *had to*. Then listen and check.**

David: [1] _____Did_____ you [2] _____have to_____ get up early?

Simon: Yes, I [3] _____. We all [4] _____ get up at half past five.
And I [5] _____ clean the floor every morning.

David: [6] _____ you [7] _____ clean the toilets?

Simon: No, I [8] _____. But I [9] _____ type a lot of letters.

David: [10] _____ you [11] _____ call the officers 'sir'?

Simon: Yes, I [12] _____. And I [13] _____ wear a uniform.

David: Was there a lot of sport?

Simon: Yes, there was. We [14] _____ be very fit.

4 **Write past simple questions. Use *have to*.**

1   he / do that?   Did he have to do that?
2   Mike and Lelia / stay late?   _____
3   what time / you / get up?   _____
4   you / clean the house today? _____
5   why / we / pay for the ticket? _____
6   she / study French at school? _____

50 Review of units 46 to 49

Grammar

1 Write sentences with *mustn't*.

1 You mustn't smoke.

2 _____

3 _____

4 _____

5 _____

6 _____

2 Read what the boss says to Josh. Write what Josh says to his friend. Use *have to, don't have to* or *mustn't*.

1 Work starts at eight o'clock.
   I have to start work at eight o'clock.

2 Don't park in my parking space.
   I musn't park in the boss's parking space.

3 Don't be late.
   _____

4 Learn the rules.
   _____

5 There's no uniform.
   _____

6 You must wear a jacket and tie.
   _____

7 It isn't necessary to call me 'sir'.
   _____

8 It isn't your job to make coffee.
   _____

3 Delia would like to be healthier. Look at her notes and write what she says with *should* or *shouldn't*.

1 drink coffee
2 drink water
3 eat doughnuts
4 do exercise
5 eat vegetables
6 drink wine

1 I shouldn't drink coffee.
2 _____
3 _____
4 _____
5 _____
6 _____

4 Complete the conversation with *did, didn't, have to* or *had to*.

A: Monday was terrible! I ¹ _had to_ start work at eight. I ² _____ phone fifty people …

B: ³ _____ you ⁴ _____ clean the toilets?

A: No, I ⁵ _____ .

B: Well, I ⁶ _____ clean the toilets.

A: That's awful.

B: Yes, it was. I ⁷ _____ be at work at six and I finished late.

A: You're joking!

B: No, I'm not.

A: But you ⁸ _____ ⁹ _____ phone fifty people.

B: That's true.

Pronunciation: *n't*

5 1.60 Listen and circle the form you hear.

1 You *must* / ⟨*mustn't*⟩ go.
2 He *should* / *shouldn't* eat healthy food.
3 You *do* / *don't* have to wear a uniform.
4 I *could* / *couldn't* play the piano.
5 We *should* / *shouldn't* call.
6 We *must* / *mustn't* leave at nine.

Vocabulary

6 Circle the word that is different.

1 beautiful great terrific ⟨awful⟩
2 boss shirt trousers uniform
3 Maths Geography homework Science
4 great horrible awful ugly
5 clean serve job cook

7 Complete the verbs with vowels (*a, e, i, o, u*).

¹C	L		²	N								

(crossword grid)

¹C L _ ² N
R ³T Y ⁴P
L ⁵D R _ N K H ⁶W
L ⁷S M K
⁸V S T N
⁹T K R
¹⁰L R N ¹¹S T ¹² D Y
K S
¹³B Y ¹⁴ T

Listen again

8 1.61 Listen and put the lines from the conversation in order.

☐ And you look terrible! You should take more exercise.

☐ And you shouldn't drink all that coffee.

☐ And you smoke? You should stop now.

☐ 1 You work too hard. You should work less.

☐ Yes, but what?

☐ You should go on holiday.

☐ And doughnuts! You should eat healthier food.

51 Present perfect

Boy: Dad, I'm going to the cinema with Jordi. Can I have £20?
Dad: Hmm. Have you cleaned the car?
Boy: Yes, I have.
Dad: Have you tidied your room?
Boy: Yes, I have.
Dad: Well, OK then.

Presentation

Use the present perfect to talk about a past action which has a present result.

I've cleaned the car. =
The car is clean now.

I haven't cleaned the car. =
The car is dirty now.

You don't say exactly when it happened. (don't say ~~I have cleaned the car yesterday.~~)

Form the present perfect with *have/has + past participle*.

Affirmative and negative

I You We They	've haven't	cleaned the car. tidied your room.
He She	's hasn't	

Past participle

- Regular past participles end in *-ed*: *borrow → borrowed*.

- Many verbs have irregular past participles: *buy → bought, break → broken*.

See page 235: Irregular verbs

Yes/No questions

Have	you we they	cleaned the car? tidied your room?
Has	he she	

Short answers

Yes,	I / you / we / they	have.
	he / she	has.

No,	I / you / we / they	haven't.
	he / she	hasn't.

Key vocabulary Daily events: do the washing-up, comb your hair, clean your shoes, clean your teeth, have a shower, iron your clothes, tidy your desk

Exercises

1 Write affirmative and negative sentences. Use the present perfect.

comb his hair

1 Mark *'s combed his hair.*
2 Rick *hasn't combed his hair.*

iron his shirt

3 Mark
4 Rick

clean his shoes

5 Mark
6 Rick

Mark   Rick

2 Complete the sentences. Use the present perfect.

1 I _____*'ve cleaned*_____ (clean) my teeth.
2 She _____ (leave) her bag on the table.
3 We _____ (not finish) our homework.
4 They _____ (have) breakfast.
5 You _____ (not do) the washing-up.
6 He _____ (tidy) his desk.
7 We _____ (buy) a new car.
8 He _____ (made) lots of mistakes.

3 Write sentences using the verbs in brackets.

1 I can't find my credit card. (lose) *I've lost my credit card.*
2 Julio's got my dictionary. (borrow) _____
3 Christina's wearing a new top. (buy) _____
4 The car was moving. Now it isn't. (stop) _____
5 I dropped my phone and now it doesn't work. (break) _____

4 ⓑ2.02 Complete the conversation with questions. Then listen and check.

Mother: Peter! It's five to nine. Are you ready?
Peter: Yes, Mum.
Mother: ¹ *Have*   you   *cleaned*   your teeth?
Peter: Yes, of course I have.
Mother: ² _____ a shower?
Peter: Yes, Mum.
Mother: ³ _____ your hair?
Peter: Yes, I have.
Mother: ⁴ _____ your shoes?
Peter: Yes, I have.
Mother: No, you haven't. They're dirty. Oh, Peter …

52 Present perfect with *just*, *already* and *yet*

A: Hi, Mum. I passed!
B: Oh, well done. Let me get your father ... Jack! It's Susie on the phone. She's just passed her driving test!

C: Are you going to tidy your room?
D: I've already tidied it!
C: Well, I don't think it's very tidy.

E: Have you talked to Mark yet?
F: No, I haven't.
E: When are you going to tell him?
F: I don't know. I haven't decided yet.

Presentation

Just, *yet* and *already* are adverbs. They add extra meaning to the present perfect.

- *Just* shows that an action is very recent. Use *just* in affirmative sentences. It usually goes before the past participle: *She's just passed her driving test.*

- *Yet* shows that something is expected. Use *yet* in negative sentences and *yes/no* questions. It usually goes at the end of the sentence: *I haven't decided yet. Have you decided yet?*

- *Already* shows that something happened sooner than expected. Use *already* in affirmative sentences. It usually goes before the past participle: *I've already tidied it.*

Key vocabulary Life events: have a baby, get married, graduate from university, move house, pass your driving test
Housework: clean the bathroom, do the shopping, do the washing-up, make dinner, make your bed, tidy the living room

Exercises

1 **Write sentences with *just*. Use the present perfect and the phrases in the box.**

> get married   graduate from university
> have a baby   ~~move house~~

1   They've just moved house.
2
3
4

2 Write questions with *yet.*

1 you / do the washing-up?   Have you done the washing-up yet?

2 he / make his bed?

3 they / clean the bathroom?

4 she / tidy the living room?

5 you / make dinner?

6 he / do the shopping?

3 Complete the sentences with *already* or *yet.*

1 They're going to be here in ten minutes and I haven't made dinner _____yet_____ !

2 Have you tidied your room _____ ?

3 I've _____ done the washing-up.

4 You don't have to tidy the living room: I've _____ done it.

5 I've haven't cleaned the bathroom and I haven't made the beds _____ .

6 The kitchen's OK. I've _____ cleaned it.

4 Tick (✓) the things on the list that Nina has done this morning. Write when she's going to do the other things.

> I've already phoned Jack. I haven't talked to Julia yet. I'm going to do that at two o'clock. I haven't emailed Brad yet. I'm going to do that this afternoon. I've already texted Leo. I've already talked to Anthony.

1 phone Jack   ✓
2 talk to Julia   at two o'clock
3 email Brad
4 text Leo
5 talk to Anthony

5 (🔊**2.03**) Look at Martin's list and write what he says. Use *going to* or the present perfect with *already* or *yet.* Then listen and check.

1 phone Angelina at four o'clock
2 phone Tom ✓
3 talk to Kevin ✓
4 email Sharon this afternoon
5 talk to Martin after lunch

> I haven't phoned Angelina yet. I'm going to do that at four o'clock.

53 Present perfect with *for* and *since*
How long ...?

Woman: Where do you live?
Man: In London.
Woman: How long have you lived there?
Man: For five years.
Woman: And you've started your own business.
Man: Yes, I have. I've had the business for two years.

Presentation

Use the present perfect to talk about actions that started in the past and continue in the present.

> *I've lived in London for five years* (and I live there now).
>
> moved to London
> five years ago   NOW
>
>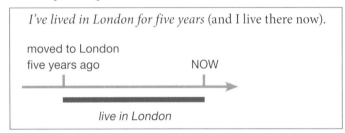
>
> *live in London*

for and *since*

- Use *for* with the present perfect to show the duration of a present situation.

  My brother's a doctor. He became a doctor five years ago: *He's been a doctor for five years.*

- Use *since* with the present perfect to show the starting point of a present situation.

  I support Real Madrid. I started supporting them since 1995: *I've supported Real Madrid since 1995.*

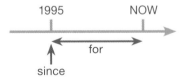

How long ...?

Use *How long ...?* with the present perfect to ask about the duration of a present situation.

How long have you lived there? For five years.

Key vocabulary Life events: become/be a (doctor), buy/have a car, get/be married, meet/know somebody, move to / live in a town, start/have your own business, start supporting / support a football team, make/have a million dollars

Exercises

1 Complete the phrases with *for* or *since*.

1 _____since_____ 1972

2 _____ Tuesday

3 _____ two weeks

4 _____ eleven o'clock

5 _____ I was fourteen years old

6 _____ August

7 _____ four days

8 _____ two hours

2 Answer the questions about Sarah.

1 Sarah got married when she was 24. She's been married for four years. How old is she now?

She's _____28_____ .

2 Her husband's name is Jeff. She met him at university when she was 21 years old. How long has she known him?

For _____ .

3 She became a teacher when she was 22. How long has she been a teacher?

For _____ .

4 Sarah and Jeff have lived in London for three years. How old was she when they moved to London?

She was _____ .

5 She's supported Chelsea FC since she moved to London. How long has she supported Chelsea FC?

For _____ .

6 She's got an old Volkswagen. She's had it for ten years. How old was she when she bought it?

She was _____ .

3 ⊘2.04 Choose the correct words and complete the interview with the present perfect of the verbs. Then listen and check.

Penny: Hi, Dmitri. Thanks for talking to us. First of all, how long [1] ___have you lived___ (live) in California?

Dmitri: I [2] _____ (be) here [3] *for / since* six years. I came from Russia when I was 24 years old. I love it here.

Penny: And how long [4] _____ (have) your own business?

Dmitri: [5] *For / Since* I was 25. I started it one year after I arrived here.

Penny: And now you're a millionaire.

Dmitri: That's right. In fact I [6] _____ (be) a millionaire [7] *for / since* I was 27.

Penny: What's the best thing about being rich?

Dmitri: My car. It's a yellow Porsche Carrera. I [8] _____ (have) it [9] *for / since* I was 28. But the best thing in my life is Ana. We [10] _____ (be) married [11] *for / since* about a year but I [12] _____ (know) her [13] *for / since* I was 26.

4 Answer these questions. Use *for* or *since*.

1 How long have you lived in your home?

2 How long have you studied English?

3 How long have you known your best friend?

117

54 *Have you ever ...?*
been and *gone*

A: Have you ever eaten sushi?
B: No, never. Is it nice?
A: It's delicious.

C: Have you ever been to the USA?
D: Yes, we have. We went to Florida last year.
C: Was it nice?

E: Have you ever played badminton?
F: Yes, I have. I played it on holiday. It's brilliant.
E: Is it hard to play?

Presentation

Have you ever ...?

Use *Have you ever ...?* questions to ask about life experiences:

Have you ever been to the USA?

ever and *never*

You often use *ever* with present perfect questions. It means 'at any time' in the past. *Never* means 'at no time'.

A: *Have you ever eaten sushi?*

B: *No, never.*

been and *gone*

Use *been* to talk about a place you went to but you are back now: *I've been to the USA three times.*

Use *gone* to talk about a person who is away and hasn't returned yet: *He's gone to the USA.*

TIP The present perfect and the past simple talk about the past.
With the past simple you know (or say) when the action happened.
I've been to Florida.
I went to Florida last year.

Exercises

1 Look at the photos. Write six questions with *Have you ever …?* Use the verbs and nouns in the boxes.

> **verbs:** ~~be~~ drink eat see play ride
>
> **nouns:** Red Bull basketball ~~to Australia~~
> a James Bond film a motorbike Greek yoghurt

1 Have you ever been to Australia?
2 ....
3 ....
4 ....
5 ....
6 ....

2 Match the responses a–f to the questions in exercise 1.

a No, I haven't. I don't like fizzy drinks. ☐
b No, I haven't. I prefer tennis. ☐
c No, I haven't. I haven't got a licence. ☐
d No, I haven't, but my sister went to New Zealand last year. ☐ 1
e No, I haven't. I don't like action films. ☐
f No, I haven't. I can't eat milk products. ☐

3 Write sentences with *never.*

1 Canada ✓   the USA ✗   I've been to Canada but I've never been to the USA.
2 Coca-Cola® ✓   Pepsi-Cola® ✗ ....
3 table tennis ✓ tennis ✗   ....
4 bicycle ✓   motorbike ✗   ....
5 French ✓   Spanish ✗   ....
6 piano ✓   guitar ✗   ....
7 sushi ✓   curry ✗   ....
8 dolphin ✓   blue whale ✗   ....

4 (🔊2.05) Write conversations. Then listen and check.

1 Canada? → yes: Montreal last year
   A: Have you ever been to Canada?
   B: Yes, I have. I went to Montreal last year.

2 rugby? → yes: when I was at school
   A: ....
   B: ....

3 curry? → yes: in London last summer
   A: ....
   B: ....

4 *Romeo and Juliet?* → yes: at the Globe Theatre in May
   A: ....
   B: ....

55 Review of units 51 to 54

Grammar

1 Complete the sentences with the correct form of *have*. Add *n't* where necessary.

1 You ___haven't___ cleaned your shoes. They look terrible.

2 Let's go inside. It _____ started raining.

3 She's hungry. She _____ had breakfast yet.

4 We're just in time. The film _____ started yet.

5 Oh no! It's my girlfriend's birthday and I _____ bought her anything.

6 They _____ left their books in my car.

7 He was really tired so he _____ gone to bed.

8 Oh, no! I _____ broken my camera.

2 Complete the letter with *just, yet* or *already*.

Hi Jenny,

We've been in New York for one day and we've [1] ___already___ visited the Empire State Building! We haven't been to the Statue of Liberty [2] _____ – we're going there this afternoon.

Peter's [3] _____ taken about 100 photos. I haven't taken any – I lost my camera and I haven't bought a new one [4] _____.

Right now we're in a Japanese restaurant. We've [5] _____ had lunch – it was great. Have you ever had sushi?

See you soon,

Gaz

3 Write sentences with *since* or *for*. Use the present perfect of the verb in brackets.

1 My cousin Tom's a dentist. He became a dentist fifteen years ago. (be)
   He's been a dentist for fifteen years.

2 He's from London but he lives in Edinburgh. He moved there five years ago. (live)
   _____

3 He supports Arsenal FC. He started supporting them when he was five. (support)
   _____

4 He's got a BMW. He bought it when he was eighteen. (have)
   _____

5 His wife's name is Meg. He met her eight years ago. (know)
   _____

6 They got married in January. (be)
   _____

7 Rosey's got her own business. She started it in 2005. (have)
   _____

4 Write questions with *Have you ever ...?* and the correct form of the verbs in the box.

| drink read play ~~be~~ eat |

1 Have you ever been _____ to Canada?
2 _____ Greek wine?
3 _____ golf?
4 _____ *Hamlet*?
5 _____ caviar?

5 **Match responses a–e to questions 1–5 in exercise 4.**

a   No, I haven't. But I've played tennis. ☐

b   Yes, I have. I saw it last month at the theatre. ☐

c   Yes, I have. I drank it in Athens on holiday. ☐

d   No, I haven't. Is it delicious? ☐

e   Yes, I have. I went there last year. ☐

Pronunciation: *have*

6 **⊘2.06 Listen to the sentences. Do you hear the full form or the contracted form of *have*?**

1	have	've
2	have	've
3	have	've
4	have not	haven't
5	have not	haven't
6	has	's
7	has	's
8	has not	hasn't

Vocabulary

7 **Match the verbs with the life events phrases.**

1	buy	b	a	a baby
2	get	☐	b	~~a car~~
3	graduate	☐	c	your driving test
4	have	☐	d	house
5	move	☐	e	married
6	pass	☐	f	from university

8 **Complete the daily events and housework with the verbs in the box.**

~~clean~~   comb   do   have   iron
make   ride   tidy

1 _____clean_____ your shoes / your teeth / the bathroom

2 _____ a shower / lunch / an idea

3 _____ your shirt / clothes

4 _____ the washing-up / the shopping

5 _____ the bed / dinner / money

6 _____ your hair

7 _____ your room / your desk

8 _____ a bicycle / a motorbike

Listen again

9 **⊘2.07 Listen and answer the questions.**

1   Has he phoned Angelina yet?
    No, he hasn't.

2   When is he going to phone her?
    At four o'clock.

3   Has he phoned Tom yet?
    _____

4   Has he talked to Kevin yet?
    _____

5   Has he emailed Sharon yet?
    _____

6   When is he going to email her?
    _____

7   Has he talked to Martin yet?
    _____

8   When is he going to talk to him?
    _____

121

56 Past continuous

IT WAS EIGHT O'CLOCK ON A MONDAY MORNING IN SAN FRANCISCO AND THE SUN WAS SHINING. PEOPLE WERE DRIVING TO WORK, CHILDREN WERE GOING TO SCHOOL AND NO ONE WAS LOOKING AT THE SKY. A SPACE SHIP WAS FLYING OVER THEIR HEADS.

IT WAS …

THE DAY THE ALIENS CAME!!

IN CINEMAS FROM FRIDAY

Presentation

Use the past continuous to talk about …

- actions and events around a time in the past: *It was eight o'clock. People were driving to work.*

- background events: *The sun was shining.*

It was eight o'clock. People were driving to work. (People started driving before eight o'clock and continued after eight o'clock.)	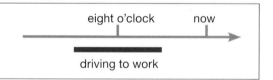

Affirmative and negative

I He She	was wasn't	driving to work. going to school.
You We They	were weren't	

Yes/No questions

Were	you they	driving to work? going to school?
Was	he she	

Wh- questions

What	were	you / we / they	doing?
	was	I / he / she	

TIP You don't normally use state verbs (e.g. *be, like, believe*) in the continuous form.

Short answers

Yes,	I / he / she	was.
	you / we / they	were.

No,	I / he / she	wasn't.
	you / we / they	weren't.

Key vocabulary Background events: the moon/sun was shining, it was raining, the wind was blowing, a dog was barking, bells were ringing, snow was falling

Exercises

1 Write affirmative and negative sentences. Use the past continuous.

1 the snow / fall / and the children / play / in it
The snow was falling and the children were playing in it.

2 the telephone / ring but Mike / work / in the garden

3 the students / not / do their work when the teacher came in

4 the baby / cry / because / a dog / bark

5 it / not / rain / so we ate outside

6 I / not plan / to go out but my friend was bored

2 Read the first part of the story. Then answer the questions.

It was midnight and the moon was shining in the sky. The church bell was ringing and dogs were barking. The wind was blowing but it wasn't raining. A baby was crying but her parents were sleeping ...

1 Was the sun shining?   *No, it wasn't.*
2 Was the church bell ringing?
3 Were the dogs barking?
4 Was it raining?
5 Were the baby's parents watching TV?

3 ⓐ2.08 Complete the conversation with the past continuous of the verbs.

A: I loved Paris. I was there in 1999.

B: Really? How long ¹ ___were you living___ (live) there?

A: For six months. I was a student.

B: What ² _____ (you study)?

A: Art.

B: That's amazing. My two brothers ³ _____ (study) art in Paris in 1999. Maybe you know them.

A: Which part ⁴ _____ (they live) in? I was in Montmatre.

B: No, I ⁵ _____ (not talk) about Paris in France.
They ⁶ _____ (live) in Paris in Texas!

A: Oh, I see.

57 Past simple and past continuous
while, when and *suddenly*

WHO KILLED LORD HUNTER?

LORD HUNTER was reading in the library when he died. Only three people lived with him. Detective Blane was looking at them – Lord Hunter's brother, his wife and his butler. First, the detective asked Lord Hunter's brother, Richard Hunter, a question.
'What were you doing this evening, Mr Hunter?'
'I was having dinner in the dining room at eight o'clock.'
'And were you having dinner, Lady Hunter?'
'No, I wasn't. I was sleeping in my bedroom at eight o'clock because I was tired.'
'What about you?' The detective was looking at the butler.

'I was tidying the library at eight o'clock. Suddenly I found Lord Hunter on the floor.

'It's interesting,' said Blane. 'When Lord Hunter died at eight o'clock, you were having dinner and you were sleeping. But I didn't say eight o'clock. In fact, Lord Hunter died at half past eight.'

Presentation

You often use the past continuous and the past simple together to talk about two actions in the past.

- Use the past continuous to talk about an action that was in progress around a time in the past.
- Use the past simple to talk about an action that 1) happened during, or 2) stopped the action in the past continuous.

When Lord Hunter died at eight o'clock, you were having dinner.

past   Lord Hunter died
having dinner

The butler found Lord Hunter's body while/when he was tidying the library.

The butler was tidying the library when he found Lord Hunter's body.

past   found body
tidying the library

while, when and *suddenly*

- You often use *while* with the past continuous: *He died while I was sleeping.*
- Use *when* with the past continuous and past simple: *He died when I was sleeping. I was sleeping when he died.*
- Use *suddenly* to describe an immediate change: *The sun was shining. Suddenly, it started raining.*

Key vocabulary   Rooms: bedroom, dining room, kitchen, library, living room, study

124

Exercises

1 Choose the correct forms.

1 I was cooking when the doorbell (rang)/ was ringing.

2 I watched / was watching my favourite TV programme when the baby started to cry.

3 The dogs barked / were barking. Suddenly, they were quiet.

4 When we were tidying the study, we found / were finding my old school photographs.

5 I was waiting at the train station when I saw / was seeing my brother.

6 While I had / was having lunch my friend called.

7 We were driving home. Suddenly, the car engine stopped / was stopping.

8 While she was cleaning the kitchen, another guest arrived / was arriving.

2 ⊙2.09 Complete the conversation with the past simple or past continuous of the verbs. Then listen and check.

Detective: What ¹___were___ you ___doing___ (do) here at midnight?

Witness: I ²_____ (drive) along this road when my car suddenly ³_____ (stop). So I walked to the house and rang the doorbell.

Detective: Did you see anyone while you ⁴_____ (wait)?

Witness: No. It ⁵_____ (rain) and a dog ⁶_____ (bark). Suddenly the door ⁷_____ (open) but no one was there.

Detective: ⁸_____ you _____ (enter) the house?

Witness: Yes. And while I ⁹_____ (walk) through the house, I ¹⁰_____ (see) the woman. She was crying.

Detective: What ¹¹_____ you _____ (do) next?

Witness: I asked her name.

3 Make sentences. Use the past continuous and past simple.

1 I / meet / old friend / while / wait / at the bus station
  I met an old friend while I was waiting at the bus station.

2 they / not work / when / we / arrive
  _____

3 when / she / call, I / have / a bath
  _____

4 everyone / look / at the sky. Suddenly, they / see / the aliens!
  _____

5 while / we / eat / breakfast, my taxi / arrive
  _____

6 I / read / my book when / the lights / go out
  _____

7 while / we / watch / TV / Molly / tell us / her / news
  _____

8 my parents / live / Italy / when / I / born
  _____

58 Conjunctions
and, or, but, before, after, while, when, because and *so*

Rome, 17th April

Dear Megan
We're in Rome at last. The trip began in London. I didn't like England but I loved
Scotland. There wasn't time to see Ireland or Wales so we went straight to Paris.
And guess what? While we were visiting the Eiffel Tower, we met some old college
friends. We travelled with them in their car to Spain because it was cheaper than
the train. After we reached Barcelona, we took a boat to Italy.

Presentation

Use *and, or, but* to connect words or parts of sentences.

- Use **and** to add information or to talk about a sequence: *We visited Austria and Russia. We left England and crossed to France.*

- Use **or** for choices and alternatives: *Which do you prefer: England or Scotland?* Also use *or* for two negative facts: *There wasn't time to visit Ireland or Wales.*

- Use **but** to talk about differences: *The hotel was good but expensive. I liked Paris but I didn't like London.*

Use *before, after, while, when, because, so* to connect two parts of a sentence.

- Use **before**, **after** and **when** to show a sequence: *Before we went to Pairs, we visited London. We were in London before we went to Paris.*

- Use **while** and **when** to talk about two actions at the same time: *While I was travelling, I met an old friend. I often meet old friends when I go to Paris.*

- Use **because** to give a reason: *We travelled in their car because it was cheaper than the train.*

- Use **so** to show a result: *They were driving to Spain so we travelled in their car.*

> **Key vocabulary** Travel verbs: begin (in), go, visit, travel, drive, reach, take (a boat, a taxi, a train)
> Places to visit: museum, art gallery, palace, park, monument, beach

Exercises

1 Choose the correct conjunctions.

1 (*After*) / *When* we visited the museum, we went to the park.
2 We didn't go to the palace *so / because* it was too expensive.
3 They visited the museum *and / or* the monument on the same day.
4 I didn't see the palace *but / or* the museum.
5 *And / Before* we went to the park, we visited the museum.
6 *When / While* we reached Sicily, we spent two days on the beach.
7 The gallery was closed *so / and* we sat in the park.
8 *While / After* I was waiting for the boat, I had lunch.
9 The hotel wasn't very nice *when / but* the restaurant was great.

2 🔊 **2.10** **Complete the conversation with the words in the boxes. Then listen and check.**

| ~~and~~ after but so while |

A: Have you ever been to Australia?

B: Yes, in fact I went when I was sixteen [1] _____and_____
again when I was twenty. I went the second time
[2] _____ I was taking a gap year.

A: Wow! Did you go to New Zealand, too?

B: Yes … [3] _____ Australia, I went to New Zealand
[4] _____ I only travelled round the North
Island. I was only there for a week [5] _____
I didn't have time for the South Island as well.

| because or when |

A: So which did you prefer, Australia [6] _____
New Zealand?

B: I suppose Australia but only [7] _____
we had problems at the airport in New Zealand.
[8] _____ we were leaving for Los Angeles,
there was a 36-hour delay!

NEW ZEALAND

NORTH ISLAND

Auckland

Wellington

Christchurch

SOUTH ISLAND

3 **Join the sentences. Use the conjunction in brackets.**

1 We went to London. We went to Paris. (and)
We went to London and Paris.

2 We didn't have time to visit the palace. We didn't have time to visit the park. (or)
_____

3 We booked tickets. We went to the theatre. (before)
_____

4 We had dinner. We went to the theatre. (after)
_____

5 She liked the theatre. She didn't enjoy the opera. (but)
_____

6 I was waiting for a taxi. My friend arrived with his car. (while)
_____

7 The art gallery closed. I went for a drink. (when)
_____

8 We didn't go to the palace. We were hungry. (because)
_____

9 The museum was closed. He went shopping. (so)
_____

59 *used to*

Fred: Is that really you?
Mandy: Yes, I used to have pink hair.
Fred: Amazing! And did you use to wear uniforms?
Mandy: Yes, we did. I hated it.
Fred: Where's your hat?
Mandy: I didn't use to wear mine. My teachers used to get really angry with me.

Presentation

Use *used to* to talk about states or habits in the past.

- State: *I used to have long hair.*
- Habit: *I used to get up at six o'clock.*

Affirmative and negative

I / You / He / She / We / They	used to	have pink hair.
	---	wear a uniform.
	didn't use to	

Questions and short answers

| Did | I / you / he / she / we / they | use to | have pink hair? |
| | | | wear a uniform? |

| Yes, | I / you / he / she / we / they | did. | No, | I / you / he / she / we / they | didn't. |

TIP The past simple is also correct for states and habits in the past but you often use *used to*.
With *used to*, you don't need to give a particular time.

I worked in my father's shop when I was young.
I used to work in my father's shop.

Exercises

1 Correct the mistakes. Two sentences are correct.

1 I use to work in a shop.   I used to work in a shop.

2 My grandparents used to visit us every Sunday.

3 We didn't use to have aeroplanes.

4 Television didn't used to be in colour.

5 I used to loved chocolate!

6 Did you used to live here?

2 (⏴2.11) **Complete the conversation with *used* or *use*. Then listen and check.**

Child: Grandfather, did you ¹_____ to go to school?

Grandfather: Yes, I did. But I ²_____ to walk. We didn't have a car in those days.

Child: How long did it ³_____ to take?

Grandfather: I ⁴_____ to get up at six o'clock and my sisters and I walked for an hour. The school was in the next village.

Child: What was your favourite subject?

Grandfather: Well, I didn't ⁵_____ to like school very much. The teachers didn't ⁶_____ to be very nice. But I suppose reading books was my favourite lesson. I ⁷_____ to enjoy that and I still do!

3 **Complete the sentences. Use the correct form of *used to*.**

1 She _didn't use to wear lots of make up._

2 He _____

3 He _____

4 They _____

4 **Complete the sentences so that they are true for you.**

1 I used to _____ but I don't now.

2 I didn't use to _____ but I do now.

129

60 Review of units 56 to 59

Grammar

1 Complete the sentences with the past continuous of the verbs in the box.

> have not look ~~run~~ study talk not work

1 I met some friends while I <u>was running</u> in the park.

2 Who _____ you _____ to on the phone just now?

3 I tried to call you earlier but my phone _____ .

4 I've just seen my sister and Jamie. They _____ lunch in a café.

5 _____ Karen _____ for her exam last night?

6 John took a photo of me while I _____ .

2 Complete the texts with the past simple or past continuous of the verbs.

Matthew ¹ <u>was sleeping</u> (sleep) but suddenly
he ² _____ (wake up).
He ³ _____ (look) out of the window
and on the hillside a strange dog ⁴ _____
(bark).

I ⁵ _____ (cycle) to the supermarket
when a car ⁶ _____ (drive) in front of
me. I shouted: 'You '⁷ _____ (not look)
where you were going!' The driver ⁸ _____
(say) he was sorry.

3 Complete the conjunctions.

1 I always like to eat chocolate a<u>fter</u> an evening meal.

2 Roger a_____ Betty are married.

3 I left the cinema early b_____ the film was boring.

4 B_____ you go to bed, please tidy your room.

5 Normally, I like any music b_____ this is awful!

6 Would you like tea o_____ coffee?

7 I was tired s_____ I went to bed.

8 We were talking w_____ the teacher came in.

9 What were you doing w_____ I was working?

4 Rewrite the sentences using the correct form of *used to*.

1 I lived in Beijing when I was a child.
<u>I used to live in Beijing when I was a child.</u>

2 What did you do when you worked there?
_____

3 He didn't like carrots before he left home.
_____

4 They had long hair in 1975.
_____

5 She didn't drive before last year.
_____

6 As a student, when did you go to bed?
_____

Pronunciation: /s/ or /z/

5 (🔊 2.12) **Listen to these sentences. Do you hear /s/ or /z/ in _used_ or _use_?**

1 I used all the cheese for my sandwich. /z/

2 He didn't use to be lazy. /s/

3 Did she use to live here?

4 We used dictionaries in the exam.

5 It used to be harder to travel abroad.

6 I didn't use your mobile phone.

Vocabulary

6 **Write the words for rooms.**

1 b~dr~~m   _bedroom_

2 d~n~ng r~~m

3 k~tch~n

4 l~br~ry

5 l~v~ng r~~m

6 st~dy

7 **Complete the postcard with the words in the box.**

gallery ~~palace~~ monument beach park

Hi Felicity
From my hotel room I can see the King's
1 _palace_ but I haven't seen him
yet! Yesterday we visited the national art
2 _____ . After that we ate bread and
cheese in the 3 _____ next to a large
4 _____ of another king on his horse.
Tomorrow, we're leaving the city for a few days.
We want to sit on a 5 _____ for a
few days after all this sightseeing!
See you soon
Andrew

Listen again

8 (🔊 2.13) **Listen and write in the missing words.**

A: Have you ever been to Australia?

B: Yes, in fact I went
1 _____ and
again when I was twenty. I went the second time
2 _____ a gap
year.

A: Wow! Did you go to New Zealand too?

B: Yes … . 3 _____ ,
I went to New Zealand
4 _____
round the North Island. I was only there for a
week 5 _____
for the South Island as well.

B: So which did you prefer,
6 _____ ?

A: I suppose Australia but only
7 _____ at the
airport in New Zealand.
8 _____ for
Los Angeles, there was a 36-hour delay!

61 *all, most, some, none*

Report

Students: January and February

In January, none of the students was female. All of them were male.

In February, some students were male but most of them were female.

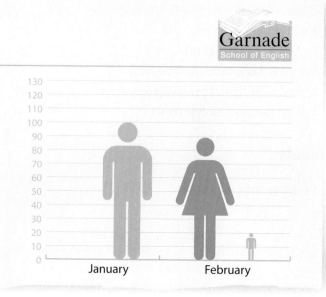

Presentation

all

All	students the students	are	married.
All of	the students them		

most and some

Most Some	students	are	married.
Most of Some of	the students them		

none

None of	the students them	is	married.

100%	all
75%	
	most
50%	
	some
25%	
0%	none

Use *all, most* or *some* without *of*, to talk about people or things in general:

Some people don't like cats. Most people like ice cream.

Key vocabulary   **Learning a language:** listening, speaking, reading, writing, grammar, vocabulary, literature

Exercises

1   Look at the charts. Complete the sections from the report with *all, most, some* or *none*.

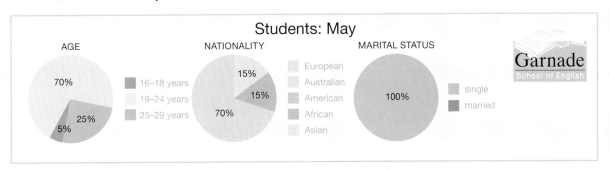

CHART 1: AGE

1   _None_ of the students is younger than 16 years old or older than 29.

2   _____ of them are between 25 and 29 but ³ _____ of them are between 19 and 24.

CHART 2: NATIONALITY

4   _____ of the students are European. ⁵ _____ of them are Asian or African.

6   _____ of them is American or Australian.

CHART 3: MARITAL STATUS

7   _____ of the students is married. ⁸ _____ of them are single.

2   Add *of* to the sentences where necessary.

1   All ___Ø___ students are older than 15.

2   None ___of___ the students is older than 29.

3   Most _____ students are between 19 and 24.

4   Some _____ them are from Africa.

5   Some _____ students are from Asia.

6   Most _____ them are from Europe.

7   None _____ the students is from Australia or America.

8   All _____ them are single.

3   (♪2.14) Put the phrases in order to make a report about the chart. Then listen and check.

☐   is Literature: none of

☐   studying Grammar and Vocabulary (70%). Some of

☐   the students has chosen it.

☐   the students have chosen it. Most of them are also

☐   them are studying Reading and Writing (30%). The worst

☐ 1 Listening and Speaking has been a success: all

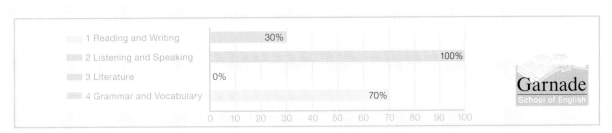

62 any-, every-, no-, some- / -thing, -where, -body, -one

Boss: Did anyone call for me while I was at lunch?
Secretary: Oh, yes. Everybody wants you today! First of all, somebody rang about your car – it's ready to collect. Then, you need to call your wife back. And finally, your friend Malcolm rang. He wants to meet somewhere for a drink this evening.
Boss: Were there any calls about work?
Secretary: No, nothing like that.

Presentation

	-thing	-where	-one	-body
any-	anything	anywhere	anyone	anybody
every-	everything	everywhere	everyone	everybody
no-	nothing	nowhere	no one	nobody
some-	something	somewhere	someone	somebody

Use these pronouns with the verb in the singular form: *Everybody wants you today.*

- Use *any-* in questions: *Is there anything to do?*
- Use *not any-* in negative sentences: *There wasn't anything to do.*
- Note that *not any-* = *no-*: *There was nothing to do.*

You can use these pronouns before adjectives to add more detail: *She's cooking something special for dinner.*

TIP You can use *one* instead of *body: anyone, everyone, no one, someone.*

Exercises

1 Complete the sentences with the words in brackets.

1 (nothing, everybody) ___Everybody___ was hungry but there was ___nothing___ to eat.
2 (nobody, everybody) There's _____ in the house. _____ has gone to the beach.
3 (anything, anybody) There isn't _____ good on at the cinema. Does _____ want to go out for a meal?
4 (anybody, somebody) There's _____ at the door – are you expecting _____?
5 (nobody, everything) I phoned but _____ answered. Is _____ OK?

2 Complete the sentences with the pairs of words in the box.

somewhere + nowhere	something + somebody	everywhere + anywhere
anything + nothing	~~anybody + anywhere~~	

1 Has ___anybody___ got José's number? I can't find it ___anywhere___ .
2 I've got _____ exciting to tell you about _____ you know.
3 We didn't do _____ interesting all weekend – we stayed at home and did _____ .
4 I've lost my keys. I've looked for them _____ but I can't find them _____ .
5 I'm looking for _____ to park, but there's _____ in this street.

3 Rewrite the sentences. Change *no-* to *not any-* and *not any-* to *no-*.

1 There's nobody in the house. There isn't anybody in the house.
2 There isn't anything to do. There's nothing to do.
3 There's nowhere to go. _____
4 There's nothing on TV. _____
5 There isn't anybody I want to phone. _____
6 There isn't anywhere worse than here. _____

4 ⏏2.15 Complete the conversations. Then listen and check.

Conversation 1

A: Polly, I've got [1] ___something___ to tell you. I'm leaving.
B: But why John? I did [2] _____ for you.
A: I know you did. But it will never work between us.
B: Oh, John. Is there [3] _____ I can do to change your mind?
A: No, [4] _____ .

Conversation 2

C: Did you hear that?
D: No, I didn't. I didn't hear [5] _____ .
C: I think there's [6] _____ downstairs.
D: No, there isn't. There's [7] _____ downstairs. Go to sleep.
C: Then what was THAT?

Conversation 3

E: Your travel photos are wonderful. You've been [8] _____ .
F: Not really. Only to India and Thailand.
E: Well, it's more than me. I haven't done [9] _____ with my life and I haven't been [10] _____ .
F: That's not true. What about your camping holiday last year, for example?

63 *both, neither* and *either*

Presentation

both and *neither*

Use *both* and *neither* to say that two things or people are the same. *Both* is positive. *Neither* is negative.

Both of them are happy.
Both students are happy.

Neither of them is happy.
Neither student is happy.

either

Use *either* to say that the choice between two people or things is not important:

Either of them is fine. (= I like both of them. I don't mind which one I have.)

TIP not + either = neither: *I don't want either of them. = I want neither of them.*

* *Both* is plural: *Both of them are students. Both teenagers are students.*
* *Either* is singular: *Either of them is fine.*
* *Neither* is singular: *Neither of them is British. Neither student is British.*

TIP You can use these words with a noun: *both students, neither country, either drink.*

Exercises

1 Look at the interview notes. Complete the sentences with *both* or *neither*.

What's your name?	Hans	Carlo
Where are you from?	Austria	Uruguay
Where do you live?	In London	In London
How old are you?	I'm 21.	I'm 21.
What do you do?	I'm a student.	I'm a student.
How tall are you?	I'm 1m 85.	I'm 1m 86.
Have you got a car?	No, I haven't.	No, I haven't.
Do you like rock music?	Yes, I do.	Yes, I do.
Do you like jazz?	No, I don't.	No, I don't.
Do you play tennis?	Yes, I do.	Yes, I do.
Do you play basketball?	No, I don't.	No, I don't.
Can you speak French?	No, I can't.	No, I can't.
Can you speak Italian?	Yes, I can.	Yes, I can.

1 _____Both_____ of them are tall.
2 _____ of them are 21.
3 _____ of them can speak French.
4 _____ of them like rock music.
5 _____ of them likes jazz.
6 _____ of them can speak Italian.

7 _____ of them play tennis.
8 _____ of them plays basketball.
9 _____ of them is British.
10 _____ of them live in London.
11 _____ of them are students.
12 _____ of them has got a car.

2 Write sentences with *either* and *neither* and the words in the box.

| country   language   sport   ~~type of music~~ |

1 I don't like jazz and I don't like rock music.
   I don't like either type of music.
   I like neither type of music.

2 I haven't been to Austria and I haven't been to Uruguay.
   _____

3 I can't speak French and I can't speak Italian.
   _____

4 I don't play tennis and I don't play basketball.
   _____

3 (2.16) Complete the sentences with *both, either* or *neither*. Then listen and check.

1 Oh, no! I've lost _____ of my earrings.

2 _____ of those men is my husband.

3 I haven't tried _____ of these drinks.

4 _____ of the women were in the train station at eight o'clock.

5 You can take the bus or go by train. _____ is just as fast.

6 _____ of my parents is English.

137

64 *much, many* and *a lot*
Countable and uncountable nouns

A: OK. How much rice have we got?
B: We've got a lot. We've got 10,000 kilos.
A: And how many tins of vegetables?
B: Not many. Just 2,500 tins.
A: That's not good. How much flour have we got?
B: Not much. Just 1,000 kilos.

Presentation

Countable and uncountable nouns

- Some nouns are countable: *one tin, two tins, three tins …*
  Countable nouns have singular and plural forms.

- Some nouns are uncountable: *rice, flour …*
  Uncountable nouns are always singular.

much, many and *a lot*

- Use *much* with uncountable nouns.

- Use *many* with countable nouns.

- Use *much* and *many* in questions (with *how*) and in negatives: *How much rice? There isn't much rice.*
  How many tins? There aren't many tins.

- Use *a lot* with both countable and uncountable nouns: *a lot of tins, a lot of rice.*

Exercises

1 Are these things countable or uncountable? Write *C* or *U*.

1	rice	U	9	air	
2	flour		10	light	
3	tin of soup		11	space	
4	people		12	window	
5	money		13	CD	
6	time		14	book	
7	petrol		15	DVD	
8	oil		16	milk	

2 **2.17** **Complete the conversations with *much* or *many*. Then listen and check.**

Conversation 1

A: How ¹ _much_ time have we got?

B: We've got about an hour before everyone arrives.

A: How ² _____ people are coming?

B: Not ³ _____ – about twenty.

A: Twenty? And how ⁴ _____ money have we spent?

Conversation 2

C: Is the car ready?

D: Well, we haven't got ⁵ _____ petrol.

C: OK, and how ⁶ _____ oil have we got?

D: Not ⁷ _____ and there isn't ⁸ _____ air in the tyres.

Conversation 3

E: Did you like the apartment?

F: No, I didn't. There wasn't ⁹ _____ light.

E: Really?

F: No, and there weren't ¹⁰ _____ windows. And there wasn't ¹¹ _____ space either.

Conversation 4

G: How ¹² _____ CDs are there?

H: About five hundred.

G: What about books? How ¹³ _____ books are there?

H: About a thousand.

G: And how ¹⁴ _____ DVDs are there?

H: About two hundred.

3 **Correct the sentences. Five are correct.**

1 There are a lot of tins in that cupboard.   _correct_

2 We don't have many salt.   _We don't have much salt._

3 How many milk do you need?

4 I have a lot of information about it.

5 There isn't a lot time. Let's go!

6 How much rooms do you need?

7 There aren't many chairs.

8 How a lot of rice do you want?

9 How much sugar have we got?

10 There aren't much milk in the fridge.

11 Are there much people at the party?

12 A lot of people is vegetarians these days.

65 Review of units 61 to 64

Grammar

1 Complete the second sentence with *all, most, some* or *none*.

1   100% of the students are studying English.
    All the students are studying English.

2   30% of them are studying Chinese.
    _____ of them are studying Chinese.

3   75% are studying business.
    _____ are studying business.

4   0% are studying Latin.
    _____ is studying Latin.

5   100% of the students are between 14 and 18 years old.
    _____ of the students are between 14 and 18 years old.

6   80% are older than 16.
    _____ are older than 16.

7   70% of them are from Europe.
    _____ of them are from Europe.

8   25% are from Asia.
    _____ are from Asia.

9   0% are from America.
    _____ is from America.

2 Complete the sentences with *everybody, somebody, anybody* or *nobody*.

1   _Everybody_ in my family likes ice cream.

2   Is there _____ in the house?

3   I'm sure I saw _____ in the garden.

4   _____ came to my party – it was terrible.

5   _____ came to my party – it was wonderful.

6   _____ knows where they went on holiday. They didn't tell us.

7   Has _____ seen my car keys?

3 Complete the sentences with *everywhere, somewhere, anywhere* or *nowhere*.

1   Are you going _anywhere_ this weekend?

2   I've looked _____ and I can't find my keys.

3   There's _____ nicer than home.

4   There isn't _____ to park here.

5   Every year we go _____ different for our holidays.

6   The café was really busy and there was _____ for me to sit.

7   I've seen that man _____ before, I just can't remember where.

4 Complete the sentences with *everything, something, anything* or *nothing*.

1   Wait a minute – I've got _something_ in my shoe.

2   There isn't _____ on TV.

3   I'd like to do _____ fun today.

4   We have to go to the shops: there's _____ to eat in the house.

5   Don't worry. _____ is going to be OK.

6   He wasn't hungry, so he didn't have _____ to eat.

7   There was _____ in the room. It was completely empty.

5 Complete the sentences with *both, either* or *neither*.

1 I've got two brothers. ____Both____ of them live in London.

2 _____ of my parents speaks English.

3 _____ of us wants to go out tonight.

4 We can see _____ film, I don't mind.

5 Hmm, apple pie or ice cream … Could I have _____ , please?

6 I don't like _____ of these CDs very much.

7 We tried two hotels but _____ of them had any rooms.

8 I can't decide. _____ of them is fine.

6 Choose the correct options.

1 How *much* / *many* petrol *is* / *are* there?

2 How *much* / *many* time *is* / *are* there?

3 How *much* / *many* books *is* / *are* there?

4 How *much* / *many* DVDs *is* / *are* there?

5 How *much* / *many* money *is* / *are* there?

6 How *much* / *many* space *is* / *are* there?

7 How *much* / *many* people *is* / *are* there?

8 How *much* / *many* CDs *is* / *are* there?

Pronunciation: *of*

7 **2.18** We often pronounce *of* like this: /əv/. Listen and repeat each line.

All of

All of the students

All of the students have a lot of

All of the students have a lot of homework

All of the students have a lot of homework but none of

All of the students have a lot of homework but none of them has done it.

Vocabulary

8 What are the students learning in English? Match the words in the box to the sentences.

> listening ~~speaking~~ reading writing
> grammar vocabulary literature

1 How do you say this word? ____speaking____

2 Sorry, I didn't understand. Can you play it again, please? _____

3 What is the opposite of 'happy'? _____

4 What's the past tense of 'do'? _____

5 I don't understand what Shakespeare means. _____

6 What does this sentence mean? _____

7 How do I finish a letter? _____

Listen again

9 **2.19** Listen and answer the questions.

Conversation 1

1 How much time have they got?
About an hour.

2 How many people are coming?

Conversation 2

3 How much oil have they got?

Conversation 3

4 Was there much light in the apartment?

5 Were there many windows?

Conversation 4

6 How many CDs are there?

7 How many books are there?

8 How many DVDs are there?

66 *a/an* (indefinite article)

… and have a huge car …

I'd like to be a pop star …

… and live in an enormous house.

Presentation

a or an?

Use *a* before a consonant sound: *a doctor, a celebrity, a university.*

Use *an* before a word beginning with a vowel sound: *an animal, an hour.*

Use *a/an* (indefinite article) with …

- singular countable nouns: *a girl*
- adjective + noun: *a small dog*
- occupations: *I'd like to be a pop star.*
- possessions and residences: *I've got a huge car. She lives in an enormous house.*

TIP Don't use *a/an* with plural nouns (*a girls*) or uncountable nouns (*an information*).

Key vocabulary Occupations: actor, celebrity, chef, composer, engineer, pop star, shop assistant, teacher

Exercises

1 Complete the phrases with *a* or *an* where possible.

1	*an* actor	7		Australian rock band
2	Ø exercises	8		shop assistants
3	German actor	9		beautiful place
4	water	10		cheese
5	difficult exercises	11		old car
6	engineer	12		rock band

2 🔊 **2.20** **Complete the conversations with *a* or *an*. Then listen and check.**

Conversation 1

A: What would you like to be when you leave school?

B: I'd like to be ¹___a___ great composer.

A: Really? Do you play music?

B: No, but I got ²_____ guitar for my birthday so I'm going to learn.

Conversation 2

C: Did you read about Robbie?

D: Yes, he's bought ³_____ enormous house in Hollywood.

C: Can you believe it? I remember when he was ⁴_____ assistant in our local shop.

Conversation 3

E: Is there ⁵_____ library in the centre of town?

F: Yes, it's straight ahead and on the right. It's ⁶_____ huge building and it's got ⁷_____ sign outside. You can't miss it.

Conversation 4

G: How was the interview? Did they offer you ⁸_____ job?

H: Yes, and I get ⁹_____ office with my own computer!

G: Sounds great. How much holiday do you get?

H: I think I have ¹⁰_____ holiday after two years.

G: What?!

3 **Correct the sentences.**

1 He lives in ~~an~~ ᵃsmall apartment.

2 Maria was ᵃ Maths teacher for three years.

3 They've got a tickets for the match.

4 My uncle is a engineer.

5 That's beautiful bracelet!

6 Would you like table for two?

7 Robert De Niro is a American actor.

8 Have you seen a umbrella anywhere?

9 I'm going to be a chefs when I'm older.

10 Is there an bank near here?

4 **Read the text. The indefinite articles are missing. Write them in.**

Why do we love celebrities? Perhaps it's because our favourite star is ᵃ singer or ᵃⁿ actor. But what about celebrities who are famous because they are 'famous'? For example, Paris Hilton grew up in rich family. Then, as adult, she was always in magazine. She spent all her time at parties with other famous people. She has had many different jobs. She was model for a while. She made album, worked as actress in some TV commercials and films and has also written book. But her most successful job is as celebrity – whatever that is!

143

67 *the* (definite article)

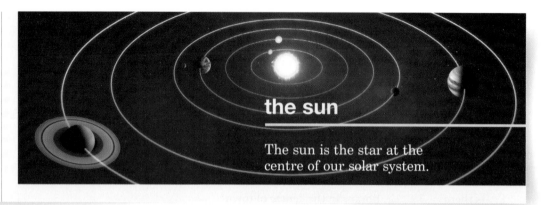

the sun

The sun is the star at the centre of our solar system.

The White House

The White House is the official home and workplace of the President of the United States of America.

blue whale

Blue whales are the largest animals in the world. They lived in all the oceans before the twentieth century. Nowadays, they normally live in the Antarctic, the Indian Ocean, the ...

Presentation

Use *the* (definite article) with …

- singular and plural countable nouns: *the house, the houses*.
- unique things (where there is only one): *the world, the White House, the Indian Ocean*.
- superlatives: *Blue whales are the largest animals in the world*.
- groups of countries or countries which are plural: *the United Kingdom, the European Union, the United States of America, the Philippines*.
- locations: *in the middle, on the left/right, in the north/south/east/west*.
- musical instruments: *I play the saxophone*.

Key vocabulary **The world:** the Earth (the world), the sun, the moon, the Indian Ocean, the United States of America (USA), the Netherlands, the Philippines, the United Kingdom (UK), the European Union (EU), the Indian Ocean, the Black Sea, the Atlantic Ocean, the North Pole, the Arctic, the Suez Canal, the Mediterranean Sea, the Red Sea
Places to visit: the White House, the Eiffel Tower, the Statue of Liberty, the Atomium monument

Exercises

1 **The definite items are missing. Write them in the sentences.**

1 This is Anouk. She's from ^*the* Netherlands.

2 Sri Lanka is in Indian Ocean.

3 Cheetahs are fastest animal on land.

4 Harald V is King of Norway.

5 Earth is 384,000 km from moon.

6 My mother cooks best cakes in world!

7 Can you play piano?

8 Paris is famous for Eiffel Tower.

9 That was worst film I've ever seen!

10 Black Sea used to be part of Atlantic Ocean.

11 There are twenty-seven countries in European Union.

12 I love to listen to violin.

2 ⏯2.21 **Write sentences. Add the definite article and make any other necessary changes. Then listen and check.**

tortoise

1 tortoises / live / longest

<u>Tortoises live the longest.</u>

2 Yuri Gagarin / be / first man in space

3 / Atomium monument / be / Brussels

4 / North Pole / be / in / Arctic

Suez canal

5 / Suez canal connects / Mediterranean Sea to / Red Sea

6 Ferdinand Magellan / go round / world in 1519

68 *a/an* and *the*

Presentation

- Use *a/an* for things in general and *the* for specific things.

  A: *Can I borrow a pen?* (any pen)

  B: *Sorry, this is the only pen I've got.* (a specific pen)

- Use *the* for things you know about.

  A: *The exams start next week.*

  B: *Yes, I know.*

- Use *a/an* for the first mention. Use *the* for the second mention.

  A: *Is there a football match tonight?*

  B: *No, there isn't. The next match is on the 25th.*

Exercises

1 Complete the sentences and questions with *a/an* or *the*.

1 Can I have ____*a*____ drink, please?

2 Is this _____ only pen you've got?

3 We'd like _____ table for two, please.

4 When does _____ History exam start?

5 What time is _____ last bus?

6 Is there _____ airport near your town?

7 What's _____ name of your new teacher?

8 Could you close _____ back door, please?

9 Who's _____ girl with long hair?

10 I've got _____ terrible headache.

2 Match the responses to a–j to the questions in exercise 1.

a   Mr Baines.   ☐

b   At midnight, I think.   ☐

c   Sure. Tea or coffee?   ☐ 1

d   My sister.   ☐

e   Yes, there's one about fifteen kilometres away.   ☐

f   Of course.   ☐

g   Would you like an aspirin?   ☐

h   Yes, it is.   ☐

i   At nine thirty.   ☐

j   Certainly. There's one by the window.   ☐

3 🔊 **2.22** Choose the correct options. Then listen and check.

Conversation 1

A: It's hot in here. Can I open ¹ *a* / *the* window?

B: Yes, but open ² *a* / *the* window in the middle. The other two don't open.

Conversation 2

C: Is there ³ *a* / *the* hotel near here?

D: Yes, there's ⁴ *a* / *the* Hilton down there.

C: Thanks.

Conversation 3

E: Have you got ⁵ *a* / *the* computer at home?

F: Yes, I have. In fact, I've just bought ⁶ *an* / *the* Apple Mac.

E: What's it like?

F: It's fantastic. ⁷ *A* / *The* screen is enormous and it's really easy to use.

Conversation 4

G: Hello. I'm on ⁸ *a* / *the* ten-thirty flight to ⁹ *a* / *the* USA.

H: Can I see your ticket and passport?

G: Sure.

H: Would you like ¹⁰ *a* / *the* window or ¹¹ *an* / *the* aisle seat?

G: Window, please.

Conversation 5

I: Who's ¹² *a* / *the* man on the bicycle? He's very good-looking.

J: I'm not sure, but I think he's one of ¹³ *a* / *the* new teachers.

I: Oh.

Conversation 6

K: Can I have ¹⁴ *a* / *the* coffee?

L: Sure. There's ¹⁵ *a* / *the* cup in ¹⁶ *a* / *the* kitchen cupboard.

K: Thanks.

Conversation 7

M: ¹⁷ *A* / *The* film I told you about is on TV tonight.

N: Really? I was going to relax and read ¹⁸ *a* / *the* book this evening.

M: You should watch ¹⁹ *a* / *the* film. It's ²⁰ *a* / *the* best film I've ever seen.

Conversation 8

O: I haven't had ²¹ *a* / *the* good meal in ages.

P: We should try ²² *a* / *the* new Italian restaurant in town. I've heard ²³ *a* / *the* pizzas are great.

O: Good idea. Let's go tonight.

4 Write articles in the boxes. Then complete the sentences so that they are true for you.

1   ☐ The ☐ most famous place in my country is ....

2   My birthday is on ☐ ....

3   I've got ☐ ....

4   Next week, I'm going to ☐ ....

5   I'm ☐ ....

6   ☐ best holiday I had was in ....

7   ☐ leader of my country is ....

8   My favourite musical instrument is ☐ ....

147

69 No article

Travel to Peru and experience history

For tourists who love history, there is no better destination than Peru. When you arrive in Lima, you can easily tour the old city on foot and visit its museums. Then go by bus to Lake Titicaca and Machu Picchu. Peruvians are friendly people and many of them speak English, but try to learn some Spanish before you go.

Presentation

You don't often use an article with plural and uncountable nouns: *There are buses to every destination. For more information, contact us.*

Don't use an article ...

- to talk about things in general: *I like cats. English people drink tea in the afternoon.*
- for many place names: *I live in Lima.*
- for languages, countries and subjects: *Take a holiday in Peru. Learn to speak Spanish. I like studying Geography.*
- with geographical features: *Lake Titicaca, Mount Everest.*
- with forms of travel and transport: *Travel through the mountains on foot or by bicycle.*

TIP Don't use an article for these special cases: *at school/home.*

Key vocabulary Travel: by bicycle, on foot, by car, by train, by taxi, tour, destination, arrive, travel round by bus, by subway, take a taxi, tourist

Exercises

1 **Choose the correct options.**

1 *The Italian food /* Italian food is the best in the world!

2 *The people / People* over there are from Germany.

3 Try *the sandwiches / sandwiches* at this café.

4 Who is *the girl / girl* on the bike?

5 I like *the rock music / rock music*.

6 There's never enough *the time / time*.

7 Are *the elephants / elephants* really afraid of mice?

8 *The life / Life* is harder for children these days.

9 I prefer to travel round cities on *the foot / foot*.

10 Do you speak *the Chinese / Chinese*?

2 **Cross out the *the* where it isn't necessary.**

1 We visited the Eiffel Tower last year. ✓

2 Have you ever been to ~~the~~ Disneyland?

3 I go to the school at eight o'clock.

4 My father works at the home.

5 She goes to work by the bicycle.

6 I would love to see the Mount Everest.

7 I hate the golf. I never play it.

8 We study the Urdu at school. It's a great language.

9 The Spanish people are very friendly.

10 My mother works at the hospital in Oxford.

11 My grandmother lives in the Berlin.

12 I eat a lot of the apples.

3 **Choose the correct answers.**

1 I love ___c___ dogs. I have three of them.
   a a   b the   c Ø

2 I live in _____ .
   a United States b United Kingdom c Uruguay

3 Do you speak _____ local language?
   a a   b the   c Ø

4 You can only travel to the village on _____ foot.
   a a   b the   c Ø

5 There's _____ bus every fifteen minutes.
   a a   b the   c Ø

6 There are always _____ taxis outside the station.
   a a   b the   c Ø

4 🎧 **2.23** **Complete the text with *the, a, an* or Ø (no article). Then listen and check.**

Travel tips for visitors to Beijing

Transport

¹ __Ø__ Beijing's metro and buses are often crowded so visitors should take ² _____ taxi. Don't worry if you don't speak Chinese – many taxi drivers are now learning ³ _____ English.

Sightseeing

⁴ _____ Great Wall of ⁵ _____ China is about two hours by ⁶ _____ car from ⁷ _____ Beijing. Or you can see ⁸ _____ panda in Beijing Zoo and then have ⁹ _____ excellent meal in ¹⁰ _____ CCTV (China Central Television) Tower restaurant.

Eating

You can buy ¹¹ _____ cheap Chinese food in the street or there are ¹² _____ international restaurants in ¹³ _____ centre. Try Peking duck.

Grammar

1 Choose the correct options.

International Space Station

Anousheh Ansari

[1](The)/ A space tourism industry is now open for [2] *the / Ø* business! Tickets cost $20 million for [3] *a / an* ten-day stay in space. Dennis Tito was [4] *the / Ø* world's first space tourist. [5] *Ø / A* Russia took [6] *an / the* American businessman into space in [7] *the / a* rocket. It arrived at [8] *an / the* International Space Station on [9] *Ø / the* 30th of April, 2001. In 2006, Anousheh Ansari, who is [10] *a / Ø* telecommunications entrepreneur, became [11] *a / the* first female space tourist.

As [12] *Ø / a* space travel becomes more and more normal, travel companies are planning to offer [13] *a / Ø* regular flights. They are also designing hotels in space and holiday resorts on [14] *Ø / the* moon.

2 Complete the second sentence so that it means the same as the first. Use an article.

1 Elephants are larger than any other land animals.
  Elephants are ___the largest___ land animals.

2 Pam is a US citizen.
  Pam lives in _____ of America.

3 My uncle plays football.
  My uncle is _____ player.

4 Your town is small.
  You come from _____ .

5 Julia has two younger brothers. She's 24 and they're 23 and 21.
  Julia is _____ in her family.

6 My degree is in Spanish.
  I have _____ degree.

7 Coffee for me, please.
  I'd like _____ , please.

8 My head aches.
  I have _____ .

9 Hollywood's most popular actress is currently Nicole Kidman.
  Nicole Kidman is currently _____ in Hollywood.

10 History starts at three.
   _____ lesson starts at three.

11 My sister's flat is in Berlin.
   My sister has _____ in Berlin.

12 There are two red cars and my car is between them.
   There are two red cars and my car _____ middle.

13 This machine washes dishes.
   This is _____ washer.

14 This song is by Abba.
   This is _____ by Abba.

Pronunciation: *the*

3 **⊘2.24** **There are two ways to pronounce *the*. Say /ðiː/ before words that start with a vowel sound. Say /ðə/ before words that start with a consonant sound. Listen.**

/ðiː/ the elephant

/ðə/ the panda

Now listen and tick /ðiː/ or /ðə/.

1	the address	/ðiː/ ✓	/ðə/
2	the mountain	/ðiː/	/ðə/
3	the school	/ðiː/	/ðə/
4	the umbrella	/ðiː/	/ðə/
5	the celebrity	/ðiː/	/ðə/
6	the ocean	/ðiː/	/ðə/
7	the town	/ðiː/	/ðə/
8	the bicycle	/ðiː/	/ðə/
9	the Eiffel Tower	/ðiː/	/ðə/
10	the White House	/ðiː/	/ðə/

Vocabulary

4 **Complete the crossword with travel words.**

Across

1 place you travel to
5 go _____ train
6 opposite of *leave*
7 a good way to travel around a crowded city
8 _____ the old city

Down

2 a train under the ground
3 a person who visits places (on holiday)
4 you walk _____ foot

5 **Match to make six occupations.**

1	com	brity	composer
2	pop	acher	
3	ch	ef	
4	cele	poser	
5	engi	star	
6	te	neer	

6 **Match to make places around the world.**

1	the Indian	Pole
2	the United	House
3	the European	Union
4	the North	Liberty
5	the White	Ocean
6	the Statue of	Kingdom

Listen again

7 **Test your general knowledge!**

Quiz

1 Which animal lives the longest?

2 Who was the first man in space?

3 Where is the Atomium monument?

4 Is the North Pole in the Arctic or the Antarctic?

5 Which canal connects the Mediterranean Sea to the Red Sea?

6 Who travelled round the world in 1519?

⊘2.25 **Listen and check your answers.**

71 *will* (for future and predictions)

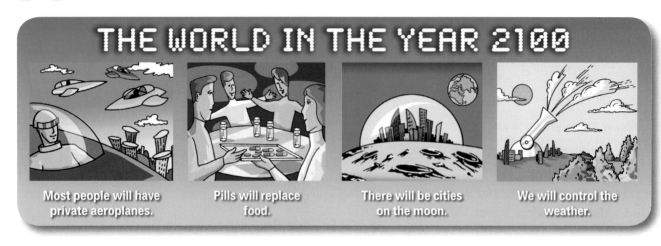

THE WORLD IN THE YEAR 2100

Most people will have private aeroplanes.

Pills will replace food.

There will be cities on the moon.

We will control the weather.

Presentation

Use *will* to …

- talk about facts in the future: *I was born in 1975. I'll be 75 in the year 2050.*
- make predictions about the future:

   Pills will replace food. (= It's certain.)

   Pills won't replace food. (= It's certain not to happen.)

   I (don't) think pills will replace food. (= It's my opinion.)

Affirmative and negative

I / You / He / She / It / We / They	will ('ll) ——————— will not (won't)	be	75 in the year 2050.

Yes/No questions

Will	I / you / he / she / it / we / they	be	75 in the year 2050?

Short answers

Yes,	I / you / he / she / it / we / they	will.	No,	I / you / he / she / it / we / they	won't.

Exercises

1 Add *'ll* or *will* to the sentences.

1   Tomorrow ᴡⁱˡˡ be a beautiful day.

2   One day I be famous.

3   We be in Rome tomorrow so meet us there.

4   Your new girlfriend be at the party?

5   I think John pass all his exams.

6   When you be eighteen?

7   Who win: Real Madrid or AC Milan?

8   Don't worry: I'm sure you get better.

9   Next week it be the summer holidays!

10   Do you think it rain tomorrow?

11   Nobody be in the office tomorrow so don't call.

12   We ever find a cure for cancer?

2 Are the sentences in exercise 1 facts in the future (F) or predictions about the future (P)? Write *P* or *F*.

1 [P] 2 [ ] 3 [ ] 4 [ ] 5 [ ] 6 [ ]
7 [ ] 8 [ ] 9 [ ] 10 [ ] 11 [ ] 12 [ ]

3 Put the words in order to make predictions.

1 become China country in richest the the will world
China will become the richest country in the world.

2 buy everything internet on people the will

3 get hotter the will world

4 English everybody speak will

5 reach in 2020 Mars humans will

6 a hundred will everybody for years live

4 ⊘2.26 Complete the conversation with *will, 'll* or *won't*. Then listen and check.

A: ¹ ___Will___ you be here tomorrow?

B: Yes, I ² _____ . I ³ _____ be in the Sol Café at eleven o'clock.

A: ⁴ _____ you be alone?

B: Yes, I ⁵ _____ .

A: What about Cassia?

B: She ⁶ _____ be here.

A: Where ⁷ _____ she be?

B: She ⁸ _____ be in Amsterdam with Henri.

5 ⊘2.27 Complete the conversation. Then listen and check.

A: Cassia? This is Bernardo. Can you talk?

C: Yes, of course.

A: When ¹ ___will you be___ in Amsterdam?

C: ² _____ in Amsterdam on 1ˢᵗ August.

A: ³ _____ alone?

C: No, ⁴ _____ . ⁵ _____ with Henri.

A: Which hotel ⁶ _____ in?

C: ⁷ _____ in the Four Seasons.

A: Be careful.

C: Don't worry. ⁸ _____ very, very careful.

72 *will* (offers, promises and requests)

Presentation

Use *will* for …

- offers: *I'll come and pick you up.*
- promises: *I'll be there in twenty minutes.*
- requests: *Will you lend me your car?*

Exercises

1 Add *'ll* or *will* to the conversations.

1 A: This exercise is difficult!

   B: Don't worry. I 'll help you.

2 A: Have we got a cake for Nell's birthday?

   B: No, but I make one.

3 A: This suitcase is heavy!

   B: I carry it for you.

4 A: I don't want to go to bed without a story.

   B: I read you one, I promise.

5 A: Are you going to the party tonight?

   B: I don't know yet. You pick me up?

6 A: I can't find my tennis racket.

   B: I lend you mine.

7 A: I help you if you like.

   B: No, thanks. I can do it.

8 A: Should I text you to remind you about the meeting?

   B: Don't worry. I remember.

9 A: I bought this from your shop but it doesn't work.

   B: That's OK. We change it.

10 A: You send the books by post?

    B: Yes, of course. What's your address?

2 Write offers with *will*.

1 I'm thirsty! (make / a cup of tea)   I'll make you a cup of tea.
2 I'm hungry! (make / a sandwich)
3 I've just arrived at the station. (pick up)
4 I'm going to be late. (wait for)
5 I haven't got any money! (lend some)
6 I'm hot! (get / glass of cold water)

3 Eddie and Flo have just got married. Complete their promises with *I'll always* or *I'll never*.

1   I'll always   love you.
2 _____ leave you.
3 _____ be there for you.
4 _____ look at another woman.
5 _____ speak to James again.
6 _____ put you first.
7 _____ forget your birthday.

Eddie and Flo

4 🔊 2.28 Write the son's requests. Then listen and check.

1 lend me / car?

No, I need it.

2 drive me to / party?

No, I'm busy.

3 pay for / taxi?

No, I won't.

4 give me money / bus ticket?

Here. Take the car.

73 *will* and *going to* (for decisions)

Woman: What are you going to have?
Man: I'm not sure. I think I'll have the fish. What about you?
Woman: Oh, I've already decided. I'm going to have the steak with fried potatoes.
Man: That sounds nice. Maybe I'll have steak too …

Presentation

Use *will* to show you are making a decision at that moment. (You often use it with *I think*.)

The man isn't sure what he wants so he uses *will*: *I think I'll have the fish*.

Use *going to* to show that you have already made a decision.

The woman has decided so she uses *going to*: *I'm going to have the steak*.

> **Key vocabulary** Adjectives: beautiful, bored, cold, hot, hungry, thirsty, tired
> Food: chicken, fish, fried potatoes, pasta, pizza, salad, sandwich, steak, tomato, soup

Exercises

1 Put the words in order.

1 have I I'll soup the think tomato   I think I'll have the tomato soup.
2 a have I I'll pizza think   ....
3 a chicken have I I'll sandwich think   ....
4 have I I'll salad steak the think with ....

2 Make decisions for the situations. Use *go*, *have* or *turn on* and the phrases in the box.

| home   the air conditioning   ~~some pasta~~   for a walk   a glass of water   the heating   to bed |

   Situations   Decisions
1 I'm hungry.   I think I'll have a some pasta.
2 I'm cold.   ....
3 I'm thirsty.   ....
4 I'm tired.   ....
5 I'm hot.   ....
6 It's a beautiful day. ....
7 It's started raining. ....

3 Complete the sentences with *I'm going to* or *I think I'll.*

1 _____I'm going to_____ see Real Madrid play AC Milan: I've got tickets.

2 The sun's come out. _____ go to the beach.

3 I've sold my car. _____ buy a new one.

4 It's getting dark. _____ turn on the light.

5 I'm going to Tokyo for six months. _____ study Japanese.

4 🎵2.29 **Put the conversation in order. Then listen and check.**

☐ I don't know. I think I'll travel around India for six months.

☐ What about you? Mark said you've got a job.

☐ 1 What are you going to do when you finish university?

☐ That sounds interesting.

☐ Yes, I have. I'm going to work for a bank.

5 **Look at the pictures. Tick what the person says.**

1 I'm going to pay for it.
  I'll pay for it. ✔

4 I'll be a doctor like my father.
  I'm going to be a doctor like my father.

2 I'm going to have a holiday in Florida!
  I'll have a holiday in Florida.

5 I'll get it.
  I'm going to get it.

3 I'll help you.
  I'm going to help you.

6 I'll have a dinner party tonight.
  I'm going to have a dinner party tonight.

74 *going to, will* and the present continuous

Woman:	What do you see?
Fortune teller:	I can see a tall man. He's walking towards you. You're going to meet him.
Woman:	Oh, I know who that is! I'm meeting my boyfriend for lunch.
Fortune teller:	And now I see you in a strange place full of people you don't know.
Woman:	I know what that is. We're going to visit Paris soon.
Fortune teller:	Wait! I think you will take a long journey together in the middle of the night.
Woman:	That'll be the train to Paris.
Fortune teller:	Is there anything about your future you don't know?!

Presentation

will or *going to* for predictions?

You can use either *will* and *going to* for making predictions.

- You can use *will* without a clue or evidence: *I think you will take a long journey together in the middle of the night.*

- You can also use *going to* when there is a clue or evidence: *The man is walking towards you. You're going to meet him.*

going to or present continuous for plans and arrangements?

You often use the present continuous and *going to* in similar ways but …

- use the present continuous to talk about future arrangements: *I'm meeting my boyfriend for lunch.*

- use *going to* to talk about a plan or intention: *We're going to visit Paris soon.*

TIP You normally use the present continuous, not *going to*, with the verbs *go* and *come*.
Say *We're going to the restaurant.* (don't say ~~We're going to go to the restaurant.~~)
Say *They're coming later.* (don't say ~~They're going to come later.~~)

See Units 33 and 34 and page 236: Summary of future forms

Exercises

1 Match predictions 1–5 to the evidence a–e.

1	You're going to hurt yourself.	☐	a	The traffic is really bad.
2	We're going to arrive late.	☐	b	There isn't a cloud in the sky.
3	It's going to be sunny today.	☐	c	He eats chocolate every day.
4	I'm going to pass this exam.	☐	d	I studied all last week.
5	Billy is going to get really fat.	☐	e	That knife looks dangerous.

2 (2.30) **Look at the pictures and write sentences. Use *going to*, *will* or the present continuous. Then listen and check.**

1   Rita and I / play / on

_____

2   It's OK. I / pay / lunch

_____

3   This year / I / learn

_____

3   Complete the conversations with the present continuous or *will* form of the verbs.

1   A: What are you doing on Tuesday?
    B: _____I'm having_____ (I have) lunch with Jerry.

2   A: Do you think Martin _____ (get) married?
    B: No, I don't think so.

3   A: _____ (it snow) tomorrow?
    B: Yes, I think it will.

4   A: When _____ (you get) married?
    B: On the 25th of June.

5   A: Where _____ (you go) for your holidays this year?
    B: To Greece.

6   A: _____ (I like) this book?
    B: No, it's boring.

4   Choose the correct options. Sometimes both forms are possible.

1   Mike and I *will have / are having* a drink at five. Would you like to come too?

2   I've only got a few pages to read. I *'ll / 'm going to* finish my book in a minute.

3   A: What does Johnny plan to see in London?
    B: He *'ll see / 's going to see* a musical and also visit a few museums.

4   What time *are you coming / are you going to come* to my house?

5   When *are you telling / are you going to tell* me your answer?

6   We *'re going to / 're going to go to* the cinema at ten o'clock.

5   Write about your plans and arrangements for these times. Use *going to* or the present continuous.

1   (this evening) _____

2   (next weekend) _____

3   (next month) _____

4   (next year) _____

75 Review of units 71 to 74

Grammar

1 Complete the sentences. Write one word in each gap.

1 We _____'re_____ going to see you later.

2 They _____ coming I'm afraid. They're busy.

3 What _____ you doing this evening at eight?

4 I think I _____ meet you after the film.

5 I don't think flying cars _____ replace normal cars in the future.

6 He _____ going to be an engineer when he leaves school.

7 He _____ having his birthday in a nightclub this year.

8 _____ you give me a lift to the party tonight?

9 It's an early flight. Promise me you _____ be late.

2 There is one extra word in each section of the email 1–7. Cross it out.

E-mail

New   Reply   Forward   Print   Delete   Send & Receive

From: Pablo
To: Lorraine
Subject: News

▶ Attachments:

Hi
Great news! I passed my final exam. ¹What ~~do~~ are you doing tonight? ²I'm to celebrating at the Irish Pub. ³Please will come. ⁴I'll be being there at eight o'clock. ⁵Also my dad is are going to pay for a holiday. ⁶I think I'll going travel to somewhere like Spain or Greece. ⁷Anyway, I'll am see you tonight I hope.
Pablo

3 Choose the correct forms.

¹ Are you being / Will you be here next week?

No, I ² 'm not. / won't. I ³ 'm being / 'll be in Paris.

What ⁴ are you doing / will you do tonight?

We ⁵ 're going / 'll go to the opera – Jamie's given us tickets for *Faust*.

Will we ⁶ see / seeing you later?

I'm afraid not. I ⁷ 'm going / will go to bed early tonight.

Is it ⁸ going to snow / snowing tonight?

Maybe. The temperature is dropping.

4 Complete these sentences so that they are true for you.

1 **prediction**
   In 2050, I _____

2 **fact in the future**
   In 2050, I _____

3 **intention**
   Next year I'm going _____

4 **arrangement**
   At the weekend, I'm _____

5 **promise to a friend**
   I'll _____

Pronunciation: 'll

5 (●2.31) **Listen and tick the sentence you hear.**

1   a   The plane leaves at five.
     b   The plane'll leave at five.

2   a   Pills replace food.
     b   Pills'll replace food.

3   a   I have tea in the morning.
     b   I'll have tea in the morning.

4   a   We pick you up from the airport.
     b   We'll pick you up from the airport.

5   a   Prices go up before Christmas.
     b   Prices'll go up before Christmas.

6   a   They learn the piano.
     b   They'll learn the piano.

7   a   Don't worry. I open it.
     b   Don't worry. I'll open it.

8   a   We always have lunch together.
     b   We'll always have lunch together.

Vocabulary

6   **Match the adjectives in the box to the sentences.**

difficult   hot   hungry
~~thirsty~~   cold   tired   bored

1   'I need a drink.'   thirsty

2   'This is really hard. Can you answer it?'

3   'Turn the heating up!'

4   'I didn't have any lunch today. Let's have something to eat.'

5   'I just need to sit down for a minute and have a little rest.'

6   'Can we open the window?'

7   'This is really uninteresting.'

7   Write the food words.

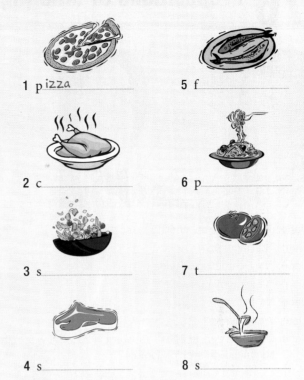

1   p izza

2   c

3   s

4   s

5   f

6   p

7   t

8   s

Listen again

8   (●2.32) **Listen and put the conversation in order.**

☐   Be careful.

1   Cassia? This is Bernardo. Can you talk?

☐   I'll be in Amsterdam on 1st August.

☐   I'll be in the Four Seasons.

☐   No, I won't. I'll be with Henri.

☐   When will you be in Amsterdam?

☐   Which hotel will you be in?

☐   Will you be alone?

☐   Yes, of course.

☐   Don't worry. I'll be very, very careful.

76 Prepositions of time *(in, on, at)*

Jane: Jeff and Sue are coming to my party!

Dan: That's great.

Jane: They're coming on Friday. They're arriving at 6.30.

Dan: In the morning?

Jane: No, in the evening.

Dan: When did we last see them?

Jane: Oh, years ago, in 2004 – or was it in 2005? It was in the summer. Don't you remember?

YOU ARE INVITED TO

Jane's 30th birthday party

ON 27TH JUNE
AT 8.30
IN THE RED LION

Presentation

- Use *in* with months, years, seasons and times of day: *in February, in 2005, in spring, in the afternoon.*
- Use *on* with days and dates: *on Friday, on 28th November, on my birthday.*
- Use *at* with times: *at 8.30, at midnight.*
- **TIP** Special uses of *at: at the weekend, at night.*

> **Key vocabulary** **Seasons:** spring, summer, autumn, winter
> **Months:** January, February, March, April, May, June, July, August, September, October, November, December
> **Dates:** Use ordinal numbers (*1st, 2nd, 3rd,* etc.) for dates, e.g. 1st January, 3rd March, 25th May

Exercises

1 Write the time expressions in the correct column.

> ~~New year's day~~   29th February   1999   half past ten   the evenings
> the third Friday of the month   Sundays   August   midday   summer   the middle of winter
> night   5 p.m.   the 1990s   the early morning   weekdays   the same time   the weekend

in	on	at
	New Year's day	

2 **Complete the sentences with expressions from exercise 1 and *in*, *on* or *at*.**

1 My birthday's ___on 29th February___ so I only celebrate once every four years!

2 I really don't like Britain _____. The days are so short and there's so little light.

3 I like to get to bed fairly early. I'm usually in bed _____ on week days.

4 I love studying _____. It's so quiet. Everyone else is still in bed and I can really concentrate.

5 Most small, local shops are closed all day _____.

6 There's a street market in the main square once a month, _____.

7 We will be holding our next meeting at the community centre _____ in the morning next week.

8 The world wide web was created _____.

3 **Match 1–6 to a–f to make sentences.**

1	I get up at ☐	a August.
2	I don't like going to the gym in ☐	b the same time every day.
3	Our book club meets on ☐	c 15th July 2005.
4	I have lunch really early. I often eat at ☐	d the evening. It's too busy.
5	I moved to London on ☐	e midday.
6	I always go on holiday in ☐	f the third Friday of every month.

4 **②2.33 Choose the correct prepositions. Then listen and check.**

Conversation 1

A: When's your birthday?

B: It's [1] *in /* (*on*) *at* 15th March.

A: When were you born?

B: [2] *In / On / At* 1988.

A: What time were you born?

B: I'm not sure. [3] *In / On / At* around eleven, I think.

A: [4] *In / On / At* the morning?

B: No, [5] *in / on / at* night.

Conversation 2

C: When do you usually get up?

D: [6] *In / On / At* weekdays, I get up [7] *in / on / at* about seven thirty, but [8] *in / on / at* the weekend I get up [9] *in / on / at* any time, whenever I wake up, really.

C: When do you usually go to bed?

D: It depends. During the week I usually go to bed [10] *in / on / at* eleven thirty. [11] *In / On / At* the winter I go to bed a bit earlier.

5 **Answer the questions with true answers for you.**

1 When's your birthday? _____

2 When were you born? _____

3 What time were you born? _____

4 When do you usually get up? _____

5 When do you usually go to bed? _____

77 Prepositions of place

The swimming pool is on the left, and the changing rooms are on the right. The gym is behind the stairs. There's a sauna between the gym and the tennis courts. There are regular aerobic classes in the gym, and yoga classes in the dance studio on the first floor. There is information about all the classes on the table at the front door. At the top of the stairs there's a solarium and a terrace bar. So, here's your card and welcome to the club!

Presentation

in, on and *at*

in the gym

on the table

at the front door

Expressions with *in, on* and *at*

in the corner

in the middle

on the left

on the right

at the corner

at the top

at the bottom

More prepositions of place

next to

under

in front of

behind

opposite

between

Key vocabulary Sports centre: (open air) swimming pool, aerobics classes, changing rooms, dance classes, dance studio, gym, sauna, solarium, tennis courts, yoga classes

Exercises

1 Match the places on the plan a–f to the words.

1 changing rooms [a]
2 gym ☐
3 tennis courts ☐
4 dance studio ☐
5 swimming pool ☐
6 reception ☐
7 solarium ☐
8 café ☐

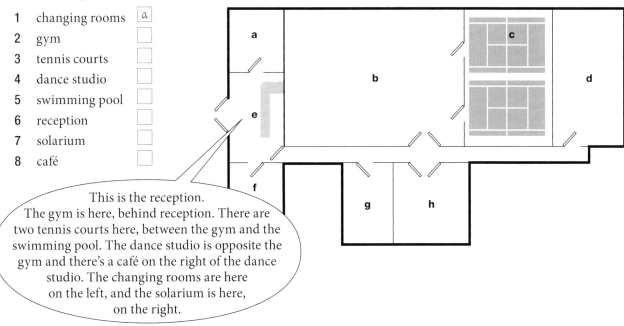

This is the reception.
The gym is here, behind reception. There are
two tennis courts here, between the gym and the
swimming pool. The dance studio is opposite the
gym and there's a café on the right of the dance
studio. The changing rooms are here
on the left, and the solarium is here,
on the right.

2 Complete the conversations with *in, on* or *at*.

Conversation 1

A: See you later?
B: Yes, I'll be ¹ _at_ the corner of the
street at 8.30.

Conversation 2

A: Where's the bus stop?
B: It's ² _____ the bottom of the street
³ _____ the left, you can't miss it.

Conversation 3

C: Where's your office?
D: It's ⁴ _____ the third floor, ⁵ _____
the middle, between a dentist and a lawyer.

Conversation 4

E: Can I use the phone, please?
F: Yes, sure. It's ⁶ _____ the table, ⁷ _____
the corner of the living room.

3 🔊 2.34 Complete the description with the expressions in the box. Then listen and check.

| behind   in front of   in the corner   ~~in the middle~~   next to   on the left   on the right   under |

This is my family. This is my mum, sitting ¹ _in the middle_ .
That's my brother ² _____ sitting
³ _____ her. That's me ⁴ _____
with my husband. ⁵ _____ us is my dad and
⁶ _____ us are our two children.
⁷ _____ the table ⁸ _____ you
can see my dog.

78 Relative clauses 1 *(who, which, that)*

Presentation

Relative pronouns introduce relative clauses. Relative clauses give information about a person or thing.

- Use *who* for people: *Bob is the person who does the repairs.*
- Use *which* for things: *A plunger is a thing which unblocks sinks.*
- Use *that* for people or things: *She's the person that works in reception. It's a thing that helps you do your job.*

> **Key vocabulary** Nouns ending in *-er*: banker, bottle opener, cleaner, computer, dancer, dishwasher, DVD player, gardener, hairdryer, lighter, plunger, printer, supporter, teacher, tennis player, writer

Exercises

1 Match the pictures to the definitions.

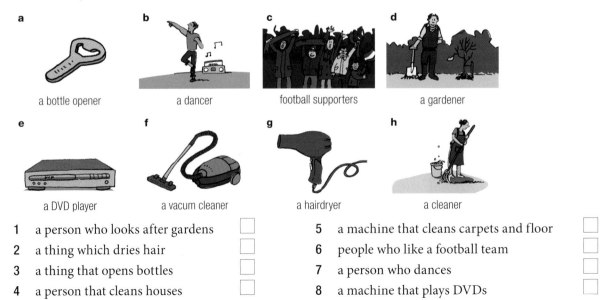

a a bottle opener	**b** a dancer
c football supporters	**d** a gardener
e a DVD player	**f** a vacum cleaner
g a hairdryer	**h** a cleaner

1 a person who looks after gardens ☐
2 a thing which dries hair ☐
3 a thing that opens bottles ☐
4 a person that cleans houses ☐

5 a machine that cleans carpets and floor ☐
6 people who like a football team ☐
7 a person who dances ☐
8 a machine that plays DVDs ☐

2 **Cross out the incorrect pronoun.**

1 A tennis player is a person *who / which / that* plays tennis.

2 A lighter is a thing *who / which / that* lights a cigarette.

3 A printer is a machine *who / which / that* prints pages from a computer screen.

4 A primary school teacher is someone *who / which / that* teaches young children.

5 A computer is a very complicated machine *who / which / that* can do any number of things.

6 A writer is a person *who / which / that* spends a long time in front of a computer screen.

7 A banker is a person *who / which / that* works in a bank.

8 A dishwasher is machine *who / which / that* washes dishes.

3 **2.35** **Complete the conversations with *who* or *which*. Then listen and check.**

Conversation 1

A: What kind of films do you like?

B: I like films ¹____which____ make me laugh.

A: Me too, but I like films ²_____ make me think as well.

B: Or films ³_____ tell really good stories.

A: And of course, the actors are really important.

B: Yeah, I don't like the big Hollywood stars ⁴_____ always seem to make the same film.

A: Or those actors ⁵_____ always seem to play the same character.

Conversation 2

C: Let me introduce you to Briony. She's the person ⁶_____ runs the marketing department.

D: How do you do? I'm Marsha.

E: Pleased to meet you, Marsha. Where were you before?

D: I worked for a company ⁷_____ sold holidays online.

E: Oh, that's interesting. The internet is something ⁸_____ we're using more and more here. Maybe you could meet Matt ⁹_____ 's in charge of that. I'm sure you have lots of experience ¹⁰_____ we could use.

D: That sounds great.

4 **Correct the mistakes. Three sentences are correct.**

1 I know someone who knows Rafael Nadal.   ✓

2 I don't like food ~~who~~ has a lot of salt in it.   which/that

3 A biologist is a person which works in a laboratory.   ....

4 He bought a new bike who cost him over two thousand euros. ....

5 Yesterday I met someone who went to school with me.   ....

6 I've always liked people which laugh really loudly.   ....

7 We stayed in a hotel who was over 200 years old.   ....

8 Have you seen the bag which I left in the kitchen?   ....

9 This is a machine who translates words into English.   ....

79 Relative clauses 2

Presentation

Combining sentences

You can use relative pronouns to combine sentences.

*I'm reading a book. The book has won an award. = I'm reading a book **which** has won an award.*

Omitting the relative pronoun

Always use a relative pronoun when it is the subject of the relative clause (i.e. when it is followed by a verb).

*This is the woman **who wrote** the book.*

*This is the DVD **that goes** with the book.*

*This is the photo **which won** first prize.*

You don't have to use a relative pronoun when it is the object of the relative clause (i.e. when it is followed by a noun or pronoun).

*This is the book (which) **I** read on holiday.*

*This is the woman (who) **Jack** was telling you about.*

*This is the CD Rom (that) **the boss** gave me.*

Key vocabulary Collocations: read/write a book, see/make a film, sing a song, take a photo, win an award / a prize

Exercises

1 Complete the conversation with *who* or *which*.

A: Have you seen the film [1] _____which_____ won the Oscar?

B: Is it the film about the couple [2] _____ lived in Japan?

A: No, it's the one about the man [3] _____ survived a plane crash.

B: Oh, is it the one [4] _____ took five years to make?

A: Yeah, that's right. With the great ending [5] _____ everyone's talking about. You know …

B: No, don't tell me! I haven't seen it yet!

A: Sorry!

2 Combine the sentences using *who* or *which*.

1 This is my new car. My parents gave it to me.
   This is my new car which my parents gave me.

2 This is my friend. She helped me with my exam.
   _____

3 This is the book. I was reading it last week.
   _____

4 This is the film. I went to see it last night.
   _____

5 These are the CDs. I bought them online.
   _____

6 This is the song. They sang it at our wedding.
   _____

3 Cross out the pronouns which are not necessary.

1 Would you like to see the photos ~~that~~ I took on my holiday?

2 This is the guide who took us around the ruins.

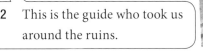

3 And this is the couple that we met on the plane. They were great fun.

4 He's the one who fell and broke his leg! Poor guy. We had to call an ambulance. It was really expensive.

5 This is one of the hotels that we stayed at. It was really nice.

6 And this is the swimming pool that they had on the roof.

7 Oh, yes, and this is rooftop garden which had the most amazing views.

80 Review of units 76 to 79

Grammar

1 Complete the notes using *in*, *on* or *at*.

I've made an appointment for you with the dentist
¹ __on__ Friday
² _____ 9.30.

I'm playing tennis ³ _____ 4pm tomorrow, so I won't be at home ⁴ _____ the afternoon.

Dave called. He says they're coming to town ⁵ _____ the summer. Can they come and stay?

2 Complete the conversations with the prepositions in the box.

| at | at | behind | between | in | in |
| in | in | of | ~~on~~ | on | to |

A: Where's the bathroom?
B: It's over there, ¹ __on__ the left, next ² _____ the living room.

A: Where are the keys?
B: They're ³ _____ the table ⁴ _____ the kitchen.

A: Where's my coat?
B: It's ⁵ _____ the corner, ⁶ _____ the door.

A: Where's the chair?
B: There, ⁷ _____ the middle, look, ⁸ _____ the window and the table.

A: Where shall I meet you?
B: How about ⁹ _____ the top of the street?

A: Where did you leave your bike?
B: ¹⁰ _____ the bottom of the stairs, ¹¹ _____ front ¹² _____ the door.

3 Correct the mistakes in the crossword clues. Four clues are correct.

1 a person ~~which~~ follows a particular team or sport _who_
2 a person who plays football or tennis _____
3 a person which works in a school _____
4 a thing who you use to light a fire _____
5 a person who writes books _____
6 a person which looks after plants _____
7 a machine which you use when your hair is wet _____
8 a person who cleans your house _____
9 a machine who prints things from your computer _____

Tick (✓) the clues which don't need the relative pronoun.

4 Combine these sentences. Omit the relative pronoun where possible.

1 I loved the film. The one we saw last night.
   I loved the film we saw last night.
2 My favourite actor was the woman. She stole the car.
   _____
3 These are the photos. I took them at the party.
   _____
4 This is the photo. It won an award.
   _____
5 Do you like the CD? My brother gave it to me.
   _____
6 I like the singer. She sings in Spanish.
   _____

5 Correct the mistakes. Four sentences are correct.

1 This is the song which I really like. ✓

2 She's the woman ~~which~~ sings that song.
   who

3 The sauna is on the right of the gym.

4 This is a book that you should read.

5 Put her CD at the player.

6 I think they're arriving in eight.

7 Are you the person has the big black dog?

8 We always meet on Sundays for lunch.

9 Take the lift and his office is on the top of the building.

10 Sit on between Mike and me and tell us what happened.

Pronunciation: sentence stress

6 ⊘2.36 Listen and complete the sentences.

1 The dance studio is at the _____ of the stairs.
2 He's waiting at the _____ of the street.
3 Put it down in the _____ of the room.
4 The changing rooms are on the _____ .
5 The bar is _____ to the pool.
6 You're standing in _____ of the TV!

7 ⊘2.37 Listen and repeat. Notice the stress on the bold words.

1 at the **top** of the **hill**
2 at the **corner** of the **square**
3 in the **middle** of the **street**
4 on the **right**
5 **next** to the **bar**
6 in **front** of the **door**

Vocabulary

8 Write the words from a sports centre.

1 sw~mm~ng p~~l   swimming pool
2 ch~ng~ng r~~ms
3 s~~n~
4 d~nc~ st~d~~
5 t~nn~s c~~rts
6 ~~r~b~cs cl~ss~s
7 s~l~r~~m
8 y~g~

9 Complete the crossword with words ending in -er. Use the clues in exercise 3.

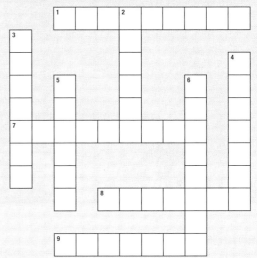

Listen again

10 ⊘2.38 Listen and answer the questions.

1 When is his birthday?

2 When was he born?

3 What time was he born?

4 When does she usually get up on weekdays?

5 When does she usually go to bed on weekdays?

81 *If/When* + present simple, present simple

- If you weigh 50 kg on Earth, you weigh 13,200kg on Jupiter.
- If you add the numbers 1–100 consecutively (1 + 2 + 3 ... + 100), the total equals 5050.
- When a bat leaves a cave, it never turns right.
- If a mosquito bites you, it's usually a female.
- It's illegal to chew gum if you live in Singapore.
- When you sneeze, it travels at over 150 kilometres per hour.

Amazing facts!

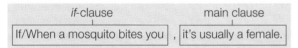

Presentation

Use *if/when* + present simple, present simple to talk about facts or things which are generally true.

if-clause		main clause
If/When a mosquito bites you	,	it's usually a female.

The *if/when* clause can come before or after the main clause.

TIP This is sometimes called the zero conditional.

if or *when*?

In sentences about general facts, there is little or no difference in meaning between *if* or *when*.

If a mosquito bites you, it's usually a female. = *When a mosquito bites you, it's usually a female.*

(See also note on *if* and *when* in Unit 83.)

Punctuation

When the sentence begins with the *if*-clause, put a comma after the *if*- clause:

If you heat water to 100 degrees, it boils.

When the sentence begins with the main clause, don't use a comma:

Water boils if you heat it to 100 degrees.

Exercises

1 Write the facts. Use *you*.

1	heat ice + melt	When you heat ice, it melts.
2	go into space + float	If
3	press this button + computer starts	When
4	have a headache + an aspirin helps	If
5	you sneeze + always close your eyes	When
6	add two and two + get four	If

2 Write clauses a–e in the adverts 1–5 from a supermarket.

> **a** when you buy two.   **b** When you visit our website,   **c** We pay you the difference
> **d** please return it within 28 days.   ~~e If you spend over £50,~~

If you spend over £50,   we enter you into our free competition.

if you find the same product for less money in another shop.

If you are not happy with a product,

You receive one extra,

you can shop online.

3 ⑥2.39 Complete the conversations with the affirmative or negative form of the verbs in brackets. Then listen and check.

Conversation 1

A: I have a problem, Doctor. If I drink coffee, I ¹ ___don't sleep___ (sleep) at night.

B: Well, stop then.

A: But if I don't drink coffee, I ² _____ (get) tired.

B: OK. Take this medicine and if you ³ _____ (have) any more problems, come back and see me.

Conversation 2

C: I'm out of the office for the week. If you have any problems, call me but ⁴ _____ (ask) Roger.

D: Why not?

C: He won't know the answer. If I ⁵ _____ (be) there, then wait until I am!

82 *If/Unless* + present simple, imperative

In case of fire

If you hear the fire alarm, leave your classroom by the nearest exit.

If you notice smoke on the stairs, take a different exit.

Do not re-enter the school unless your teacher says it's safe.

Presentation

Use *if* + present simple, imperative for instructions or giving advice:

If you hear the fire alarm, leave your classroom by the nearest exit.

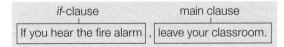

if-clause	main clause
If you hear the fire alarm	, leave your classroom.

Unless

Unless = if not

Do not re-enter the school if your teacher doesn't say it's safe. = Do not re-enter the school unless your teacher says it's safe.

Key vocabulary Phrasal verbs: call back, put back, put in, tidy up, turn off

Exercises

1 Complete the house rules with the phrases in the box.

turn it off ~~close it~~ tidy it up put it back mend it don't use it

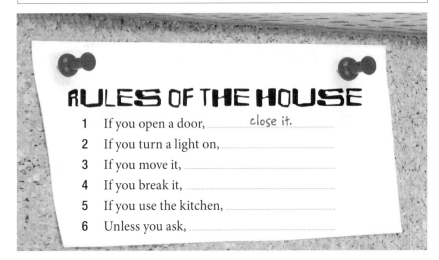

RULES OF THE HOUSE

1 If you open a door, *close it.*

2 If you turn a light on,

3 If you move it,

4 If you break it,

5 If you use the kitchen,

6 Unless you ask,

2 🔘 **2.40 Put this answer machine message in order. Then listen and check.**

☐	I'm at work. Call me there on 020 7998 1234. If it isn't urgent,
1	Hello, this is Braxton. Sorry, but I can't answer the
☐	email me at braxton51@hotmail.com. Bye!
☐	phone at the moment. If it's between nine and five,
☐	leave your name and number and I'll call you back. Or call me
☐	on my mobile if you like. That's 0770 879 3345. Or you could

3 **Look at the pictures. Write sentences with *if* + present simple, imperative.**

1 need help / ring / bell
   If you need help, ring this bell.

2 light / red / not cross / road

3 'd like / apply for job / complete / form

4 not have / a security badge / not enter

5 want / drink / put some money in slot

6 not feel better / tomorrow / phone / doctor

4 **Rewrite the sentences using *unless*.**

1 If you don't hear from me, don't wait.
   Unless you hear from me, don't wait.

2 Don't call the police if it isn't an emergency.

3 If it isn't important, don't spend time on it.

4 Meet at five if Rachel doesn't change the time again!

83 *If/When* + present simple, *will*

Presentation

Use *if* + present simple to talk about a possible future action.

Use *will/won't* in the main clause to talk about the result of that action.

if-clause	main clause
If we go this way	, we'll (will) get to the campsite.

TIP Say *If I have time, I'll help you.* (don't say *If I'll have time, I'll help you.*)

If or *when*?

When + future action = certain future action

If + future action = possible future action

TIP This is sometimes called the first conditional.

Key vocabulary Verb phrases: leave someone a message, hear from someone, see someone, ask someone something, leave someone alone

Exercises

1 Complete the sentences with the correct form of the verbs in brackets.

1   If you _____leave_____ (leave) a message with your number, I _____'ll call_____ (call) you back.

2   If you _____ (not give) it to me now, I _____ (tell) your mum!

3   I _____ (pay) you five dollars if you _____ (help) me.

4   When he _____ (phone), I _____ (say) you're busy.

5   You _____ (not pass) your exams if you _____ (not work) harder.

6   If you _____ (go) now, you _____ (catch) the train.

7   When the police _____ (arrive), they _____ (ask) you some questions.

8   _____ (they visit) us if they _____ (have) time?

9   What _____ (Jane do) if she _____ (not hear) from Jacob?

2 Write sentences with *if* + present simple, *will*.

1 work hard at school, go to university
If you work hard at school, you'll go to university.

2 catch the bus, run
You'll catch the bus if you run.

3 not get a job, not have any money

4 the police stop you, drive too fast

5 not tell me the answer, not be your best friend

6 give me your email address, send you the attachment

3 ⟨♫2.41⟩ **Write in the missing *'ll* or *will* for each line of the conversations. Then listen and check.**

Conversation 1

A: [1]If you turn left, you ^'ll see the house on the left.

B: [2]But it's a one-way street. If I turn left, the police stop me.

Conversation 2

C: [3]If my plane lands at three, you pick me up?

D: [4]Sure, but if it's delayed, you call?

Conversation 3

E: [5]I send you to your bed if you hit your brother again!

F: [6]I stop if he stops hitting me!

E: [7]If you ignore him, he leave you alone.

Conversation 4

G: [8]If I tell you a secret, you keep it?

H: [9]Sure. It be between you and me.

4 Complete the sentences with *if* or *when*.

1 I'll tell you all about it _____when_____ we meet at three.
2 _____ I don't see you before I leave, I'll call you after my holiday.
3 _____ you get the job, will you call me?
4 We're coming down on Christmas Day so we'll see you _____ we arrive.
5 _____ my son passes all his exams, he'll go to university.
6 I'll let you know _____ dinner is ready.
7 We'll see you on Tuesday _____ we don't see you before.
8 _____ you run, you'll probably catch the train.
9 Let's talk about this again _____ you get back from your holiday.
10 _____ you help me, I'll help you.

177

84 *If* + present simple, modal verb

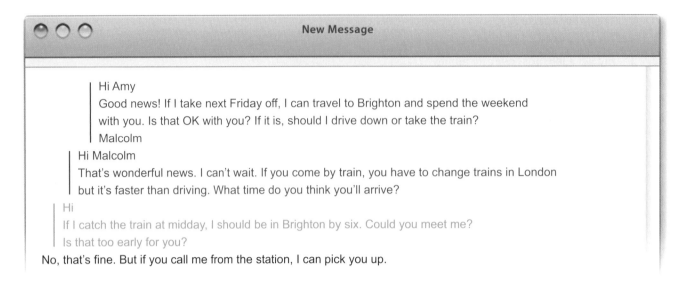

New Message

Hi Amy

Good news! If I take next Friday off, I can travel to Brighton and spend the weekend with you. Is that OK with you? If it is, should I drive down or take the train?

Malcolm

Hi Malcolm

That's wonderful news. I can't wait. If you come by train, you have to change trains in London but it's faster than driving. What time do you think you'll arrive?

Hi

If I catch the train at midday, I should be in Brighton by six. Could you meet me?

Is that too early for you?

No, that's fine. But if you call me from the station, I can pick you up.

Presentation

Use *if* + present simple, modal verb to talk about future choices or options.

If the bus is late,	she**'ll** get a taxi. (certain)
	I **can** give you a lift. (possibility)
	you **must / have to** call me. (obligation)
	you **should** take a taxi. (strong advice)
	he **might** miss the film. (possibility)
	she **could** walk. (possibility)

Key vocabulary Phrasal verbs: check out, get around, pick someone/something up

Exercises

1 Complete the sentences about the hotel signs.

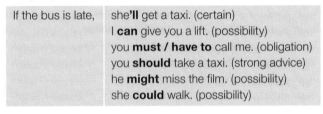

1   When you leave, you must *check out before 10 a.m.*

2   If you pay by credit card, you can

3   Unless you work here, you cannot

4   If there is a fire, you have to

5   If you want room service, you should

2 Choose the correct modal verbs.

1 If the light is red, you *have to* / *can* stop.

2 You *could* / *must* study medicine if you want to be a doctor.

3 You *might* / *can* see James if you go to the party. I think he's going.

4 If I finish my homework, *can* / *must* I watch TV? My favourite programme is on at eight.

5 You *mustn't* / *don't have to* eat the meat if you don't like it.

6 We *have to* / *might* go away this weekend if the weather's good.

7 *Should* / *Must* I call you on your home number or your mobile number when I arrive?

8 If you join the army, you *could* / *have to* wear a uniform.

9 I *'ll* / *have to* join you for a drink later if I'm free.

3 Correct the sentences.

1 If you're late, you should to call me.
   If you're late, you should call me.

2 He cans come later if you want.

3 If you have stay another day, that's fine.

4 She can learns French if she uses this computer program.

5 We take a break now if you will like.

6 The taxi can to pick you up if you want.

7 We must to meet up for dinner when you come to England.

8 You can stay with Lars if you will visit Stockholm.

4 ⊘2.42 Match the two halves of the sentences giving advice on travel to New York. Then listen and check.

1 If you want to enter the United States,	c	a you might need to reserve a ticket in advance.
2 If you want to travel around New York,	☐	b you can use a credit card anywhere.
3 If you don't have cash,	☐	c you must have a passport with a visa.
4 If you have some free time,	☐	d you have to be careful in the street.
5 If you're out late at night,	☐	e you could visit Times Square.
6 If you want to see a show on Broadway,	☐	f you should take taxis. It's the fastest way to get around.

5 Write three pieces of advice for a visitor to your country. Use modal verbs.

1 If ....

2 If ....

3 If ....

85 Review of units 81 to 84

Grammar

1 Choose the correct forms.

1 If you need some money, *go* / *goes* to a cash machine.

2 You *dream* / *will dream* when you sleep.

3 If it *rains* / *will rain*, use your umbrella.

4 If you leave a message, I *call* / *'ll call* you back this evening.

5 We *stay* / *'ll stay* at home if there's something good on TV tonight.

6 *Don't* / *Won't* enter the building unless the police say you can.

7 If I get an A grade, my parents *give* / *will give* me 100 euros!

8 When I ask you to do something, *do* / *does* it!

9 When the cake *is* / *will be* ready, take it out of the oven.

10 If you *don't* / *won't* agree, we won't do it.

11 What *do* / *will* you usually do when you go on holiday?

12 What *do* / *will* you study if you go to university?

2 Match the two halves of the sentences.

1	Press 1	9
2	Walk out of the building	
3	They'll meet you	
4	I won't come	
5	I'll come with you	
6	I'll eat the last one	
7	You have to pass a test	
8	Bill and Sally can play	

a if you say what time your flight lands.

b if they want to.

c if you leave now.

d unless my girlfriend comes too.

e unless someone else wants it.

f if you want to drive a car.

g ~~if you'd like to speak to an operator.~~

h when you hear the fire alarm.

3 Complete the recipe with *when*, *if* or *unless*.

fruit crumble

- 1,000g of fruit
- 100g butter
- 100–150g sugar
- 150g flour

Fruit crumble is probably the quickest and most delicious dessert in the world!

[1] **If** you like apples they are good but any fruit will do. [2] _____ you have cut the fruit, put it in a large dish. Then mix the flour, butter and, [3] _____ you are on a diet, add lots of sugar. [4] _____ you've mixed it, you have the 'crumble'. Put it on top of the fruit. Switch on the oven and [5] _____ it's at 200°C, put the dish in. Cook for about 30 minutes or 40 minutes [6] _____ you want the top to be brown.

It will serve about six friends, [7] _____ you are eating it on your own! Pour some cream on or, [8] _____ you have some, vanilla ice cream tastes good with it.

4 Complete the conditional sentences with the correct form of the verbs.

1 When you press this button, the machine ___starts___ (start).

2 If you are happy with his work, _____ (tell) him!

3 When the light _____ (come) on, the machine is ready.

4 If you _____ (not tidy) your room, I won't give you a lift to the party.

5 When we reach the top of the mountain, we _____ (have) some lunch.

6 If you don't know the answer, your teacher _____ (not be) angry.

7 I _____ (pick) you up if you tell me what time you finish.

8 If she _____ (want) to travel abroad, she'll need a passport.

Pronunciation: intonation

5 **⊘2.43 In conditional sentences, the intonation rises on the *if-* clause and falls on the main clause. Listen to these sentences and repeat.**

1 If you want to enter the United States, you must have a passport with a visa.

2 If you want to travel around New York, you should take taxis.

3 If you don't have cash, you can use a credit card anywhere.

4 If you have some free time, you could visit Times Square.

5 If you're out late at night, you have to be careful in the street.

6 If you want to see a show on Broadway, you might need to reserve a ticket in advance.

Vocabulary

6 **Complete the phrasal verbs with the words in the box.**

> back   back   off   up   ~~around~~   up

1 When you are in Amsterdam, get ___around___ on a bicycle. It's the best way to see the city.

2 Turn that noise _____. It isn't music!

3 Can you put my keys _____ in my bag, please?

4 Did you tidy _____ that mess you made?

5 Can I call you _____ in five minutes?

6 Tell me your flight times and I'll pick you _____.

Listen again

7 **⊘2.44 Listen and write the missing words.**

Hello, this is Braxton. Sorry, but I [1]_____ the phone at the moment. If [2]_____ between nine and five, I'm at work. Call me there on 020 7998 1234. If [3]_____ urgent, [4]_____ your name and number and [5]_____ you back. Or [6]_____ me on my mobile [7]_____. That's 0770 879 3345. Or you [8]_____ me at braxton51@hotmail.com. Bye!

86 *-ed* and *-ing* adjectives

ENJ

http://www.ENJ.com/

Google

www.ENJ.com

Read what our clients say:
'I was surprised how much money I could really make.'
'There were so many interesting careers I never knew about at ENJ.'
'Before I discovered my job at ENJ, life was boring!'
Get excited with ExcitingNewJobs.com!

Click here now

Presentation

- Use an adjective that ends in *-ed* to describe how a person feels.

  *Are you **bored**?*

  *I was **surprised**.*

- Use an adjective that ends in *-ing* to describe the thing that causes the feeling.

  *We have 1,000 **exciting** new jobs.*

  *Life was **boring**.*

Key vocabulary Adjectives: annoyed/annoying, bored/boring, embarrassed/embarrassing, excited/exciting, frightened/frightening, interested/interesting, relaxed/relaxing, surprised/surprising, tired/tiring, worried/worrying

Exercises

1 **② 2.45** **Choose the correct forms in the job interview. Then listen and check.**

A: So, you're [1] *interesting / interested* in our advert for a shop assistant. Is that correct?

B: That's right. I think sales is a really [2] *exciting / excited* career.

A: But you work for a sales company now. I'm [3] *surprising / surprised* you want to leave.

B: It's really [4] *bored / boring*. I'm [5] *tiring / tired* of answering the phone all day and I want to meet people. Also, my boss is really [6] *annoying / annoyed*.

2 How do these people feel? Match the words in the box to the pictures.

annoyed bored embarrassed excited frightened ~~interested~~ relaxed surprised tired worried

1 _interested_ 2 _____ 3 _____ 4 _____ 5 _____

6 _____ 7 _____ 8 _____ 9 _____ 10 _____

3 Complete the sentences with the *-ing* form of the adjectives in exercise 2.

1 These test results are ___worrying___ . How can we improve them?

2 This book is so _____ . Nothing happens.

3 I love snowboarding! It's _____ because you go so fast.

4 My little sister is _____ . She never stops talking and she steals things from my bedroom.

5 We were driving home when a lorry turned and nearly hit our car. It's was really _____ .

6 My father is a security guard and works at night. It's _____ work and he always goes straight to bed in the morning.

7 It's _____ how much people spend on clothes these days. I can't believe it!

8 The most _____ subject at school is history. I like reading about kings and queens.

9 There is nothing more _____ for me than lying in bed on a Sunday morning with the newspapers. I love it.

10 It was so _____ when I dropped my lunch on the floor. Everybody was looking at me.

4 Complete the sentences so that they are true for you.

1 It's annoying when people _____

2 I think TV quiz shows are _____

3 The most exciting thing I have ever done was _____

4 I get worried when _____

5 At school I am/was interested in _____

6 The last time I was surprised was when _____

7 The most boring thing I have to do is _____

8 The last time I was embarrassed was when _____

87 *looks, sounds, tastes, smells, feels*
Sense verb + adjective

There are two faces in this picture. Which face can you see?

She looks young.

She looks old.

Presentation

You often use an adjective after these verbs: *look, sound, feel, smell, taste.*

She looks young. He sounds unhappy. This feels really soft. This air smells really fresh. This soup tastes awful.

TIP Don't use an adverb after these verbs.

Say *She looks beautiful.* (don't say ~~She looks beautifully.~~)

> **Key vocabulary** Adjectives: awful, beautiful, cool (= fashionable/attractive), delicious, fluent, fresh, great (= really good), lovely, old, polluted, relaxing, rough, sad, smooth, soft, sweet, well (= healthy), young

Exercises

1 Complete the adverts with the phrases in the box.

> look younger   ~~feel smoother~~   smell fresh   taste delicious   sound fluent

With our **RAZORS** you'll
1 *feel smoother.*

2
by ten years with
magic
SKIN CREAM

Does your breath
3
24 hours a day?
Be certain. Chew
minty
gum day and night!

Visiting London?
4
in English in only
7
days!

Doesn't your cooking 5
?
It does now with
Mr Cook's
sauce.

2 Complete the sentences about the photos with the words in the box.

awful cool delicious lovely old polluted relaxing rough sad sweet

1 He looks _____cool_____.
2 This feels _____.
3 That music sounds _____!
4 My dinner tastes _____.
5 It smells _____.

6 Why does he look so _____?
7 The air smells _____.
8 That feels _____.
9 It tastes _____.
10 That sounds _____.

3 ⏱2.46 Write in the missing verbs. Then listen and check.

Conversation 1
A: Are you OK?
B: I don't [1] _____feel_____ very well. I think I need a doctor.

Conversation 2
C: I haven't seen you for ages.
D: I know. You [2] _____ great! How do you do it?
C: I go to the gym every day.

Conversation 3
E: This is Mozart.
F: It [3] _____ beautiful.

Conversation 4
G: That [4] _____ nice. Is it Chanel?
H: Yes, Number 5.

Conversation 5
I: How does it [5] _____?
J: Really good. Did you cook it?

Conversation 6
K: That boy shouldn't be driving a car. He [6] _____ too young.
L: Don't worry. I'm sure he's over seventeen.

Conversation 7
M: Something [7] _____ bad. What is it?
N: I was making toast but I burnt it.

Conversation 8
O: This [8] _____ spicy. Is it Indian?
P: Yes, it's a new recipe from my cook book.

Conversation 9
Q: Let's go to the beach this weekend.
R: That [9] _____ great!

Conversation 10
S: Can you massage my shoulders?
T: Sure. How does that [10] _____?
S: Great, thanks.

88 Order of adjectives

Two small, old, English, oil paintings of local countryside from the nineteenth century. Call 635 8875.

Round, wooden dining table with chairs. Seats six. £100 or nearest offer.

Elegant, black, Tuscan lamp bought in Florence. £45. Call 0778 767 7331 after 6 p.m.

Presentation

Adjectives usually go in this order before a noun:

opinion	size	shape	age	colour	origin	material	noun
	small		old		English	oil	paintings
		round				wooden	dining table
elegant				black	Tuscan		lamp

TIP In conversation, you rarely use more than two adjectives before a noun.

- With long lists of adjectives, you often write commas between adjectives: *It's an elegant, black, Tuscan lamp.*
- Numbers go before adjectives: *two small oil paintings.*

Key vocabulary Furniture: armchair, chair, cooker, curtains, desk, lamp, table, vase
Adjectives: ancient, beautiful, black, blue, brown, comfortable, cool, cotton, nineteenth-century, elegant, fast, French, green, huge, Italian, Japanese, Korean, large, long, lovely, new, old, metal, modern, plastic, practical, red, round, Russian, square, stylish, tall, white, wooden, yellow

Exercises

1 Put the adjectives in the correct order.

1	large white metal	a	*large, white, metal*	cooker
2	plastic practical square	a		garden table
3	red comfortable two			armchairs
4	tall Japanese ancient	a		vase
5	wooden stylish brown	a		office desk
6	cotton yellow long			curtains

2 Use the adjectives in the sentences to complete the descriptions.

1   I love your new shirt! It's cotton, isn't it?

2   This car is Korean. It's very fast.

3   That's a lovely necklace. Is it Russian?

4   Have you seen my old jeans? You know, the black ones.

5   This painting is French I think, probably from the eighteenth century.

6   They're building a huge office block. It looks very modern.

7   I've seen some garden chairs for sale. They're made of plastic and green.

8   I bought these sunglasses at an Italian market. They're so cool!

1   _a new cotton_ shirt

2   _____ car

3   _____ necklace

4   _____ jeans

5   _____ painting

6   _____ office block

7   _____ garden chairs

8   _____ sunglasses

3 Describe the following with some of the adjectives in the box.

> Australian   beautiful   diamond   ~~elegant~~   enormous
> eighteenth-century   Italian   modern   plastic   tiny   ugly

1   She's a(n) ___elegant___ _____ actress.
OPINION   ORIGIN

2   The Queen of England lives in a(n) _____ _____ palace.
SIZE   AGE

3   I'd like a(n) _____ _____ necklace.
OPINION   MATERIAL

4 Complete the sentences so that they are true for you. Use two adjectives each time.

1   I live in a(n) _____

2   Today, I'm wearing a(n) _____

3   My favourite possession is a(n) _____

187

89 Adjectives with prepositions

lonelyheartsclub

Name: **Nigel**
Age: 26

I'm good at snowboarding and interested in travel. I would like to meet someone who is keen on dangerous sports and is different from other women.

Name: **Manuella**
Age: 37

Are you tired of your boring life? Let me change your world. I'm keen on theatre, live music and cinema. I'm not bad at cooking either.

Presentation

Many adjectives are followed by particular prepositions:

*I'm **good at** snowboarding.*

*Are you **tired of** your boring life?*

TIP You often use the verb *to be* with *adjective* + preposition: *I'm keen on dangerous sports.*

> **Key vocabulary** Adjectives with prepositions: annoyed with, bad at, bored with, different from, excited about, frightened of, good at, interested in, keen on, married to, surprised by, tired of, worried about

Exercises

1 **2.47** **Choose the correct prepositions. Then listen and check.**

Name: **Lisa**
Age: 41

Name:
Prescott
Age: 56

Name: **Pam**
Age: 28

I'm good ¹ *at / of / about* art and very keen ² *from / on / at* painting. I love nature and the countryside but I'm frightened ³ *with / by / of* spiders. I need a man to protect me.

I'm divorced and bored ⁴ *with / on / at* being alone. I love fast food and I'm bad ⁵ *at / by / on* sport but I'm loving and caring.

Are you annoyed ⁶ *of / on / with* the world? I'm really worried ⁷ *on / at / about* global warming and tired ⁸ *by / of / on* pollution. I want to meet someone with similar beliefs. Let's change the world together!

2 Complete the sentences with prepositions.

1 She's bored _____ with _____ this programme.
2 They were surprised _____ the news.
3 Are you tired _____ your job?
4 He isn't excited _____ his fortieth birthday.
5 Is she annoyed _____ her mother?
6 We aren't very good _____ Maths.
7 Is he frightened _____ anything?
8 He's really different _____ his brothers.
9 Who is Tom Cruise married _____ now?
10 Why are the police interested _____ what you're doing?
11 We're really bad _____ painting but we enjoy it.
12 There's nothing to be worried _____ .

3 Complete the conversation with the adjectives and prepositions in the boxes.

| interested   different   married   ~~excited~~   good   worried | | to   ~~about~~   in   at   about   from |

A: So, are you [1] _____ excited _____ about _____ the big day?
B: Actually, I'm really [2] _____ it.
A: Why?
B: Well, what if Sharon doesn't want to get [3] _____ me. She might change her mind on the day. My last three girlfriends all left me.
A: Don't be ridiculous! Sharon is [4] _____ all those others. She really loves you!
B: I know. But what happens when she finds out I'm no [5] _____ anything. I don't have a good job and I have no money.
A: But she isn't [6] _____ that kind of thing. She's only in love with you.
B: Do you really think so?

4 Rewrite the sentences using an adjective and preposition.

1 Flying really frightens me!   I'm really frightened of flying.
2 History interests me.   I'm _____
3 Your news surprised everyone.   Everyone was _____
4 This TV show is boring for the kids. The kids _____
5 Why is your new job worrying you?   Why are you _____
6 Saffron is annoying Peter.   Peter _____

5 Complete the sentences so that they are true for you.

1 I'm good at _____
2 I'm keen on _____
3 I'm bad at _____
4 I'm frightened of _____
5 I'm excited about _____

90 Review of units 86 to 89

Grammar

1 Complete the adjectives.

1 You look very bor ed . What's the matter?

2 Your holiday sounds gre_____ .

3 It's really annoy_____ when people telephone and try to sell you something.

4 My father flies round the world for his job. It's very tir_____ .

5 I don't think the children should watch that horror film. It's too frighten_____ .

6 Are you worr_____ about your exam?

7 Did you watch the final? It was so excit_____ !

8 Your perfume smells beauti_____ !

9 Roy is marr_____ to Rita.

10 Your Spanish is quite flu_____ , isn't it?

11 That want to close the factory because the air is pollut_____ .

12 The programme is aw_____ . Turn it off.

13 She's really interest_____ . Have you ever spoken to her?

14 This cake is delici_____ . How did you make it?

15 I'm not surpris_____ that he's leaving his job.

2 Complete the conversation with the verbs in the box. There is one extra verb.

| looks | ~~sounds~~ tastes feel smells |

A: So, I'm happy to tell you we have a new product for Christmas.

B: That [1] sounds good! What is it?

A: It's a perfume for young professional women. Here it is. What do you think of the bottle?

B: It [2]_____ wonderful – very stylish. There's only one problem.

A: What's that?

B: It [3]_____ disgusting!
   I [4]_____ sick!

3 Correct the sentences. Five are correct.

1 He's interested in football. ✓

2 I have a ~~white new~~ fridge for sale.
  I have a new white fridge for sale

3 They're keen at golf.

4 There's an elegant, diamond necklace in the window.

5 Emily is really excited at her birthday.

6 Who does that frightening brown big dog belong to?

7 I'm really bad with Maths. Can you help me?

8 I feel ill. Can I go home?

9 He looks intelligently.

10 That smells nice. What is it?

11 They look very happy together!

12 I was surprised on his new haircut.

13 This is a really romantic annoying film.

14 Those flowers smell delicious.

15 Why are you worried for your results?

Pronunciation: syllables and word stress

4 (♪2.48) Listen. How many syllables are there in each word?

1	<u>in</u>teresting	3	9	tiring
2	interested		10	tired
3	boring		11	annoying
4	bored		12	annoyed
5	exciting		13	frightening
6	excited		14	frightened
7	worrying		15	surprising
8	worried		16	surprised

Listen again and underline the stress in words with more than one syllable.

Vocabulary

5 Write the adjectives in the columns.

> <s>ancient</s> beautiful boring brown cool
> cotton elegant large metal modern
> old orange plastic red round small
> square wooden yellow young

size/shape	age	colour
	ancient	

material	opinion

6 Reorder the letters to make furniture words. Then match them to the pictures.

a   b   c

d   e   f

1	cokero	cooker	c
2	hiarmcar		
3	bleta		
4	save		
5	sked		
6	palm		

Listen again

7 (♪2.49) Listen and complete the notes about Lisa, Prescott and Pam.

Lisa	Prescott	Pam
Age:	Age:	Age:
Interests:	Marital status:	Concerns:
	Likes:	
Dislikes:	Dislikes:	

91 Verb + *to*-infinitive

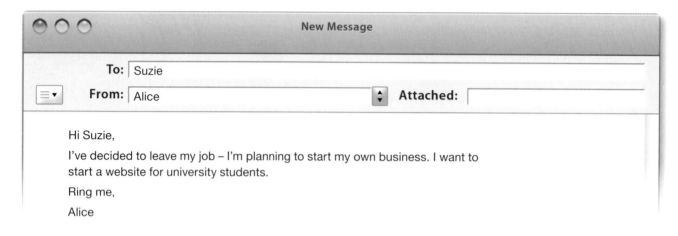

New Message

To: Suzie

From: Alice   Attached:

Hi Suzie,

I've decided to leave my job – I'm planning to start my own business. I want to start a website for university students.

Ring me,

Alice

Presentation

After many common verbs, you can use the *to*-infinitive form of another verb:

*I've decided **to leave** my job.*

decide plan agree refuse want hope would like	*to*-infinitive

You often use verbs with *to*-infinitive to talk about hopes, intentions and decisions.

- There are two possible negatives. They often have different meanings.

  I haven't decided to go. = I haven't made a decision yet.

  I've decided not to go. = I've made a decision. It was negative.

- Don't use the *to*-infinitive form after modal verbs (*can, could, will, would, shall, should, may, might, must*):

  Say *She can't drive.* (don't say *She can't to drive.*)

Exercises

1 ⏱2.50 **Match 1–6 to a–f to make a text. Then listen and check.**

1	First, I want to travel around	b	a	Save the Children.
2	Then, I hope to work for		b	~~the world.~~
3	If possible, I'd like to help		c	married.
4	One day, I hope to get		d	happy.
5	I'd like to have		e	two children.
6	But basically, I just want to be		f	children in the developing world.

2 Put the words in order.

1 hoping I'm marathon New York run the to

....

2 at Economics decided I've study to university

....

3 after degree I'm immediately my not planning to work

....

....

4 me refused she talk to to

....

5 agreed not police tell the to we

....

6 an don't I to in office want work

....

3 Read the situations. Then complete the sentences.

1 A: Can we meet at nine?
  B: OK. Nine is fine.
  They agreed *to meet at nine.*

2 'I won't wear my red dress!'
  Matilda refused ....

3 'After school, I'm going to study medicine.'
  He plans ....

4 'It would be nice to leave early.'
  Richard would like ....

5 A: We can catch the train.
  B: No. Let's take a taxi.
  A: Good idea.
  They decided ....

6 'I'd like to have my own TV show one day.'
  Sasha hopes ....

7 'Can I come with you all tonight?'
  Richie wants ....

4 Write in the missing *to* in the sentences.

1 We're planning ^to^ go to Greece for our holidays.

2 She's agreed not tell David.

3 I hope move house in September.

4 I've agreed work late on Tuesday.

5 The bank refused lend me the money.

6 Carrie's decided not go to university.

7 Would you like borrow my dictionary?

8 I plan go on a diet.

9 We invited them but they refused come.

10 We decided not go to the cinema.

5 Write about your hopes, intentions and decisions.

1 One day, I hope to ....

2 I'd also like to ....

3 But basically I just want to ....

92 Verb + -*ing*, -*ing* nouns

A: What time shall we leave?

B: Let's get on the road at three o'clock.

A: That's very early.

B: I don't like driving at night.

A: Why not?

B: Driving at night is dangerous. I worry about having an accident.

A: OK. We'll leave at three.

Presentation

Verb + -*ing*

After many verbs, you use the -*ing* form of another verb: *I don't like **driving** at night.*

Common verbs followed by -*ing* are: *like, dislike, love, hate, enjoy* and *(not) mind.*

Nouns

The -*ing* form of the verb is often a noun:

***Driving** at night is dangerous.*

Verb + preposition + -*ing*

You also use the -*ing* form after a preposition:

*I worry about **having** an accident.*

See page 234: spelling rules

Key vocabulary Leisure activities: camping, eating out, sunbathing, skiing, surfing, swimming

Exercises

1 Write what these people like or don't like doing. Use the words in the box.

> camp   do homework   eat out   ~~ski~~   sunbathe   surf

1 She *doesn't like skiing.*

2 He

3 We

4 She

5 He

6 They

2 Complete the sentences using the -ing form of the verbs in the box.

| be   clean   eat   learn   park   ski   ~~smoke~~   steal   swim   watch |

1 ___Smoking___ is bad for you.
2 _____ in the sea is nicer than in a pool.
3 _____ TV all evening is boring.
4 _____ is wrong.
5 _____ a policeman is a dangerous job.
6 _____ too much chocolate makes you fat.
7 It's a big car. _____ it is difficult.
8 It's a big house. _____ it takes a long time.
9 The violin is a difficult instrument. _____ to play it can take years.
10 _____ is more dangerous than playing football.

3 (🎧2.51) Complete the sentences with the correct form of the phrases in the box. Then listen and check.

| buy a guitar   fly   get old   go on a diet   ~~learn languages~~   not phone |

1 She speaks French, English, Italian and Mandarin. She's very good at ___learning languages___ .
2 Could you help me? I'm interested in _____ .
3 I'm getting fat. I'm thinking about _____ .
4 Do you ever worry about _____ ?
5 John rarely goes abroad. He's afraid of _____ .
6 I'm sorry for _____ . I forgot my mobile.

4 Put the words in the correct order.

1 mind you I helping don't   ___I don't mind helping you.___
2 enjoy sports do playing you?   _____
3 is exercise good swimming   _____
4 about worry at driving they night _____
5 are at skiing you good?   _____
6 like computer they playing games _____
7 sunbathing for is bad your skin _____

5 Make any necessary changes to these sentences to make them true for you.

    don't mind
1 I ~~love~~ watching TV.

2 Smoking is a really nice habit.

3 My friends and I often go sunbathing.

4 Making time to study English is difficult.

5 I'm thinking about getting a new job.

6 I'm not afraid of flying.

7 Camping is something I enjoy.

8 I prefer eating out to eating at home.

93 Verb + -ing or verb + to-infinitive?

Presentation

When there are two verbs in a sentence, they can follow two patterns ...

- verb + -ing: *I **enjoy helping** old people and children.*

The *-ing* form also follows these verbs: *dislike, finish, give up, mind, miss, practise, suggest.*

- verb + *to*-infinitive: *I'**d like to help** old people and children.*

The *to*-infinitive form also follows these verbs: *agree, decide, plan, want, need, refuse, hope, promise, want, would like.*

verb + -ing or to-infinitive?

These verbs can follow either pattern with little or no change in meaning: *like, prefer, love, hate.*

*What do you **like doing** in your free time?*

*What do you **like to do** in your free time?*

Exercises

1 **Choose the correct forms. Sometimes both forms are possible.**

1 They miss *to live / living* in France.

2 I hate *to wash / washing* dishes.

3 We've decided *to move / moving* house.

4 Can't they agree *to go / going* next week instead?

5 We suggest *to apply / applying* for a job as soon as you can.

6 She prefers *to live / living* in the city to the country.

7 They refused *to give / giving* us the money back.

8 Have you practised *to play / playing* your guitar today?

9 Michelle and Marty want *to have / having* dinner at Tortelli's.

10 Why do you think Jack loves *to surf / surfing* so much?

11 When did you give up *to eat / eating* meat?

12 They promised *to help / help* me this afternoon. Where are they?

2 ⊘2.52 **Complete the questions with the correct form of the verbs in the box. Sometimes more than one form is possible. Then listen and check.**

> bring   drink   ~~sit~~   try

1 Would you like ___to sit___ by the window?

2 Which do you prefer _____, red, or white?

3 May I suggest _____ the steak?

4 Would you mind _____ me a different fork?

3 **Read the situations. Then complete the sentences. Use the correct form of the <u>underlined</u> verb in the first sentence. Sometimes both forms are possible.**

1 '<u>Playing</u> tennis is great.'
Jane loves _playing / to play tennis._

2 'Can I <u>go</u> tonight, too.'
Bill would like _____, too.

3 'I'll <u>call</u> her back.'
He promised _____

4 'I've <u>painted</u> your picture. It's finished.'
The artist has finished _____

5 A: Did you <u>listen</u> to that new CD?
B: Yes, it was good.
She enjoyed _____

6 A: Can we <u>watch</u> a film?
B: What sort? I have comedy and horror films.
A: Oh, a horror film, definitely.
He prefers _____

94 *stop + -ing* or *stop + to*-infinitive?

Presentation

You can follow some verbs with the *-ing* form or *to*-infinitive, but there is a difference in meaning.

We've just stopped to have something to eat.
= We were driving. We wanted something to eat.
We stopped driving.

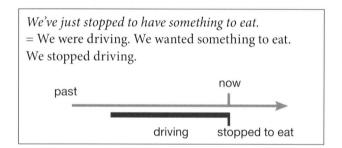

She's stopped feeling sick. = She felt sick. Then she got better. She doesn't feel sick now.

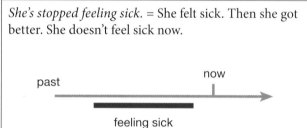

> **Key vocabulary** Health and illness: break a leg, feel sick, get better, have a headache, lose weight, stop smoking, take regular exercise

Exercises

1 Choose the correct forms.

1 We drove 300 kilometres and then stopped *to eat* / *eating*.

2 We had an argument and he stopped *to write* / *writing* to me.

3 I had to stop *to play* / *playing* tennis after I broke my leg.

4 I stopped *to smoke* / *smoking* ten years ago.

5 On way to my mother's house I stopped *to buy* / *buying* her flowers.

6 I've stopped *to eat* / *eating* chocolate. I want to lose weight.

7 I was early so I stopped *to have* / *having* a coffee.

8 Can we stop for a few minutes *to smoke* / *smoking* a cigarette?

9 I read a negative article about that company and I've stopped *to buy* / *buying* their products.

10 The doctor gave me a new medicine and I've stopped *to have* / *having* headaches.

2 Complete the sentences with *stop* or *stop to* and the correct form of the verbs in the box.

drive   eat   relax   ~~smoke~~   spend   take   watch

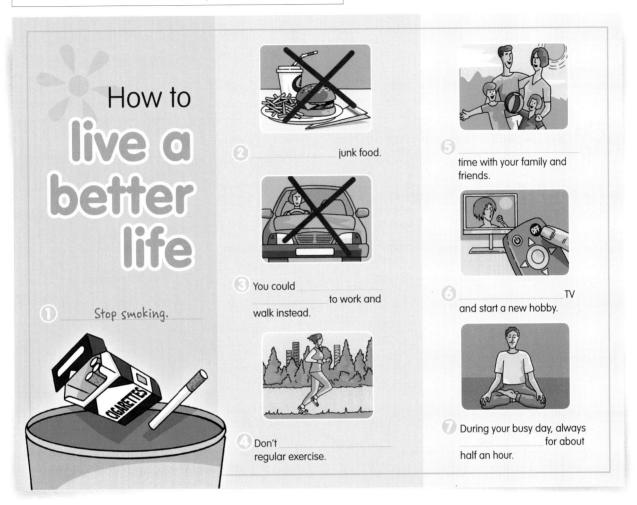

How to **live a better life**

① _____ *Stop smoking.* _____

② _____ junk food.

③ You could _____ to work and walk instead.

④ Don't _____ regular exercise.

⑤ _____ time with your family and friends.

⑥ _____ TV and start a new hobby.

⑦ During your busy day, always _____ for about half an hour.

3 (2.53) Complete the conversation with the correct form of the verbs. Then listen and check.

A: Happy New Year! How are you?

B: A bit tired. I went to a party last night.

A: What did you do?

B: Well, first we stopped ¹ _____*to pick*_____ (pick) Mel up from her house.

A: Doesn't she still work at the restaurant?

B: No, she stopped ² _____ (work) there ages ago. Anyway, we all went to a great party and at midnight everyone stopped ³ _____ (watch) the fireworks. But this morning I feel terrible. I must stop ⁴ _____ (smoke).

A: That could be your New Year's resolution.

B: What do you mean?

A: Well, lots of people often stop ⁵ _____ (do) something on January the first.

B: Really? So, what's your resolution?

A: I've stopped ⁶ _____ (eat) fast food and I think I'm also going to stop ⁷ _____ (watch) TV. I need to do more exercise.

B: Sounds a bit boring to me!

95 Review of units 91 to 94

Grammar

1 Choose the correct forms.

1. Did you hate *go / to go / going* to school?
2. *Snowboard / To snowboard / Snowboarding* is quite dangerous.
3. Would you like *try / to try / trying* this dish?
4. I enjoy *try / to try / trying* dishes from different countries.
5. Have you stopped *do / to do / doing* your course?
6. Are you interested in *come / to come / coming* out tonight?
7. I want you *help / to help / helping* me with something.
8. Could you *help / to help / helping* me?
9. Ask William. He's good at *fix / to fix / fixing* computers.
10. We can't *agree / to agree / agreeing* with you, I'm afraid.
11. We'd like you *be / to be / being* in our team.
12. We hope *meet / to meet / meeting* at five.
13. She's not bad at *cook / to cook / cooking* actually.
14. Did the President agree *change / to change / changing* the law?
15. He didn't stop *say / to say / saying* hello. Why not?
16. He's decided *take / to take / taking* the job.

2 Complete the email with the correct form of the verbs in brackets.

					E-mail			
New		Reply		Forward	Print	Delete	Send & Receive	

Dear Rich

I wanted ¹ <u>to call</u> (call) you on your mobile today but I couldn't ² _____ (find) your number. Anyway, you know I promised ³ _____ (have) a drink with you this evening? Well, do you mind ⁴ _____ (meet) at the weekend instead? The problem is that I haven't finished ⁵ _____ (prepare) for a job interview on Friday. I really want ⁶ _____ (get) the job so I need ⁷ _____ (spend) some time on it. Hope that's OK.
See you later this week.
Mindy

3 Look at the pairs of sentences. Which one is correct? Sometimes both are correct.

1. a The decided to leave their jobs and go travelling. ✓
   b The decided leaving their jobs and go travelling. ✗
2. a Mark prefers listening to rock music.
   b Mark prefers to listen to rock music.
3. a They're annoyed about to miss the concert.
   b They're annoyed about missing the concert.
4. a We love trying new restaurants.
   b We love to try new restaurants.
5. a I promise working harder in the future.
   b I promise to work harder in the future.
6. a We've become vegetarians so we've stopped eating meat.
   b We've become vegetarians so we've stopped to eat meat.
7. a Do your children hate eating vegetables?
   b Do your children hate to eat vegetables?

4 Complete the second sentence so that it means the same as the first.

1 I'm not going.
   He's decided ___not to go.___

2 I won't talk to you.
   She refused _____ me.

3 Can you photocopy this?
   I'd like you _____

4 Don't smoke. It's bad for you.
   You should _____

5 On my way to work I met Jules. We talked.
   I stopped _____ to Jules.

6 Sorry but I'm not good at making things.
   Sorry but I'm bad _____

7 We're going to travel around Europe this summer.
   They plan _____
   this summer.

8 You shouldn't drink a lot of coffee. It's bad for you.
   Drinking _____ is bad for you.

Pronunciation: intrusive /w/

5 Ⓑ**2.54** When we say *to* before a verb that begins with a vowel sound, you can hear a /w/ sound. Listen to these examples. Then listen again and repeat.

to /w/ apply   to /w/ eat   to /w/ include
to /w/ open   to /w/ understand

6 Ⓑ**2.55** Write in the /w/ sound in these sentences. Then listen and check.

1 I'd like to /w/∧ ask for a pay rise.

2 He promised to answer my call.

3 Do we need to employ anyone else?

4 Would you like to order now?

5 When do they want to interview you?

Vocabulary

7 Match to make six leisure activities.

1 cam ——— ing   ___camping___
2 eatin ⟍⟋ ping   _____
3 sunb   g out   _____
4 ski   ming   _____
5 sur   fing   _____
6 swim   athing   _____

8 Complete the sentences with a verb and a noun from the boxes.

| break   feel   get   have   lose   ~~stop~~   take |

| better   exercise   headache   leg   sick
~~smoking~~   weight |

1 I've tried to ___stop___ ___smoking___ three times now. But after three days I always start again.

2 My dog is so fat. He really needs to _____ some _____ !

3 A: How did Mike _____ his _____ ?
   B: He was playing football and fell badly.

4 I know that I should have a good diet and _____ regular _____ but it's so hard.

5 I _____ a terrible _____ . Can I have a paracetamol?

6 What's the matter? Do you _____ _____ ? We can stop the car if you want.

7 Take this medicine and it will help you to _____ .

Listen again

9 Ⓑ**2.56** Listen and number these events in order.

☐ have children   ☐ be happy
☐ travel   ☐ marry
☐ help children   ☐ work

96 Verb + object + *to*-infinitive

Presentation

You can ask someone to do something using verb + object + *to*-infinitive.

verb	object	*to*-infinitive
Tell Ask	him her them	to photocopy this report.

	verb	object	*to*-infinitive
I You We They	want need 'd like	me you him	to photocopy this report.
He She	wants needs 'd like	her us them	

TIP Say *I want you to …* (don't say ~~I want that you …~~)

Key vocabulary Office tasks: book somebody a room, meet somebody at the airport, organise meetings, photocopy a report, send somebody a copy / an email, take somebody to the station

Exercises

1 Put the words in order.

1 him me phone tell to — Tell him to phone me.
2 ask come her my office to to
3 at be here tell them to six
4 a ask copy him me send to
5 give tell the them to money you
6 tell and her to come me see
7 photocopy Michelle to this ask
8 the station the at to driver tell stop

202

2 Choose the correct pronouns.

1 (He)/ *Him* asked *she* /(her) to send an email with this attachment.
2 *Us / We* told *them / they* to arrive at eight o'clock.
3 *I / Me* wanted *him / he* to meet *we / us* at the airport.
4 *Them / They* would like *me / I* to phone *them / they* this evening.
5 *She / Her* needs *us / we* to take *she / her* to the station.
6 *He / Him* would like *I / me* to meet *they / them* early tomorrow.
7 Do *you / your* need *I / me* to sign this?
8 How many cakes does *she / her* want *he / him* to make?

3 There are six mistakes in this email. Find and correct them.

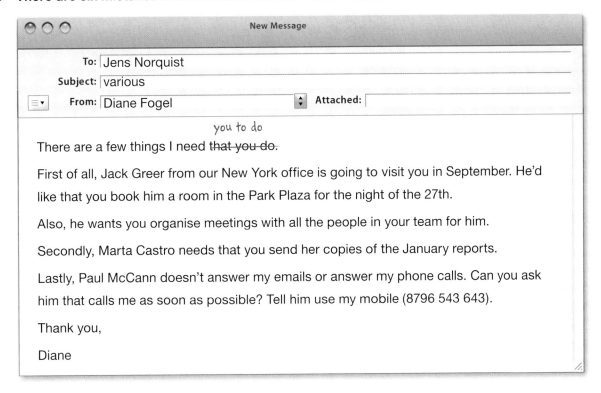

New Message

To: Jens Norquist
Subject: various
From: Diane Fogel   Attached:

you to do
There are a few things I need ~~that you do.~~

First of all, Jack Greer from our New York office is going to visit you in September. He'd like that you book him a room in the Park Plaza for the night of the 27th.

Also, he wants you organise meetings with all the people in your team for him.

Secondly, Marta Castro needs that you send her copies of the January reports.

Lastly, Paul McCann doesn't answer my emails or answer my phone calls. Can you ask him that calls me as soon as possible? Tell him use my mobile (8796 543 643).

Thank you,

Diane

4 ⊙2.57 Rewrite the sentences with verb + object + *to*-infinitive. Then listen and check.

1 Photocopy this report.
   I'd like you to photocopy this report.
2 Mike, I spoke to the boss. Send a copy of the letter to him.
   The boss wants ....
3 Your secretary hasn't booked the hotel room. Can she do it now?
   Please ask ....
4 Meet us at the café on the corner and invite Jerry.
   Tell Jerry ....
5 Bring me another steak. This one tastes awful.
   I'd like ....
   This one tastes awful.

97 Infinitive of purpose

Presentation

You use the infinitive of purpose (*to* + verb) to say why a person does something.

*All passengers must go to gate 20 immediately **to board** the plane.*

*I'm going to Florida **to meet** some clients in Miami.*

*I want to go Orlando **to see** Disneyland.*

*I'd like some perfume **to give** to my daughter for her birthday.*

TIP The infinitive of purpose often answers the question *Why?*
In spoken English, you can answer the *Why?* question with *To*.

*Why do you want to go to Orlando? **To see** Disneyland.*

Exercises

1 **⊘2.58 Match 1–8 to a–h to make sentences. Then listen and check.**

1	I'm going to Buckingham Palace	b	a	to buy some meat.
2	They went to the butcher		b	to see the Queen.
3	You need to study hard		c	to put petrol in the car.
4	Leave early in the morning		d	to wear to the party.
5	I want to buy an mp3 player		e	to avoid the traffic.
6	I stopped at the garage		f	to learn a language.
7	We'd like a menu		g	to take on holiday.
8	You should buy a new dress		h	to see what's for lunch.

2 The word *to* is missing six times in the text. Write it in.

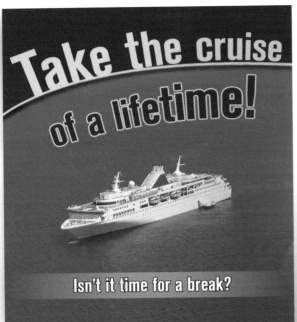

Take the cruise of a lifetime!

Isn't it time for a break?

Join us on a cruise of the Mediterranean Sea to visit some of the most famous sites in the world.

DAY ONE

Fly to Venice meet the cruise liner *The Golden Angel.*

DAY TWO

Before we leave you'll have a few hours buy souvenirs from one of Italy's most famous cities. Then at midday, we leave for Athens. In the evening you can sit on the deck enjoy the sunset and the live entertainment.

DAY THREE

We arrive at the port of Piraeus take a tour of the city. We'll walk into town see the Acropolis and try some wonderful Greek food.

3 Look at the pictures and answer the questions. Use the infinitive of purpose with the verb in brackets.

1 Why is she cycling? (get) — She's cycling to get to school.

2 Why is he at the market? (buy)

3 Why is he waiting? (catch)

4 Why do you press this button? (take)

5 Why did they go to the zoo? (see)

6 Why did they fly into space in 1969? (land on)

4 Complete these sentences about you using the infinitive of purpose.

1 I'm studying English to ....

2 Last year I visited .... to ....

3 Next year I'm going to .... to ....

98 The passive: present simple

How is tea served in Japan?

A GUIDE FOR GUESTS

The tea is made by the host. Guests are invited into the room, or outside into a garden.

Hands are washed and shoes are removed.

Sometimes guests are served a simple small meal before the tea.

The table is prepared with a special tea bowl and the tea is placed in this.

A tea ceremony lasts between one and five hours.

Presentation

Use the passive form when you want to focus on the object not the subject (or person) of the active sentence. The object becomes the subject.

	subject		object
Active sentence:	The host	serves	tea.

Passive sentence:	Tea	is served by	the host.

Form the present simple passive with the verb *to be (am/is/are) + past participle*.

Affirmative and negative

Tea	is(n't)	served in the garden.
Guests	are(n't)	invited into the room.

Questions

	Is	tea	served in the garden?
Where	are	guests	invited to go?

See page 235: Irregular verbs

Key vocabulary Customs, traditions and ceremonies: birthday, cake, candles, fireworks, gifts, guests, host, meal

Exercises

1 **Complete the sentences with *is* or *are*.**

1 Gifts _____are_____ given on December 25th.
2 Candles _____ put on a birthday cake.
3 Coffee _____ served to guests.
4 Shoes _____ left outside a person's house.
5 Money _____ left when children lose a tooth.
6 Fireworks _____ lit on New Year's Day.

Which of the statements 1–6 are true for your country?

2 🔊 **2.59 Complete the text with the present simple passive form of the verbs. Then listen and check.**

IT'S A FACT!

- Four main types of tea [1] _____are grown_____ (grow) – green tea, black tea, oolong tea and white tea.
- Most tea [2] _____ (pick) by hand and then it [3] _____ (take) to a factory.
- When the leaves [4] _____ (dry) with hot air, they turn brown or black.
- Coffee [5] _____ (not drink) as much as tea around the world.
- Tea [6] _____ (use) as a medicine in some countries.

3 **Write questions in the passive.**

1 what / this machine / use for   What is this machine used for?
2 how / this computer / switch on   _____
3 what / make / with flour   _____
4 how often / these rooms / clean   _____
5 where / coffee beans / grow   _____
6 when / the post / deliver   _____
7 how / this word / pronounce   _____
8 how much / know / about dinosaurs   _____

99 The passive: past simple
The agent *by*

welovechocolate.com

Are you a chocolate lover?

How is chocolate made?

Where was it discovered?

Here are some things you might not know ...

- White chocolate is not really chocolate because it isn't made with cacao beans.
- The Mayan people grew cacao beans in 600AD. Cacao beans were used by them as a form of money.
- The Swiss eat more chocolate per person than any other country and over $13 billion per year is spent on chocolate by US consumers.
- Early explorers brought it to Europe and later it was taken to North America.

Presentation

Form the past simple passive with the verb *to be (was/were) + past participle.*

Chocolate was taken to North America.

Cacao beans were used as a form of money.

Where was chocolate discovered?

The agent

In the active form you know who did the action: ***Explorers*** *brought chocolate to Europe.*

In the passive we can say the agent (who did it) using *by*: *Chocolate was brought to Europe **by explorers**.*

The agent isn't always necessary. This sentence is also possible: *Chocolate was brought to Europe.*

You don't normally use the agent when the agent is ...

- obvious and therefore unnecessary: *White chocolate isn't made from cacao beans* ~~by chocolate makers~~.
- unknown: *A piece of chocolate was left on my desk* ~~by someone~~.

Exercises

1   Choose the correct forms.

The potato ¹ *discover /* was discovered nearly 7,000 years ago. People in the Andes in South America ² *grew / was grown* the vegetable and it ³ *ate / was eaten* as a main part of their diet. It ⁴ *arrived / was arrived* in Europe in around 1570, but by the nineteenth century it ⁵ *grew / was grown* by many countries and it ⁶ *became / was become* the main vegetable in many countries.

2 (♫2.60) Complete the text with the past simple active or passive form of the verbs. Then listen and check.

On the Road [1] ___was written___ (write) in 1951 but it [2] _____ (not publish) until 1957. In 2005, it [3] _____ (chose) by *Time* Magazine as one of the best 100 English-language novels of the last century.

Jack Kerouac [4] _____ (write) the book in only three weeks but he [5] _____ (use) notes and diaries from seven years of travel across the USA. Often the names of real people and places [6] _____ (change).

Many poets, writers and musicians [7] _____ (say) the book was important to them. Bob Dylan said: 'It [8] _____ (change) my life.'

In 2001, the original text [9] _____ (buy) for $2.4 million.

3 Complete the quiz questions with the past simple passive form of the verbs. Can you answer the questions? (See the answers at the bottom of the page.)

Quiz

1 Who ___was___ Hamlet ___written___ (write) by?
2 Where _____ gunpowder _____ (invent)?
3 How much _____ Russia _____ (pay) by the USA for Alaska in 1867?
4 What _____ the first words _____ (speak) on the moon?
5 What year _____ Mount Everest first _____ (climb)?
6 Where _____ coffee first _____ (discover)?
7 The first plane _____ (fly) by which brothers in 1903?
8 Where _____ the Olympic games _____ (hold) in 2008?
9 When _____ seatbelts first _____ (use) in cars?
10 Who _____ the ball-point pen _____ (invent) by?

4 We don't always need the agent. Which agent (a or b) is necessary?

1 The President was shot …
   a by someone. ✗
   b by a man in a black suit and dark glasses. ✓

2 Did you read the autobiography …
   a by a writer?
   b by that Hollywood actress?

3 The painting was done …
   a by a child aged nine.
   b by a painter.

4 The man was finally stopped for driving at 200 kilometres per hour …
   a by six police cars!
   b by the police.

5 Was the car made …
   a by a machine or by hand?
   b by something?

100 Review of units 96 to 100

Grammar

1 **Complete the conversation with the words in the box.**

```
go   need   something   tell   wants   to (x2)   you
```

Boss: So, is there anything else?

Assistant: Yes, Mr Braun [1] _____wants_____ us to
            pick him up at the airport at five.

Boss: I see. OK. [2] _____ Marco to
            pick him up, then.

Assistant: I'm afraid Marco is going to the station
            [3] _____ meet Ms Shimeal at
            the same time.

Boss: Well, we [4] _____ someone to
            meet Mr Braun. Ask someone else in the
            office to [5] _____ .

Assistant: And one last thing. We'd like to buy
            [6] _____ to give Rosanne.

Boss: Why?

Assistant: [7] _____ celebrate her birthday.

Boss: Really?

Assistant: Yes, and we'd like [8] _____ to
            give us some money to pay for it.

Boss: How much?

2 **Complete the sentences with the present or past simple passive form of the verbs.**

1 Every year fires _____are burnt_____ (burn)
   on November 5th in England.

2 New Year _____ always _____
   (celebrate) on a different day in China.

3 In Japan the main guest for a meal sits in the
   centre and _____ (serve) first.

4 Before 1972, Sri Lanka _____ (call)
   Ceylon.

5 The scientist Louis Pasteur _____
   (be born) in France in 1822.

6 Slovakia _____ (join) to the Czech
   Republic until 1993.

7 Tagalog _____ (spoke) in the Philippines.

3 **Write three similar facts about your country. Use the passive.**

1 _____

   _____

2 _____

   _____

3 _____

   _____

4 **Rewrite the sentences and questions using the present or past simple passive.**

1 They built the Eiffel Tower in 1889.
   The Eiffel Tower _____was built in 1889_____ .

2 You make pasta with flour and eggs.
   Pasta _____ .

3 How do you grow cotton?
   How _____ ?

4 Someone left a message on your desk.
   A message _____ .

5 When did you send the letter?
   When _____ ?

6 Brazilians don't speak Spanish. They speak
   Portuguese.
   Spanish _____ .
   They speak Portuguese.

7 My employer pays me £500 a week.
   I _____ .

8 We deliver packages all over the world.
   Packages _____

   _____ .

9 The weather was bad but it didn't delay our
   plane.
   The weather was bad but our plane _____

   _____ .

5 Correct the mistake in each sentence.

1 Tell ~~she~~ *her* to give me a call.

2 We're going to the theatre for to watch a play.

3 I need you copy this report.

4 Do you want him to send I an email?

5 Them would like to meet us at the station.

6 How many of these do you want buy from us?

7 Is Angie there? Tell to come and see me straight away.

8 Water are heated to 100 degrees.

9 How many different languages are teached in your school?

10 This building designed by a famous architect in 1999.

11 A famous architect was designed this city.

12 No one knows when the wheel was invent.

Pronunciation: past participles

6 **2.61** **Listen to the pronunciation of these past participles. Complete the table.**

~~grown~~ read brought told left lit paid
worn made said drove built taught

/əʊ/ no	/e/ met	/eɪ/ say
grown		

/ɔː/ or	/ɪ/ it

Vocabulary

7 Complete the sentences with the verbs in the box.

book   meet   ~~photocopy~~   send   take

1 Could you _photocopy_ this report and give a copy to Ms Barker?

2 Please _____ him an email with this attachment.

3 Did you _____ the room for our meeting?

4 He lands at three. Can you _____ him at the airport?

5 I need a taxi to _____ me to the station.

Listen again

8 **2.62** **Listen and answer the questions.**

1 When was the book *On the Road* published?
   _1957_

2 Which magazine chose it as one of the best novels of the last century?
   _____

3 How quickly was the book written?
   _____

4 What did Bob Dylan say it changed?
   _____

5 How much was the original book bought for?
   _____

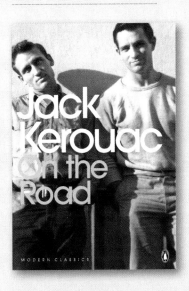

1 Progress test (Units 1 to 10)

1   I _____ from Italy.
   a am   **b** is   **c** are

2   Ray and Maria _____ eighteen.
   a am   **b** is   **c** are

3   She _____ married.
   a 'm   **b** 's   **c** 're

4   We _____ single.
   a 'm   **b** 's   **c** 're

5   This picture is nice. It _____ from Brazil.
   a 'm   **b** 's   **c** 're

6   I _____ thirty. I'm thirty-one.
   a 'm not   **b** isn't   **c** aren't

7   They _____ from Chile. They're from Argentina.
   a am not   **b** isn't   **c** aren't

8   'Is Andrew British?' 'No, he _____.'
   a aren't   **b** isn't   **c** is

9   He's _____ doctor.
   a a   **b** an   **c** Ø

10 We're _____ teachers.
   a a   **b** an   **c** Ø

11 Pablo is _____ artist.
   a a   **b** an   **c** Ø

12 The three brothers are _____.
   a engineer   **b** engineers   **c** an engineers

13 They're Chinese. They _____ Japanese.
   a no   **b** not   **c** aren't

14 _____ it three o'clock?
   a Am   **b** Is   **c** Are

15 _____ Tom and Liz from Sydney?
   a Am   **b** Is   **c** Are

16 'Are you Polish?' 'Yes, I _____.'
   a am   **b** is   **c** are

17 _____ the Eiffel tower in Paris?
   a Am   **b** Is   **c** Are

18 'Are you and Jenna married?' 'Yes, _____.'
   a it is   **b** we are   **c** they are

19 They are _____.
   a fasts cars   **b** fast cars   **c** cars fast

20 Your son _____ short. He's tall.
   a isn't   **b** is   **c** aren't

21 Matilda is _____ young nurse.
   a a   **b** an   **c** Ø

22 Leah and Monika are _____ French teachers.
   a a   **b** an   **c** Ø

23 They're _____ fast motorbikes.
   a a   **b** an   **c** Ø

24 W. B. Yeats is _____ Irish writer.
   a a   **b** an   **c** Ø

25 Where are _____ car keys?
   a a   **b** an   **c** the

26 _____ the books on the chair?
   a Am   **b** Is   **c** Are

27 The phone is _____ the table.
   a on   **b** in   **c** to

28 '_____ is the phone?' 'It's on the table.'
   a What   **b** Where   **c** Who

29 Your wallet is _____ to the bag.

a in   b on   c next

30 _____ my bags?

a Where's   b Where are   c Are where

31 There _____ two sofas in the room.

a am   b is   c are

32 No, there _____ a chair in the bedroom.

a is   b isn't   c aren't

33 _____ there a café near here?

a Are   b Is   c Am

34 There are _____ sofas in my living room.

a a   b one   c two

35 The sofa is _____ the two windows.

a in   b between   c on

36 'Is there a cash machine near here?'
'Yes, _____.'

a there's   b there is   c there are

37 There _____ any money in my wallet.

a am not   b isn't   c aren't

38 There's a chair _____ the corner of the room.

a of   b on   c in

39 There are some pens _____ my desk.

a between   b on   c in front

40 The cinema is _____ the taxi rank and the bus station.

a between   b under   c in front

41 There's a cash machine _____ Regent Street.

a in   b at   c of

42 The museum is _____ of the train station.

a between   b behind   c in front

43 There's _____ apple in my bag.

a a   b an   c some

44 There are _____ biscuits in the cupboard.

a a   b an   c some

45 Sorry, there isn't _____ milk.

a a   b some   c any

46 _____ there any bread?

a Is   b Are   c Some

47 Is there _____ banana in the kitchen?

a a   b an   c some

48 There are _____ eggs.

a any   b some   c an

49 There's a _____ on the table.

a milk   b biscuit   c bread

50 There isn't any _____.

a sugar   b apples   c eggs

2 Progress test (Units 11 to 20)

1 My brother _____ got a new bicycle.
a have   b has   c is

2 We _____ got a cold.
a 've   b 's   c is

3 He _____ got brown eyes.
a 've   b 's   c has

4 They haven't got _____ children.
a a   b some   c any

5 She _____ got a car.
a hasn't   b haven't   c isn't

6 _____ you got a bicycle?
a Is   b Has   c Have

7 'Has Michael got dark hair?'
'No, he _____ . He's got blond hair.'
a hasn't   b haven't   c hasn't got

8 I _____ 32.
a 've   b 've got   c 'm

9 That's my sister. _____ name is Ana.
a His   b Her   c Its

10 Have you got _____ camera?
a you   b you're   c your

11 My father is from Argentina but _____ parents are from Spain.
a his   b her   c their

12 _____ house is in the city centre.
a Are   b Our   c We

13 Paris is beautiful. Its famous for _____ art and museums.
a its   b it's   c it

14 _____ son's a teacher.
a Their   b They're   c They

15 _____ 've got a passport.
a I   b He   c My

16 _____ coat is Peter's.
a That   b These   c Those

17 _____ trainers are new.
a This   b That   c These

18 Is _____ your pen?
a this   b that's   c these

19 Which _____ is his car?
a one   b ones   c this

20 'Whose is it?' 'It's _____ .'
a Karen   b Karens   c Karen's

21 'Whose is this camera?' 'It's _____ .'
a my   b me   c mine

22 Karen and Fred have got a blue car. Is this _____ car?
a there   b they're   c their

23 _____ English lessons are long.
a Our   b Ours   c Our's

24 That's _____ teacher.
a Lisas   b Lisa's   c Lisas'

25 Those books are _____ .
a he's   b he   c his

26 We _____ in New York.
a live   b lives   c are live

27 She _____ work at five.
a finish   b finishs   c finishes

28 Jack _____ geography at university.

 a study   **b** studies   **c** studys

29 I _____ homework after school.

 a do   **b** does   **c** dos

30 They _____ a break at twelve o'clock.

 a has   **b** have   **c** got

31 I'm from the USA _____ I live in Australia.

 a and   **b** but   **c**

32 I _____ like pizza.

 a no   **b** don't   **c** doesn't

33 He _____ the new girl in our class.

 a like   **b** likes   **c** don't like

34 _____ sushi?

 a You like   **b** Does you like   **c** Do you like

35 Does your friend _____ horror films?

 a like   **b** likes   **c** liking

36 He likes her but she doesn't like _____ .

 a he   **b** him   **c** his

37 That music is great. I love _____ .

 a it   **b** its   **c** it's

38 _____ live next to a famous person.

 a We   **b** Our   **c** Us

39 'Do you like this picture?'
    'Yes, he's _____ favourite artist.'

 a me   **b** my   **c** mine

40 I _____ early for school.

 a always am   **b** always   **c** 'm always

41 They _____ TV.

 a never watch   **b** watch never   **c** never watches

42 Rich and Jenny don't _____ see each other now.

 a sometimes   **b** never   **c** often

43 '_____ go to the opera?' 'No, never.'

 a Do you ever   **b** Ever you   **c** Do ever

44 'What _____ the capital of Australia?' 'Canberra.'

 a is   **b** do   **c** does

45 _____ often do you go to the cinema?

 a Why   **b** How   **c** When

46 What time _____ your mother start work?

 a is   **b** do   **c** does

47 When _____ their birthdays?

 a is   **b** are   **c** does

48 Who _____ you live with?

 a are   **b** do   **c** does

49 _____ long is the Amazon River?

 a What   **b** How   **c** Where

50 _____ one do you want?

 a Which   **b** When   **c** How

3 Progress test (Units 21 to 30)

1. Can you _____ French?
   a speaks **b** speak **c** to speak

2. I can't play the piano. _____ you?
   a Can **b** Can't **c** Do can

3. Hilary can't sing but she _____ play the guitar.
   a can **b** cans **c** does can

4. She can't sing _____ .
   a not very well **b** very well **c** not well

5. Roger Federer _____ play tennis very well.
   a can **b** cans **c** does can

6. _____ she like tennis?
   a Can **b** Do **c** Does

7. They _____ play football very well.
   a don't can **b** doesn't can **c** can't

8. _____ play a musical instrument?
   a Does he can **b** Can he **c** Do he can

9. They _____ speak any languages.
   a doesn't can **b** can't **c** don't can

10. 'Can you run fast?' 'No, I _____ .'
    a can't **b** don't **c** can

11. 'Can I get _____ a drink?' 'Yes, please.'
    a me **b** you **c** my

12. Can you pass _____ the salt, please?
    a me **b** you **c** it

13. _____ ask you a question?
    a Can I **b** Can you **c** Do I

14. 'Can I have a drink?' 'Yes, _____ .'
    a please **b** certainly **c** thanks very much

15. _____ help me?
    a Can me **b** Can I **c** Can you

16. Can I _____ your car?
    a borrow **b** lend **c** would

17. Hello, we _____ a table for two, please.
    a like **b** 'd like **c** would

18. '_____ you like some sushi?' 'Yes, please.'
    a Do **b** Would **c** can

19. 'Would you like some wine?' 'No, thanks. _____ like some water.'
    a I **b** I'd **c** Please

20. '_____ the menu now?' 'Yes, please.'
    a Would you like **b** You like **c** Do you like

21. We'd like _____ tea, please.
    a a **b** some **c** any

22. The light's red. _____ !
    a Stop **b** Stop you **c** You stop

23. Come in. _____ a seat.
    a Takes **b** Take **c** Take you

24. _____ turn left here. Turn right.
    a Doesn't **b** No **c** Don't

25. I have two sisters. They are _____ than me.
    a young **b** younger **c** more young

26. This one is _____ than that one.
    a expensive **b** expensiver **c** more expensive

27. My English is _____ than yours.
    a good **b** gooder **c** better

28 Is his brother older _____ me?

    a as   **b** any   **c** than

29 A bicycle is _____ expensive than a car.

    a more   **b** less   **c** as

30 That's a really _____ idea.

    a bad   **b** badder   **c** worse

31 Are you _____ in your new home?

    a happyer   **b** happier   **c** hapier

32 It's cold here. The weather is _____ in my country.

    a hoter   **b** hotter   **c** hot

33 You are _____ beautiful than ever!

    a the   **b** most   **c** more

34 Her new book is _____ interesting than the others. I can't finish it.

    a more   **b** less   **c** most

35 Cheetahs can run _____ than crocodiles.

    a fast   **b** faster   **c** fastest

36 The tortoise lives the _____ of all animals.

    a long   **b** longer   **c** longest

37 Crocodiles are _____ .

    a dangerous   **b** more dangerous   **c** most dangerous

38 The blue whale is _____ heaviest animal in the world.

    a Ø   **b** a   **c** the

39 This was the _____ day ever!

    a good   **b** better   **c** best

40 My Spanish is _____ than yours.

    a worse   **b** worst   **c** the worse

41 This animal is the _____ heavy of the three.

    a less   **b** least   **c** more

42 This table is bigger _____ mine at home.

    a than   **b** as   **c** to

43 Normally, the nightclubs are _____ than this.

    a crowded   **b** more crowded   **c** most crowded

44 Paris is _____ beautiful than I remember.

    a most   **b** much   **c** more

45 I get up _____ than anyone else in my house.

    a early   **b** earlier   **c** earliest

46 He drives very _____ .

    a slow   **b** fastly   **c** slowly

47 They are _____ married.

    a happy   **b** happily   **c** happier

48 We'll be late. Drive _____ !

    a quick   **b** more quickly   **c** quicklier

49 How _____ do you play tennis? You can't be as bad as me!

    a bad   **b** badly   **c** worse

50 She can _____ .

    a well play   **b** play good   **c** play well

4 Progress test (Units 31 to 40)

1   Right now, I _____ cooking dinner for some friends.
    a 'm   b 's   c 're

2   At the moment, they _____ visiting friends.
    a 'm   b 's   c 're

3   She always _____ a bath in the morning.
    a has   b have   c are having

4   _____ you _____ chess?
    a Are … play   b do … playing   c Are … playing

5   'Is she reading anything interesting?'
    'No, she _____.'
    a aren't   b isn't   c isn't reading

6   What _____ he _____ now?
    a are … doing b is … doing   c is … do

7   'Are you busy?' 'No, I _____ TV.'
    a watch   b watching   c 'm watching

8   Jane _____ in a hotel near the station this week.
    a stay   b stays   c 's staying

9   Sorry I _____ late.
    a 'm   b 'm being   c being

10 It _____ today. It's sunny.
    a 's raining   b isn't raining   c doesn't rain

11 _____ rock or jazz?
    a Do you like   b Are you liking   c Liking you

12 We can't come now. We _____ some work.
    a do   b 're doing   c does

13 '_____ the children playing?' 'A computer game.'
    a What are   b Are   c What do

14 Anne and Andrew _____ the new James Bond film this evening.
    a are seeing   b see   c is seeing

15 'Can we meet on Saturday?'
    'Sure. I _____ anything.'
    a don't do   b 'm not doing   c not doing

16 _____ free next week?
    a Are you doing   b You   c Are you

17 My son and his friends are _____ travel around New Zealand.
    a go to   b going   c going to

18 Are you going _____ us tonight?
    a to join   b join   c to joining

19 What _____ do about your exam results?
    a are you going to   b do you go to   c do you

20 I have an arrangement with Bill. We _____ at six.
    a are meet   b 're meeting   c 're going meet

21 'What are you going to do when you finish school?'
    'I _____ engineering at university.'
    a 'm studying   b 'm going to study   c study

22 I _____ really busy at work last week.
    a was   b were   c am

23 They _____ at home yesterday.
    a wasn't   b weren't   c don't were

24 _____ Sam and Matt at the party?
    a Wasn't   b Was   c Were

25 'Was it your birthday last month?' 'Yes, it _____.'
    a was   b were   c am

26 Our anniversary _____ on 25th April.

a was   b were   c weren't

27 '_____ your weekend?' 'Fine, thanks.'

a What was   b How was   c Who was

28 When I was a child, _____ a park here.

a there's   b there was   c there were

29 '_____ a busy road here?' 'No, it was quiet.'

a Was there   b Were there   c Is there

30 'Were there any trees?' 'No, _____.'

a there wasn't   b there weren't   c there were

31 I think _____ some skyscrapers over here.

a there's   b there were   c there was

32 '_____ you play the piano when you were a child?' 'Yes, but not very well.'

a Can   b Could   c Do

33 Mozart _____ play the organ as a child.

a can   b were   c could

34 Sorry, I _____ hear you. Please say that again.

a could   b couldn't   c can

35 _____ Beethoven a composer?

a Could   b Was   c Can

36 How _____ Picasso paint?

a well   b far could   c well could

37 _____ you run when you were young?

a How far could   b How   c How far

38 'Could Helen Keller hear when she was a child?' 'No, she _____.'

a could   b couldn't   c wasn't

39 She _____ sing very well.

a could   b coulds   c could to

40 _____ your name, please?

a Could I have   b Could I having   c Could have

41 Could you _____ that?

a spelling   b spell me   c to spell

42 _____ you like to leave a message?

a Do   b Would   c Could

43 Would you _____ help me?

a like   b like to   c liking

44 _____ I speak to Ms Blumer, please?

a Would   b Could   c Do

45 '_____ I email the document, please?' 'Sure.'

a Would   b Do   c Can

46 Could you give _____ your number?

a I   b you   c me

47 Can you tell _____ Rosanne called?

a to him   b him   c you

48 Sorry, I _____ come to your party last week.

a can't   b couldn't   c wasn't

49 '_____ some pizza?' 'Yes, please.'

a Would you like   b Do you like   c Would you like to

50 'Would you like to come out tonight?' '_____?'

a No, I wouldn't.

b Thanks, but I can't. I'm going to the cinema.

c Yes, I'd like.

5 Progress test (Units 41 to 50)

1 My father _____ born in 1951.
   a was   **b** were   **c** could

2 The students _____ this course last May.
   a start   **b** started   **c** are starting

3 We _____ Maths for four years.
   a study   **b** studyed   **c** studied

4 The train _____ at the station.
   a stoped   **b** stopped   **c** stop

5 Could you _____ the saxophone when you were a boy?
   a play   **b** played   **c** are playing

6 Did they _____ to China last year?
   a travel   **b** travelled   **c** travelling

7 My parents _____ in a small house near Lyon in France. They love it there!
   a live   **b** lived   **c** is living

8 Sheila _____ from college with a degree in nursing in 2006.
   a qualify   **b** is qualifying **c** qualified

9 The team _____ to the hotel at midnight.
   a get   **b** got   **c** getted

10 We _____ some sightseeing after the shops closed.
   a do   **b** does   **c** did

11 At the restaurant, Norman _____ the local food but I _____ a burger.
   a eat … had   **b** ate … have   **c** ate … had

12 The girl _____ in the sun for hours and _____ red!
   a sat … went   **b** sit … go   **c** sit … went

13 I _____ see her at the lesson. Is she OK?
   a don't   **b** doesn't   **c** didn't

14 Sorry, we _____ your letter. Can you send it again?
   a didn't received **b** didn't receive **c** no received

15 Did you _____ school at sixteen or eighteen?
   a leave   **b** leaved   **c** left

16 Did Ingrid have any children? Yes, she _____ .
   a was   **b** did   **c** didn't

17 '_____ you stay at the conference?' 'At the Ritz Hotel.'
   a Where do   **b** Where did   **c** What did

18 How _____ the hotel?
   a was   **b** were   **c** did

19 Who _____ with you?
   a did you go   **b** go   **c** went

20 What _____ you do last night?
   a do   **b** were   **c** did

21 'What time _____ ?' 'She left at nine.'
   a she leave   **b** did she leave **c** she left

22 I'm afraid there _____ time to see Liza.
   a didn't   **b** wasn't   **c** did

23 Who _____ this? It's beautiful!
   a make   **b** did make   **c** made

24 'Who _____ here?' 'Picasso did.'
   a did live   **b** lives   **c** lived

25 Did you _____ the palace?
   a like   **b** likes   **c** liked

26 You _____ switch off your mobile phone here.
   a must   **b** musts   **c** must to

27 You _____ drive faster than 70 mph in the UK.
   a don't must   **b** mustn't   **c** didn't must

28 The doctors says I _____ eat more fruit and fewer sweets.

a must   b mustn't   c must to

29 All employees _____ to wash their hands.

a must   b have   c has

30 Quick! We _____ be late for the start of the film.

a don't must   b mustn't   c don't have to

31 You _____ wear a uniform. You can wear your normal clothes.

a have to   b don't have to   c don't have

32 When a customer walks in, the waiter _____ to be polite.

a has got   b have   c must

33 _____ to get up early?

a Do you have   b Have you   c Must you

34 'Does she have to come too?' 'Yes, she _____.'

a has   b does   c do

35 I like this dress. What do you think? _____ I buy it?

a Would   b Should   c Could

36 The police _____ stop those cars.

a should   b shoulds   c should to

37 You _____ do that. It's dangerous.

a don't should   b shouldn't   c shouldn't to

38 I couldn't come to the party. I _____ study for my exam.

a have to   b had to   c musted

39 We always _____ do what the teachers say at my school.

a have to   b had   c musted

40 They _____ to study. There wasn't an exam that week.

a hadn't   b didn't have   c have

41 _____ to ask Rita and Paul. They are so boring!

a Did you have   b Had you   c Have

42 _____ we eat now? I'm very hungry.

a Have   b Must   c Could

43 I _____ walk for six months when I was younger.

a mustn't   b shouldn't   c couldn't

44 They _____ turn left on that road.

a mustn't   b hadn't   c don't had

45 We _____ get a qualification. It isn't necessary for the job.

a couldn't   b mustn't   c don't have to

46 You _____ call your mother. She would like to speak to you.

a would   b had to   c should

47 '_____ I borrow my dad's car?' 'Yes, that's a good idea.'

a Must   b Should   c Would

48 'Why _____ stop?' 'There's a red light.'

a should you   b could you   c did you have to

49 Hello, Tourist Information. _____ I help you?

a Can   b Would   c Must

50 My doctor's appointment is in five minutes. We _____ leave right now.

a have   b must   c could

6 Progress test (Units 51 to 60)

1 I _____ the kitchen so you can cook dinner now.
   a 've cleaned   b clean   c 's cleaned

2 Marie _____ to meet her new boyfriend I think.
   a has went   b has go   c has gone

3 _____ you tidied your bedroom?
   a Have   b Did   c Are

4 Has the visitor arrived? Yes, he _____ .
   a has   b have   c arrived

5 Good news! Tracey called. She's _____ passed her final test.
   a yet   b already   c just

6 No, I haven't decided _____ .
   a just   b already   c yet

7 Don't worry about the ironing. Your mother's _____ done it. She was here this morning.
   a just   b already   c yet

8 Has the President made a decision _____ ?
   a just   b already   c yet

9 I'm afraid _____ yet.
   a they've arrived   b they haven't arrived
   c have they arrived

10 The police _____ to check the building.
   a have just been   b haven't just been
   c have been yet

11 The company has produced clocks _____ over fifty years.
   a for   b since   c yet

12 There haven't been any visitors _____ this morning.
   a for   b since   c yet

13 They've _____ got married. That's great news!
   a just   b for   c since

14 _____ has he been a doctor?
   a How much   b How many   c How long

15 They haven't won a game _____ 1985.
   a for   b since   c already

16 I haven't seen you _____ ages. You look well!
   a yet   b for   c since

17 _____ been to Russia?
   a How long   b Have you ever   c How

18 Have you _____ eaten tofu?
   a ever   b never   c yet

19 No, she's _____ failed an exam in her life.
   a ever   b never   c just

20 Marjorie has _____ to Scotland twice before.
   a been   b gone   c went

21 Where's Roger _____ ? I can't find him.
   a been   b went   c gone

22 My family _____ to Hawaii last month.
   a been   b gone   c went

23 I've _____ my tea. Could I have another cup, please?
   a drink   b drank   c drunk

24 _____ the show about whales on TV last night?
   a Have you seen   b Have you ever seen
   c Did you see

25 'Did you have time for a break?' 'Yes, I _____ .'
   a 've had   b did   c had

26 'Have you got a driving licence?' 'No, I _____ .'
   a haven't   b hadn't   c didn't

27 They _____ walking home when they saw the accident.
   a was   b wasn't   c were

28 The moon _____ shining in the night sky.

   a was   b were   c have

29 _____ when they called?

   a What were you doing   b What have you done
   c What are you doing

30 _____ with the pen I lent you? Have you lost it?

   a What were you doing   b What have you done
   c What are you doing

31 I was sleeping _____ they arrived.

   a when   b suddenly   c just

32 It was getting colder and colder. _____ it started
    to snow.

   a When   b Suddenly   c While

33 The butler was cleaning the bedrooms when he
    _____ a loud noise.

   a hear   b heard   c was hearing

34 He _____ on holiday since last week.

   a was   b has been   c was being

35 I _____ the house while Jake made the dinner.

   a tidied   b 've tidied   c was tidy

36 While we _____ for the bus, we met some old
    friends.

   a were waiting b 've waited   c waiting

37 So far we've seen the Eiffel Tower _____ the
    Louvre Museum.

   a but   b and   c while

38 Would you like a table by the window _____ by
    the door?

   a and   b so   c or

39 _____ we saw Big Ben, we went to Buckingham
    Palace.

   a While   b So   c Before

40 Can we meet _____ lunch? I don't have time to
    talk now.

   a after   b when   c but

41 I hated Maths at school _____ I loved Science.

   a so   b before   c but

42 _____ I was walking to work, it started to rain.

   a Before   b Because   c While

43 _____ you get to the station, give me a call.

   a Because   b When   c While

44 We took the bus _____ it was cheaper than
    the train.

   a because   b but   c so

45 The TV didn't work _____ I had to buy
    another one.

   a before   b so   c when

46 Jean _____ long hair but it's quite short now.

   a have   b was having   c used to have

47 Did you _____ walk to school?

   a used to   b use to   c use

48 My brothers _____ help in my father's shop.

   a used to   b use to   c use

49 The journey _____ to take very long.

   a didn't use   b didn't used   c no use

50 I _____ newspapers every morning when I was a
    teenager.

   a use to deliver   b deliver   c delivered

7 Progress test (Units 61 to 70)

1 .... of the students were married – about 45%.

a All   b Most   c Some

2 .... students must register at reception.

a All   b All of   c Some of

3 .... the people here is under 16.

a Some   b Most   c None of

4 Everyone passed – and .... scored over 90% as well.

a most of   b most of you   c none

5 .... of them are studying Spanish but most are studying English.

a None   b All   c Some

6 I think everyone has worked hard. .... of them was lazy.

a None   b All   c Some

7 There are lots of messages for you today. Everybody .... to speak to you.

a want   b wants   c have wanted

8 There's .... nicer than Rome for a weekend break. It's wonderful.

a everywhere   b nowhere   c anywhere

9 I think there's .... at the door. Can you go and see who it is?

a somebody   b anybody   c everybody

10 Was there .... for me in the post today?

a anything   b everything   c nothing

11 .... has seen my bag. I don't know where I left it.

a No one   b Someone   c Anyone

12 'Is there anything in the fridge?' 'No, ...'

a anything   b everything   c nothing

13 'Do you like Bryan and Bob?' 'Yes, I like .... of them.'

a any   b most   c both

14 .... apple pie or strawberry cake is fine for dessert.

a Either   b Neither   c Any

15 .... students are very happy. They passed all their exams.

a Either   b Neither   c Both

16 'Is answer A or B correct?' '........ because the answer is C.'

a Either   b Both   c Neither

17 How .... milk have we got?

a many   b much   c any

18 How .... cakes are there?

a many   b much   c any

19 Is there .... chocolate left or have we eaten it all?

a many   b much   c any

20 Look in the cupboards. There are .... tins in there.

a much   b a lot of   c any

21 .... children don't like vegetables but Billy does.

a Much   b A lot of   c Any

22 How much .... have we got?

a people   b coins   c time

23 How many .... work here?

a people   b employee   c mans

24 Do you have .... bread?

a many   b any   c a lot

25 _____ information on the internet is incorrect.

   a Many   **b** Any   **c** A lot of

26 I'm going to be _____ famous film star when I grow up.

   a a   **b** an   **c** the

27 I'm sure Madonna lives in _____ enormous house.

   a a   **b** an   **c** the

28 My doctor says I should take _____ regular exercise.

   a a   **b** Ø   **c** the

29 There's _____ Australian actor in this film.

   a a   **b** Ø   **c** an

30 _____ United States of America has 50 states.

   a A   **b** Ø   **c** The

31 Leonid Stadnyk is the tallest man in _____ world.

   a a   **b** Ø   **c** the

32 How fast does _____ sun go round _____ moon.

   a a … the   **b** the … the   **c** the … Ø

33 Would you like _____ menu?

   a a   **b** Ø   **c** an

34 Can you play _____ guitar?

   a a   **b** Ø   **c** the

35 _____ walk slowly but they live a long time.

   a Tortoises   **b** The tortoise   **c** A tortoise

36 'Can I borrow your pen?' 'Sorry, but this is _____ only one I've got.'

   a a   **b** Ø   **c** the

37 'Is there _____ train now?' 'No, the next one is at six o'clock.'

   a a   **b** Ø   **c** the

38 What time does _____ plane to Lima leave?

   a a   **b** Ø   **c** the

39 Would you like _____ window seat or _____ aisle seat?

   a a … an   **b** an … a   **c** an … an

40 Can you open _____ door for me? I haven't got a key.

   a a   **b** Ø   **c** the

41 Who's _____ man over there with black hair? He's famous, isn't he?

   a Ø   **b** the   **c** a

42 My grandmother loves _____ cats. She's got twenty-one of them!

   a a   **b** Ø   **c** the

43 We travelled for six days on _____ foot and by camel.

   a a   **b** Ø   **c** the

44 We're studying the history of the Romans at _____ school.

   a Ø   **b** the   **c** a

45 Our teacher always gives us _____ difficult exercises for homework.

   a Ø   **b** a   **c** the

46 My cousin is _____ engineer.

   a a   **b** Ø   **c** an

47 These are some of _____ oldest books in the world.

   a a   **b** Ø   **c** the

48 I'm _____ Australian citizen.

   a an   **b** Ø   **c** a

49 My degree is in _____ French and German.

   a the   **b** Ø   **c** a

50 The gallery is in the centre of _____ Berlin.

   a a   **b** Ø   **c** the

8 Progress test (Units 71 to 80)

1 I think we _____ have cars that fly in the future.
   a will   b wills   c will to

2 How old will you _____ in the year 2050?
   a are   b being   c be

3 'Will you tell them?' 'Yes, I _____.'
   a 'll   b will tell   c will

4 Sorry, but I _____ be there tonight. I have to work.
   a will   b won't   c 'll

5 What time _____?
   a will Toby arrive   b Toby will arrive
   c will arrive Toby

6 I think I _____ have the steak.
   a 'll   b 'm going   c going to

7 When Mandy leaves school, she _____ train to be a hairdresser.
   a 'll   b 's going to   c 's

8 We _____ the Rolling Stones. I've got an extra ticket. Would you like to come too?
   a 'll see   b 're going to see   c see

9 '_____ when you get to Delhi?'
   'I don't know yet. I'm still planning the trip.'
   a What are you doing   b What are you going to do
   c What you will do

10 'I didn't get the email you sent' 'Don't worry. I _____ it again.'
   a 'll send   b 'm going to send   c 'm sending

11 I _____ I'll have a cup of tea.
   a 'm think   b 'm going   c think

12 'Can I talk to Bryan?' 'Sorry, he _____ a meeting at the moment.'
   a 'll have   b 's going to have   c 's having

13 Which one _____ buy?
   a are you   b will   c are you going to

14 What's Sammy _____ when he's older?
   a going to do   b will do   c going

15 'Do you want to have lunch with me?' 'Sorry but I _____ my parents for lunch today.'
   a meet   b 'm meeting   c 'll meet

16 It's possible Mike _____ me. Can you take a message, please?
   a will call   b 's calling   c calls

17 'Tell me about your holiday. What's your plan?'
   'First, we _____ to Krakow …'
   a 're going to fly   b 'll fly   c 're fly

18 No, I _____ help! I don't want to!
   a will   b won't   c 'm not

19 There's a problem today and the bus to London _____ to stop here.
   a won't   b isn't go   c isn't going

20 _____ you tell her or do you want me to?
   a Are   b Is going to   c Will

21 My birthday is _____ 19th June.
   a in   b on   c at

22 My wedding anniversary is _____ April.
   a in   b on   c at

23 The party starts _____ nine o'clock.
   a in   b on   c at

24 The last time I saw them was _____ 2004 I think.
   a in   b on   c at

25 Everyone is arriving _____ the same time.
   a in   b on   c at

26 All the flowers come up _____ the spring.

    a in   b on   c at

27 Let's meet _____ the afternoon. How about _____ three?

    a in … at   b in … in   c at … in

28 There's a farmer's market _____ the first Saturday of each month.

    a in   b on   c at

29 Music was much better _____ the sixties.

    a in   b on   c at

30 It's too hot to go outside _____ the middle of the day in summer.

    a in   b on   c at

31 The film finishes _____ about ten thirty.

    a in   b on   c at

32 We always visit our grandparents _____ Friday afternoons.

    a in   b on   c at

33 'Where are the children?' 'I think they're _____ the bedroom.'

    a in   b on   c at

34 There's someone _____ the front door.

    a in   b on   c at

35 Your car keys are _____ the table.

    a in   b on   c at

36 Turn right and the police station is _____ the left.

    a in   b on   c at

37 There's a bag _____ the table. Is it yours?

    a between   b under   c at

38 The sauna is _____ to the solarium.

    a in front   b behind   c next

39 Go straight ahead and the swimming pool is _____ of the restaurant.

    a in front   b behind   c opposite

40 He's the person _____ does the photocopying.

    a which   b who   c he

41 Rachel is the teacher _____ likes to give tests.

    a which   b that   c she

42 'What do you call the machine _____ boils water?' 'A kettle.'

    a which   b who   c it

43 This is the cable _____ connects the computer to the printer.

    a that   b who   c where

44 This is the DVD _____ last week.

    a who we watched   b that we watched
    c which watched

45 She's the woman _____ at the local hospital.

    a works   b who works   c which works

46 Do you like the book _____ you?

    a who I gave   b I gave   c gave

47 Do you want to see the photos _____ on holiday?

    a when we took   b who we took   c that we took

48 'Who is the person _____ the Harry Potter books?' 'J.K. Rowling.'

    a which wrote   b that wrote   c wrote

49 I'm studying the same course _____ last year.

    a who you did   b you did   c which

50 Who is the man _____ that awful yellow car?

    a that owns   b owns   c which owns

9 Progress test (Units 81 to 90)

1 When you _____ this button, it switches the TV on.

a press   b will press   c pressed

2 If anyone _____ , please tell them I'm out.

a ask   b asks   c will ask

3 If the alarm goes off, _____ the building.

a please leave   b left   c you leave

4 If you heat water _____ hot.

a , it gets   b it gets   c it get

5 The engine _____ you press this switch.

a starts, if   b starts if   c start,

6 Don't cross the road _____ the policeman says you can.

a unless   b if   c when

7 _____ hear the fire alarm, walk to the nearest exit.

a Unless you   b You   c If you

8 _____ the police unless it's a real emergency.

a Call   b When you call   c Don't call

9 If you drive faster, we _____ there by this evening.

a get   b 'll get   c 're getting

10 _____ we walk this way, will we reach the top of the mountain?

a If   b When   c While

11 Unless we book it now, there _____ any tickets left for the concert.

a will be   b won't be   c are

12 If I have any free time this afternoon, _____ you.

a I help   b I'll help   c help

13 _____ at the lights if they turn red.

a Stop   b Will stop   c Stops

14 When they _____ this song, I have to dance!

a sing   b 'll sing   c 're going to sing

15 They'll meet us at the Blue Moon café _____ you know a better place.

a if   b when   c unless

16 I'm sure if the bus is late, they _____ take a taxi.

a 'll   b might   c should

17 When the teacher asks you a question, you _____ answer.

a could   b can   c have to

18 _____ you pick him up if he calls? I'm too busy to do it I'm afraid.

a Could   b Must   c Should

19 We _____ miss the film if we don't leave now. Let's go!

a have to   b might   c should

20 If they want to see the Picasso exhibition, they _____ need to reserve tickets in advance. I'm not sure.

a can   b must   c might

21 I think you _____ use a credit card or cash when you pay for the tickets. It doesn't matter.

a will   b can   c must

22 When the alarm starts, everyone _____ walk outside and wait in the car park.

a must   b can   c could

23 When you visit my country, you _____ bring warm clothing. It gets very cold at night.

a might   b could   c should

24 If you don't have any money, I _____ lend you some. It isn't a problem for me.

a have to   b can   c must

25 If you buy a lottery ticket, you _____ win a million!

a could   b have to   c won't

26 I was really _____ when Gill told me she was leaving.

a surprised   b surprising

27 They're late again. How _____ !

a annoyed   b annoying

28 This part of the film is really _____ . I've seen it six times.

a excited   b exciting

29 Look out! Here comes the _____ part with Dracula.

a frightened   b frightening

30 'Do you find this kind of book _____ ?' 'No, not very.'

a interested   b interesting

31 Don't be _____ . We'll be fine.

a worried   b worrying

32 He looks really _____ . It's time for his bed.

a tired   b tiring

33 Why do you _____ so sad? What's the problem?

a look   b smell   c taste

34 Wow! This cake _____ delicious.

a feels   b tastes   c sounds

35 'How does it _____ ?' 'Very soft.'

a smell   b feel   c taste

36 I love jazz but rock _____ awful.

a looks   b feels   c sounds

37 Your new girlfriend looks very _____ .

a beauty   b beautiful   c beautifully

38 This soup _____ hot and spicy. What's in it?

a smells   b feels   c tastes

39 Try this perfume. It _____ really fresh.

a smells   b feels   c tastes

40 I think you should buy that _____ .

a beautiful old table   b old table beautiful
c old beautiful table

41 There's a _____ bowl in the kitchen. Can you get it for me?

a wooden small round   b round small wooden
c small round wooden

42 Whose is that _____ ball in the garden?

a huge green plastic   b green plastic huge
c plastic green huge

43 My dream car is a(n) _____ sports car. What about you?

a stylish Italian red   b Italian stylish red
c stylish red Italian

44 Are you good _____ painting?

a about   b by   c at

45 I'm bored _____ this programme. Let's turn the TV off.

a about   b with   c at

46 Are people in this country very _____ from people in yours?

a different   b interested   c excited

47 We are very excited _____ our holiday.

a about   b from   c with

48 Who is Jennifer married _____ now?

a by   b with   c to

49 They aren't very keen _____ basketball. They prefer tennis.

a of   b at   c on

50 Don't ask them to do it. They're really _____ at cleaning.

a annoyed   b worried   c bad

1 Have you decided _____ your job?

 a leave   b to leave   c leaving

2 We plan _____ at about six.

 a arrive   b to arrive   c arriving

3 They didn't _____ to pay that much.

 a agree   b to agree   c agreeing

4 Would you like _____ something this weekend?

 a do   b to do   c doing

5 I really like _____ golf at the weekends.

 a play   b to   c playing

6 Why are you worried about _____ on a plane?

 a go   b to go   c going

7 _____ at night can be dangerous.

 a Drive   b You drive   c Driving

8 Matthew hopes _____ his studies at Oxford University.

 a continue   b to continue   c continuing

9 Tell _____ to borrow mine.

 a she   b her   c to her

10 My uncle is really good at _____ sushi.

 a make   b to make   c making

11 Is it true that _____ too much coffee is bad for you?

 a drink   b to drink   c drinking

12 Do you mind _____ later?

 a eat   b to eat   c eating

13 I often go _____ with friends.

 a sunbathe   b to sunbathe   c sunbathing

14 Rashish would like _____ too. Is there space in the car?

 a come   b to come   c coming

15 What do you enjoy _____ in your free time?

 a do   b to do   c doing

16 I plan _____ smoking on 1st January.

 a give up   b to give up   c giving up

17 They want _____ at eight but I think that's too early.

 a start   b to start   c starting

18 They've stopped _____ and have agreed to work together.

 a argue   b to argue   c arguing

19 We were hungry so we stopped _____ something to eat.

 a have   b to have   c having

20 They won't mind _____ late to finish this project.

 a work   b to work   c working

21 We stopped _____ junk food months ago. Why don't you stop too?

 a eat   b to eat   c eating

22 Don't stop _____ to me, please. I love _____ your letters.

 a writing … receiving   b to write … to receive
 c to write … receiving

23 We've agreed _____ for lunch at one o'clock.

 a stop   b to stop   c stopping

24 _____ her to send this, please.

 a Tell   b Say   c Want

25 My manager _____ you to send this, please.

 a says   b wants   c tells

26 We need _____ for the hotel.
    a pay   **b** to pay   **c** paying

27 I _____ to have the steak and chips, please.
    a like   **b** liking   **c** 'd like

28 What time do we need _____ ?
    a leave   **b** to leave   **c** leaving

29 I want _____ me when you get there.
    a you to call   **b** that you to call   **c** you call

30 We'd like _____ help today.
    a everyone   **b** everyone to   **c** to everyone

31 Lydia is visiting Nepal _____ Mount Everest.
    a the   **b** see   **c** to see

32 I'm calling you _____ arrange a meeting.
    a to   **b** so   **c** for

33 We need to stop at the supermarket _____ some vegetables.
    a buy   **b** buying   **c** to buy

34 The manager wants us to work late to _____ the shop.
    a clean   **b** cleaning   **c** for clean

35 Please _____ your hands before eating.
    a wash   **b** washes   **c** are washed

36 Your salary _____ into your bank account at the end of every month.
    a pay   **b** is paid   **c** are paid

37 The steak _____ with potatoes and salad.
    a serves   **b** is served   **c** is serving

38 All our coffee _____ in Ethiopia.
    a grow   **b** is grown   **c** to grow

39 The Japanese _____ really good-quality cars.
    a produce   **b** are produced   **c** is produced

40 How often _____ ?
    a are these rooms cleaned   **b** clean these rooms
    c do these rooms cleaned

41 More people _____ Urdu than English.
    a speak   **b** is spoken   **c** are spoken

42 A new type of plant _____ in the Amazon jungle last week.
    a was discovered   **b** discovered   **c** is discovered

43 Chocolate _____ first brought to Europe hundreds of years ago.
    a is   **b** was   **c** were

44 *The Lord of the Rings* _____ by J.R.R. Tolkien between 1937 and 1949.
    a wrote   **b** writes   **c** was written

45 The President was shot _____ a man on top of a building.
    a by   **b** with   **c** at

46 I _____ potatoes in my garden every year.
    a are grown   **b** was grown   **c** grow

47 Why _____ about this problem?
    a I wasn't told   **b** wasn't I told   **c** didn't I tell

48 I love this song. Who _____ it?
    a sings   **b** is sung   **c** was sing

49 All our pasta _____ by hand.
    a makes   **b** is made   **c** made

50 Why _____ that? It wasn't very nice.
    a did you say   **b** was it said   **c** said you

Appendix 1 Punctuation

Capital

Use a capital letter for …

- the first letter of a sentence.
- the names of people and places: *Wolfgang Amadeus Mozart, Helen Keller, Jackie Chan, Madrid, New York, Hong Kong.*
- the names of countries, nationalities and languages: *China/Chinese, France/French, Australia/Australian, English.*
- days of the week and months of the year (but not seasons): *Monday, Thursday, April, September.*
- school subjects: *English, Maths, Biology.*
- people's titles: *Mr Brown, Doctor Smith, President Obama.*
- the pronoun *I*: *Martha and I live in Simpson Street.*

End of a sentence

Normally, we end a sentence with a full stop:
I live in London.

Question mark

- Put *?* at the end of a question (not a full stop):
Where do you live?

Commas

Use commas for …

- lists of nouns: *I bought a pen, a book and a bag.*
- lists of adjectives: *It's an old, black, electric lamp.*
- conditional sentences when the *if*-clause comes first: *If you leave now, you'll catch the last train.*

Apostrophe '

Use an apostrophe for …

- contracted verbs forms. Here are some common examples:

Verb *to be*

I'm = I am

he's = he is

they're = they are

isn't = is not

aren't = are not

Verb *to have*

I've = I have

she's = she has

we've = we have

hasn't = has not

haven't = have not

Auxiliary verb *to do*

don't = do not

doesn't = does not

didn't = did not

would like

I'd like = I would like

I wouldn't like = I would not like

Negative modals

won't = will not

wouldn't = would not

mustn't = must not

can't = cannot

couldn't = could not

shouldn't = should not

- for possessive *'s* (see Unit 14):
Karen's mobile. My brother's T shirt.

Appendix 2   Spelling rules

Plural nouns

- Add -s to most nouns.

> dog → dog**s**
>
> desk → desk**s**
>
> house → house**s**

- Add -es to nouns ending in -ch, -o, -s, -ss, -sh, and -x.

> sandwich → sandwich**es**   class → class**es**
>
> tomato → tomato**es**   dish → dish**es**
>
> bus → bus**es**   box → box**es**

- Change nouns ending in -y (after a consonant) to -i.

> country → countr**ies**
>
> story → stor**ies**
>
> city → cit**ies**

> TIP Don't change the -y to -i after a vowel:
> *holidays, keys*

- Some nouns are irregular. For example:

> man → men
>
> child → children
>
> woman → women
>
> person → people

Present simple third person (*he/she/it*) verbs

- Add -s to most verbs in the present simple third person form.

> live → live**s**
>
> start → start**s**
>
> work → work**s**

- Add -es to verbs ending in -ch, -o, -s, -ss, -sh and -x.

> watch → watch**es**   finish → finish**es**
>
> go → go**es**   relax → relax**es**
>
> pass → pass**es**

- Change verbs ending in -y (after a consonant) to -i.

> study → stud**ies**
>
> fly → fl**ies**

> TIP Don't change the -y to -i after a vowel: *plays, buys*

- A few verbs have irregular forms.

> have → has
>
> be → is

Comparative and superlative adjectives

- Add -er to short adjectives to form the comparative. Add -est to short adjectives to form the superlative.

> young → young**er** → young**est**
>
> cheap → cheap**er** → cheap**est**

> TIP When the adjective ends in -e, add -r/-st:
> *large → larger/largest*

- Change adjectives ending in -y (after a consonant) to -i.

> happy → happ**ier** → happ**iest**
>
> angry → angr**ier** → angr**iest**

- Double the final consonant on some adjectives ending with a vowel and a consonant.

> hot → ho**tt**er → ho**tt**est
>
> big → bi**gg**er → bi**gg**est

> TIP Don't double the consonant with adjectives ending in -w or -y: *slow → slower/slowest*.

Adverbs ending in -*ly*

- You often add -ly to an adjective to form an adverb.

> quick → quick**ly**
>
> slow → slow**ly**

- Note these differences:
  Adjectives ending in -l: *beautiful → beautifully*
  Adjectives ending in -y: *happy → happily*
  Adjectives ending in -ble: *horrible → horribly*

Past simple regular verbs (-ed endings)

- Add -ed to verbs ending in a consonant.

watch → watch**ed**

visit → visit**ed**

- Add -d to verbs ending in -e.

dance → dance**d**

arrive → arrive**d**

- Double the final consonant on some verbs ending with a vowel and a consonant.

stop → sto**pp**ed

jog → jo**gg**ed

Present participles (-ing endings)

- With verbs ending in -e, delete the -e before adding -ing.

dance → danc**ing**

live → liv**ing**

- Double the final consonant on some verbs ending with a vowel and a consonant.

stop → sto**pp**ing

run → ru**nn**ing

swim → swi**mm**ing

jog → jo**gg**ing

British and American spelling

There are a few differences.

- Words ending in -re often end in -er: *centre (Br Eng) – center (Am Eng)*.
- Words with -our often delete the -u: *colour (Br Eng) – color (Am Eng), favourite (Br Eng) – favorite (Am Eng)*.
- Verbs ending with a vowel and a consonant don't double the final consonant: *travelling (Br Eng) – traveling (Am Eng)*.
- Verbs ending with -ise or -ize are always -ize: *memorise (Br Eng) – memorize (Am Eng)*.

Check your spelling!

1 Write the plural of these words.

1 cat   *cats*
2 address
3 car
4 potato
5 apple
6 dress
7 baby
8 person

2 Write the third person form of these verbs.

1 go   *goes*
2 drive
3 buy
4 try
5 push
6 marry
7 teach
8 play

3 Correct the spelling mistake in each sentence.

1 She ~~stoped~~ at the traffic lights.
   stopped

2 It's hoter inside than out.

3 I'm the happyest person in the world!

4 Where are you moveing to?

5 They love swiming.

6 We danceed all night long.

7 It's the bigest tower in London.

8 They're planing their holidays.

Appendix 3   Irregular verbs

infinitive	past simple	past participle	infinitive	past simple	past participle
be	was/were	been	learn	learnt	learnt
become	became	become	leave	left	left
begin	began	begun	lend	lent	lent
bite	bit	bitten	lose	lost	lost
blow	blew	blown	make	made	made
break	broke	broken	mean	meant	meant
bring	brought	brought	meet	met	met
build	built	built	pay	paid	paid
burn	burnt	burnt	put	put	put
buy	bought	bought	read /riːd/	read /red/	read /red/
catch	caught	caught	ride	rode	ridden
choose	chose	chosen	ring	rang	rung
come	came	come	rise	rose	risen
cost	cost	cost	run	ran	run
do	did	done	say	said	said
draw	drew	drawn	see	saw	seen
drink	drank	drunk	sell	sold	sold
drive	drove	driven	send	sent	sent
eat	ate	eaten	shine	shone	shone
fall	fell	fallen	show	showed	shown
feel	felt	felt	shut	shut	shut
fight	fought	fought	sing	sang	sung
find	found	found	sit	sat	sat
fly	flew	flown	sleep	slept	slept
forget	forgot	forgotten	speak	spoke	spoken
get	got	got	spend	spent	spent
give	gave	given	stand	stood	stood
go	went	gone/been	steal	stole	stolen
grow	grew	grown	swim	swam	swum
hang	hung	hung	take	took	taken
have	had	had	teach	taught	taught
hear	heard	heard	tear	tore	torn
hide	hid	hidden	tell	told	told
hit	hit	hit	think	thought	thought
hold	held	held	throw	threw	thrown
hurt	hurt	hurt	wear	wore	worn
keep	kept	kept	win	won	won
know	knew	known	write	wrote	written

Appendix 4   Summary of main verb forms

Summary of present tenses

Present simple

I/You/We/They **live** in Ireland.
He/She/It **lives** Ireland.

We **don't live** in Ireland.
She **doesn't live** in Ireland.

Where **do** they **live**?
Where **does** he **live**?

Present continuous

I'm **playing** basketball at the moment.
You/We/They**'re playing** basketball at the moment.
He/She**'s playing** basketball at the moment.

I'm **not playing** basketball at the moment.
He **isn't playing** basketball at the moment.
We **aren't playing** basketball at the moment.

What **are** you **doing**?
Where **is** she **playing** basketball?

Present perfect

I/You/We/They**'ve gone** to the cinema.
He/She**'s gone** to the cinema.

We **haven't gone** to the cinema.
He **hasn't gone** to the cinema.

Where **have** they **gone**?
Where **has** she **gone**?

Summary of past tenses

Past simple

I/You/He/She/It/We/They **finished** last night.

I/You/He/She/It/We/They **didn't finish** last night.

Did I/You/He/She/It/We/They **finish** last night?

Past continuous

I/He/She/It **was waiting** for a bus.
You/We/They **were waiting** for a bus.

I **wasn't waiting** for a bus.
We **weren't waiting** for a bus.

Was he **waiting** for a bus?
Were you **waiting** for a bus?

Summary of future forms

I'll **see** you tonight.
I'm **going to** see her tonight.
We**'re seeing** each other this evening.

Check your tenses!

1   **Complete the sentences with the correct form of the verbs.**

1   She always _____ (travel) by bicycle.

2   Where do you _____ (work)?

3   Sorry, we _____ (not open) the shop on Mondays.

4   Right now they _____ (do) their homework.

5   My family _____ (not eat) anything with meat in at the moment.

6   Who _____ (sing) in the shower? It's really noisy!

7   Where _____ (they live) nowadays?

8   Matilda _____ (go) out but I can give her a message.

9   I _____ (not be) to the cinema in ages!

10   We _____ (finish) cleaning the car. What's next?

11   Mary and Dick _____ (play) tennis yesterday.

12   They _____ (win) the lottery last year.

13   When _____ (you move) to Scotland? Was it a long time ago?

14   He _____ (watch) TV when we arrived.

15   What _____ (you do) when the teacher arrived?

Summary of modal verbs

Use **will** for …

- talking about the future (see Unit 71)

  I'll be in the café at six.

  She won't be here tonight.

- predictions (see Unit 71)

  I think she'll pass her exams.

  I'm sure they'll get married.

- offers, promises and requests (see Unit 72)

  I'll pick you up.

  I'll be there in ten minutes.

- instant decisions (see Unit 73)

  I think I'll have fish.

  Don't worry. I'll go and get her.

Use **can** for …

- ability (see Unit 21)

  I can speak French.

  I can't play the piano.

- offers and requests (see Unit 22)

  Can I help you?

  Can I have a drink?

would

- Use *would like* for requests and offers (see Unit 23)

  I'd like some water.

  Would you like a table for two?

- Use *would you like …* for requests and offers (see Unit 39)

  Would you like to speak to someone?

  Would you like something to drink?

Use **could** for …

- for past ability (see Unit 38)

  Mozart could play the organ.

  How well could she see?

- polite requests (see Unit 39)

  Could I speak to Shelby, please?

  Could you spell that?

Use **must** for obligation (see Unit 46 and 47)

You must be home by ten-thirty.

You mustn't be late.

Use **should** for advice (see Unit 48)

You should buy that dress.

He shouldn't go with them.

Check your tenses!

2 Choose the correct modal verbs.

1 I'm afraid I *won't / mustn't* be at the party tonight. I'm busy at work.

2 My best friend *can / could* play the piano really well. He's a musician.

3 We *'ll / 'd* like a room on the south side of the hotel, please.

4 You *can / should* take the medicine twice a day. Don't forget!

5 You *wouldn't / mustn't* take photographs at passport control. It's against the rules.

6 *Can / Would* you like something to eat?

7 You *shouldn't / couldn't* stay up late. There's school tomorrow.

8 How well *can / could* you play football when you were young?

Answer key (and tapescript)

Unit 1

1   1 c   2 e   3 d   4 a   5 b

2   1 I'm from Brazil.   4 We're from Japan.
2 I'm from the USA.   5 I'm from Egypt.
3 I'm from Italy.   6 We're from Russia.

3   1 They're from Spain.   6 I'm single.
2 We're married.   7 They're from Japan.
3 I'm from Russia.   8 She's from the UK.
4 He's single.   9 We're from Poland.
5 You're twenty-one.   10 You're from China.

4   1 Hi. I'm Andrea. I'm from Poland. I'm twenty-one
and I'm single.
2 Hi. I'm Bruno. I'm from Germany. I'm thirty-two
and I'm married.
3 Hi. I'm Marisol. I'm from Mexico. I'm eighteen
and I'm single.

5   Students' own answers.

Unit 2

1   1 a   2 an   3 Ø   4 a   5 Ø   6 a   7 an   8 a   9 a   10 an
11 Ø   12 an

2   1 She isn't a nurse.
2 I'm not a teacher.
3 You aren't an artist.
4 They aren't Russian.
5 We aren't engineers.
6 She isn't Chinese.
7 He isn't married.
8 I'm not twenty-one.
9 She isn't a musician.
10 They aren't from Peru.
11 We aren't students.
12 She isn't twenty-nine.

3   1 The Taj Mahal isn't in Pakistan. It's in India.
2 The Statue of Liberty isn't in Canada. It's in the USA.
3 Machu Picchu isn't in Mexico. It's in Peru.
4 The Eiffel Tower isn't in Italy. It's in France.
5 The Sydney Opera House isn't in the UK. It's in
Australia.

Unit 3

1   1 Are   2 Is   3 Are   4 Is   5 Is   6 Are   7 Is   8 Are
9 Are   10 Is

2   1 it isn't   2 I am   3 she isn't   4 I'm not   5 we are
6 she is   7 they aren't   8 it is   9 they are   10 he isn't

3   Students' own answers.

4   1 A: Are you Italian?   B: No, I'm not. I'm Spanish.
2 A: Is he Japanese?   B: Yes, he is.
3 A: Is she Brazilian?   B: Yes, she is.
4 A: Is he Polish?   B: No, he isn't. He's Russian.
5 A: Are they doctors?   B: No, they aren't. They're
teachers.
6 A: Are they married?   B: Yes, they are,
7 A: Are you and Jack American?   B: No, we aren't.
We're British.
8 A: Is it six o'clock?   B: No, it isn't. It's half past five.
9 A: Is she single?   B: No, she isn't. She's married.
10 A: Is he a musician?   B: No, he isn't. He's an
engineer.

Unit 4

1   1 He's short.   5 They're rich.
2 She's old.   6 They're small.
3 It's big.   7 I'm young.
4 He's tall.   8 We're poor.

2   1 a   2 Ø   3 a   4 Ø   5 Ø   6 a   7 Ø   8 a   9 Ø   10 an
11 a   12 Ø

3   1 I'm hungry.   4 I'm tired.
2 I'm cold.   5 I'm thirsty.
3 I'm hot.

4   1 John isn't happy. He's unhappy.
2 Sue isn't angry. She's happy.
3 Lee isn't unhappy. He's angry.

Unit 5

1   1 It's an expensive house.
2 They're fast cars.
3 It's a cheap car.
4 It's a big book.
5 It's a slow car.
6 They're expensive books.
7 They're small houses.
8 It's a big house.

238

2 1 ? 2 . 3 ? 4 . 5 ? 6 . 7 . 8 ?

3 1 He's a Russian doctor.
2 She's a British teacher.
3 We're Spanish engineers.
4 I'm an Italian musician.
5 They're Japanese students.
6 She's a Polish engineer.
7 He's a Brazilian artist.
8 They're American nurses.

4 1 A: Is Madonna from the USA? B: Yes, she is.
2 A: Is Tom Cruise tall? B: No, he isn't.
3 A: Is Bill Gates rich? B: Yes, he is.
4 A: Is Julia Roberts a musician? B: No, she isn't.
5 A: Are the Rolling Stones American? B: No, they aren't.
6 A: Are Ferraris expensive? B: Yes, they are.

5 1 Tom Cruise isn't tall.
2 Bill Gates isn't poor.
3 The Rolling Stones aren't American.
4 Madonna isn't from Italy.
5 Ferraris aren't cheap.
6 Julia Roberts isn't a musician.

6 1 He isn't 2 I am 3 She's 4 They're 5 We aren't
6 It is not 7 You're

7 1 artist 2 doctor 3 engineer 4 musician
5 teacher 6 student

8 1 It's quarter to eight.
2 It's ten o'clock.
3 It's half past four.
4 It's five to eight.
5 It's twenty-five past eleven.
6 It's quarter past three.

9 1 short 2 poor 3 young 4 small 5 slow 6 cheap
7 single 8 cold

10 1 T 2 F 3 F 4 T 5 T 6 F

Unit 6

1 1 Where's the phone?
2 Where's the table?
3 Where are the keys?
4 Where's the camera?
5 Where are the pens?
6 Where's the wallet?
7 Where's the bag?
8 Where are the books?

2 1 on 2 ✓ 3 in 4 under 5 ✓ 6 on

3 1 It's under 2 They're in 3 It's under 4 It's next to
5 They're on 6 They're next to 7 It's next to
8 It's on 9 They're under 10 It's in

Unit 7

1 1 There's 2 There are 3 There's 4 There's
5 There's 6 There are

2 1 B 2 A 3 B 4 A 5 B 6 A 7 B 8 A 9 B 10 A
11 B 12 A 13 A 14 B

3 1 There are two windows in the room.
2 There's a big sofa in the middle of the room.
3 There are two chairs in front of the windows.
4 There's a desk in the corner of the room.
5 There's a computer on the desk.
6 There's a television in front of the sofa.

Unit 8

1 Conversation 1: 2, 4, 5, 3, 1, 6
Conversation 2: 2, 5, 4, 1, 6, 3

2 1 Yes, there is. It's on the first floor.
2 No, there isn't.
3 Yes, there is. It's on the second floor.
4 Yes, there is. It's on the third floor.
5 No, there isn't.
6 It's on the ground floor.

3 1 Is there a cinema near here?
2 Is there a café near here?
3 Is there a taxi rank near here?
4 Is there a swimming pool near here?
5 Is there a restaurant near here?
6 Is there a cash machine near here?

4 Students' own answers.

Answer key (and tapescript)

Unit 9

1 1 milk 2 coffee 3 eggs 4 apples 5 bread
6 banana 7 sugar 8 butter 9 biscuits

2 1 e 2 g 3 d 4 c 5 f 6 b 7 a

3 1 any 2 an 3 any 4 some 5 a 6 any 7 some

4 1 Is there any coffee? Yes, there is.
2 Are there any biscuits? No, there aren't.
3 Is there any sugar? No, there isn't.
4 Are there any eggs? Yes, there are.

Unit 10

1 1 There are 2 There's a 3 There are 4 There's a
5 There's a 6 There isn't a

2

	food	drink
countable	apples bananas biscuits eggs	
uncountable	butter bread sugar	coffee milk

3 1 a, c 2 a 3 b 4 a, c 5 a, c 6 a, b 7 a 8 a
9 b, c 10 c

4 1 are 2 any 3 aren't 4 some 5 on 6 in 7 're

5 1 There isn't … 2 Where are …? 3 Are there …?
4 There's … 5 There aren't … 6 Where's …?
7 Is there …? 8 There are …

Tapescript ⦿1.11
1 There isn't any milk.
2 Where are the keys?
3 Are there any apples in the kitchen?
4 There's some butter on the table.
5 There aren't any eggs.
6 Where's the milk?
7 Is there any coffee in the kitchen?
8 There are some biscuits on the table.

6 1 desk 2 sofa 3 bed 4 television 5 table 6 shower
7 bath 8 door 9 window 10 chair

7 1 F 2 F 3 T 4 T 5 F 6 T 7 T 8 F 9 T 10 T

8 1 biscuits 2 sugar 3 shower 4 door 5 table
6 window 7 reception

9 1 T 2 F 3 T 4 T 5 F

Tapescript ⦿1.12
There's some milk and some coffee in the fridge and
there are some eggs. There are some apples under
the table. There's some bread on the table and there's
a banana. There's some sugar on the shelf. There isn't
any butter and there aren't any biscuits.

Unit 11

1 1 I've got 2 She's got 3 We haven't got 4 He's got
5 They've got 6 He hasn't got

2 1 Joe's got a nice house.
2 Annika and Ray haven't got a car.
3 Have you got a bike?
4 Has Catherine got a sister?
5 We haven't got any children.
6 I haven't got a cold. I've got the flu.

3 1 Have 2 got 3 they've got 4 I've got 5 Have 6 got
7 I haven't 8 Has 9 got 10 she's got 11 Has she got

4 1 is 2 's 3 's got 4 's got 5 's 6 's got

5 1 Johnny Depp is an actor.
2 He's 1m 79.
3 He's got brown hair and brown eyes.
4 He's got thirteen tattoos.
5 He's from the USA.
6 He's got a brother and two sisters.

Unit 12

1 1 I've got my keys.
2 You haven't got your laptop.
3 We've got our passports.
4 He hasn't got his glasses.
5 She's got her camera.
6 We haven't got our credit cards.
7 I've got my mobile.
8 They've got their tickets.

2
1 My camera's fantastic!
2 Her new motorbike is great!
3 His Dell laptop is brilliant!
4 Our old car is terrible!
5 Their old television is awful!

3
1 her 2 His 3 his 4 Her 5 her 6 His 7 Their
8 their 9 Its

4
1 her 2 Our 3 She 4 I 5 your 6 His 7 its
8 Their 9 my 10 We 11 His 12 My

5
Students' own answers.

Unit 13

1
1 Is this your watch?
2 Are these your sunglasses?
3 Is this your camera?
4 Is that your bike?
5 Are these your books?
6 Is that your phone?

2
1 These trainers are old.
2 This shirt is big.
3 These trousers are small.
4 These shoes are old.
5 That coat is big.
6 This hat is small.

3
1 A: That's my phone. B: Which one?
  A: The black one.
2 A: That's my bike. B: Which one?
  A: The blue one.
3 A: Those are my sunglasses. B: Which ones?
  A: The yellow ones.

4
1 that 2 Which 3 one 4 one 5 That

Unit 14

1
1 A: Whose mobile is this? B: I think it's Harry's.
2 A: Whose books are these? B: I think they're Lisa's.
3 A: Whose sunglasses are these? B: I think they're Harry's.
4 A: Whose camera is this? B: I think it's Tim's.
5 A: Whose laptop is this? B: I think it's Lisa's.
6 A: Whose trainers are these? B: I think they're Tim's.

2
1 It's his. 2 They're his. 3 They're hers. 4 It's hers.
5 They're his. 6 It's his.

3
1 This is mine and that is yours.
2 Those are theirs and these are ours.
3 This is hers and that is yours.
4 This is mine and that's his.

4
1 P, has 2 is, is 3 P, P 4 has, is 5 is, is 5 P, is

Unit 15

1
1 I've got blue eyes.
2 She hasn't got a motorbike.
3 Have you got a cold?
4 Yes, I have.
5 No, he hasn't.
6 We've got two children.
7 He's got a new laptop.
8 Has she got dark hair?

2
1 Serena's 2 Sofia's 3 Bob's 4 Clintons'
5 George's 6 Jane's 7 Judy's 8 Elizabeth's

3
1 my 2 its 3 her 4 their 5 your 6 Its 7 Our 8 her

4
1 They're his. 2 It's hers. 3 It's mine.
4 They're his. 5 It's theirs. 6 It's hers.
7 They're yours. 8 They're ours.

5
1 Which one is Mike's? The black one.
2 Which ones are Ellen's? The yellow ones.
3 Which one is Lauren's? The red one.
4 Which ones are Paul's? The blue ones.

6
1 /z/ 2 /s/ 3 /z/ 4 /s/ 5 /s/ 6 /z/

7
boyfriend – girlfriend
brother – sister
father – mother
husband – wife
son – daughter

8
1 passport 2 credit card 3 sunglasses 4 laptop
5 camera 6 watch

9
1 T 2 F 3 T 4 F 5 F 6 T 7 F 8 T

10
Harry: mobile, sunglasses
Lisa: books, laptop
Tim: camera, trainers
(see next page for tapescript)

Answer key (and tapescript)

Unit 16

1 1 I'm from Spain but I live in London.
  2 Alberto's from Spain and he lives in Madrid.
  3 Tessa's from Greece and she lives in Athens.
  4 Jim and I are from the UK but we live in Tokyo.
  5 Yang and Li are from China but they live in Paris.
  6 Dan is from Australia and he lives in Melbourne.

2 1 He works in a hospital.
  2 She works in a bank.
  3 She works in a school.
  4 He works in a restaurant.
  5 They work in a hospital.
  6 We work in a restaurant.

3 1 works 2 work 3 start 4 starts 5 has 6 have
  7 finishes 8 finish 9 studies 10 watch

4 1 starts 2 starts 3 have 4 finishes 5 finishes

5 Larry starts work at half past four and Dan starts at five o'clock. They have a break at half past seven. Larry finishes work at half past eleven and Dan finishes at twelve o'clock / midnight.

6 Students' own answers.

Unit 17

1 1 c 2 e 3 b 4 d 5 a

2 1 Fran 2 Nancy 3 Matt 4 Luke

3 1 A: Do you like pasta?
    B: No, I don't.
  2 A: Does your boyfriend like Chinese food?
    B: No, he doesn't but he likes Japanese food.
  3 A: Do your parents like sushi?
    B: My mother likes it but my father doesn't.

4 1 her 2 me 3 her 4 them 5 us 6 him

5 1 I don't like it.
  2 I like them.
  3 I don't like her.
  4 I love it.
  5 I like him but I prefer her.

Unit 18

1 1 Lucy never goes to the opera.
  2 John goes to the opera every month.
  3 Lucy often goes to the cinema.
  4 Chris and Sally go to the cinema every Tuesday.
  5 John goes to the cinema twice a week.
  6 Chris and Sally sometimes go to the theatre.
  7 Lucy goes to the theatre once a year.
  8 John doesn't often go to the theatre.

2 1 I play football twice ^ week.
  2 They always go to the cinema ^ Saturdays.
  3 Jenny goes to the opera once ^ year.
  4 I play basketball three ^ a month.
  5 Li ^ often go to the cinema.
  6 Anita goes to the cinema ^ weekend.
  7 I watch football once a ^.
  8 I go to the theatre ^ a year

3 1 I never go to the opera.
  2 Steve plays football once a week.
  3 Donna always plays golf on Sundays.
  4 They sometimes go to the theatre.
  5 Carlo doesn't often play tennis.
  6 I play basketball every Thursday.

4 1 ever 2 to 3 do 4 every 5 How 6 love 7 twice

5 Students' own answers.

Unit 19

1 1 do 2 is 3 does 4 is 5 do 6 does 7 is 8 does
  9 is 10 does

2 1 Where 2 Where 3 How 4 When 5 Which
  6 What 7 How 8 Who 9 When 10 What

3 1 g 2 c 3 f 4 b 5 e 6 a 7 d

4 1 What time does she have breakfast?
  2 When does she study?
  3 What does she have for lunch?
  4 What does she do in the afternoon?
  5 Where does she have dinner?
  6 How long does she watch television in the evening?

Unit 20

1
1 She lives in Paris.
2 She works in a bank.
3 She starts work at eight o'clock.
4 She finishes work at six o'clock.
5 She has sushi for lunch.
6 She studies English.
7 She plays tennis.
8 She never watches television.
9 She goes to the opera once a month.
10 She hates rock music.
11 She sleeps six hours every night.
12 She often eats in restaurants.

2
1 Yes, I do. 2 No, he doesn't. 3 No, I don't.
4 Yes, he does. 5 Yes, I do. 6 Yes, I do.
7 Yes, he does. 8 No, I don't. 9 No, he doesn't.
10 Yes, he does.

3
1 Does 2 doesn't 3 don't 4 do 5 does 6 don't
7 Does 8 does 9 do 10 Do 11 do 12 doesn't

4
1 I like hip-hop but I prefer rock.
2 We always go to the cinema on Monday.
3 She doesn't often watch television.
4 I don't like jazz.
5 My sister works in a bank in Paris.
6 Jim starts work at half past nine.
7 I play tennis once a week.
8 Do you ever go to the theatre?

5
1 I, her, she, me 2 We, him, he, us 3 They, me, I, them

6
1 When 2 Where 3 What 4 Which 5 Who

7
1 /z/ 2 /ɪz/ 3 /z/ 4 /s/ 5 /ɪz/

8
1 play 2 go to 3 have 4 have 5 play 6 go to
7 have 8 go to 9 have

9
1 brother 2 girlfriend 3 parents 4 mother
5 children

10
1 banker 2/3 doctor, nurse 4/5 chef, waiter
6 teacher

11
1 What time does she have breakfast?
2 When does she study?
3 What does she have for lunch?
4 What does she do in the afternoon?
5 Where does she have dinner?
6 How long does she watch television in the evening?

Tapescript 🔊 **1.26**
1 A: What time does she have breakfast?
  B: At eight o'clock.
2 A: When does she study? B: In the morning.
3 A: What does she have for lunch? B: A sandwich.
4 A: What does she do in the afternoon?
  B: She plays golf.
5 A: Where does she have dinner? B: In a restaurant.
6 A: How long does she watch television in the
  evening? B: For two hours.

Unit 21

1
1 c 2 b 3 a 4 e 5 d

2
1 can 2 Can 3 can't 4 can 5 Can 6 can't 7 Can
8 can 9 Can 10 can't 11 Can 12 can 13 Can
14 can't 15 can

3
1 Can 2 speak 3 can't 4 very well 5 can
6 well 7 can't

4
1 A: Can you speak Spanish?
  B: No, I can't. I can speak Chinese.
2 A: Can they play the piano?
  B: Yes, they can play very well.
3 A: Can she run fast?
  B: Yes, she can.
4 A: Can you play tennis?
  B: Yes, I can. I can also play golf.
5 A: Can he speak three languages?
  B: No, but he can speak two languages.

5
Students' own answers.

Unit 22

1
1 Can I, O 2 Can you, R 3 Can I, R 4 Can I, R
5 Can you, R 6 Can I, O 7 Can I, O 8 Can I, R
9 Can you, R 10 Can I, R

2
1 Can I borrow your car?
2 Can you speak to her?
3 Can I open the window?
4 Can I buy you lunch?
5 Can you get me a drink?
6 Can I carry your bag?
7 Can you help me?
8 Can you lend me your phone?
9 Can I use your laptop?
10 Can you answer the phone?

3 Conversation 1: 2, 4, 1, 3
Conversation 2: 3, 1, 5, 4, 2
Conversation 3: 3, 5, 4, 6, 1, 2
Conversation 4: 4, 2, 1, 3

4 1 a 2 a 3 b 4 a 5 b 6 a 7 b 8 a

Unit 23

1 1 Would you like 2 please 3 we'd like 4 Certainly
5 I'd 6 Would 7 thanks 8 like

2 1 I'd like some soup, please.
2 Would you like the menu?
3 I'd like some coffee.
4 Would you like some bread?
5 We'd like some water, please.
6 I'd like the bill, please.

3 1 A: Would you like a cup of coffee?
   B: No, thanks. I'd like the bill, please.
2 A: Would you like a table for two?
   B: Yes, please.
3 A: Would you like some soup?
   B: No, thanks. I'd like a green salad.
4 A: Would you like the menu?
   B: Yes, please.
5 A: Would you like some wine?
   B: No, thanks. I'd like some water.
6 A: Would you like some cheese?
   B: Yes, please.

Unit 24

1 1 Go 2 turn 3 go 4 stop 5 Don't 6 turn

2 1 b 2 c 3 d 4 f 5 a 6 e

3 1 c 2 d 3 g 4 e 5 j 6 b 7 h 8 i 9 a 10 f

Unit 25

1 1 you 2 you 3 you 4 me 5 you, me 6 me 7 me
8 you 9 you 10 you

2 1 He can play the piano.
2 I can't sing well.
3 Would you like the menu?
4 Does he play tennis? / Can he play tennis?
5 Stop at the traffic lights!
6 She can run fast.
7 I'd like some water, please.

8 Stop!
9 Have a drink!
10 Don't turn left.

3 1 a 2 a 3 b 4 b 5 a 6 b 7 b 8 a 9 b 10 a

4 1 R 2 O 3 Or 4 D 5 Or 6 R 7 O 8 D 9 Or 10 R

5 1 I can. Can you help me, please? Please bring a friend.
2 Can you give me a drink, please? Give me a drink
(please). Please go.
3 No, I can't. I can't play the piano. Play the piano,
please.
4 Can you lend me your phone? Lend me your
phone. Phone me at ten o'clock.
5 Yes, I would. I would not like a dessert (thank
you). Thank you very much.

6 1 /kɑːnt/ 2 /kæn/ 3 /kən/ 4 /kɑːnt/ 5 /kæn/

Tapescript ⏯**1.32**
1 Sorry, I can't play tonight.
2 Can I have a table for two?
3 You can have ice cream.
4 We can't have a table near the window.
5 Yes, they can.

7 1 sing 2 beautiful 3 please 4 map 5 coffee
6 right

8 1 speak 2 play 3 borrow 4 Close 5 get 6 speak
7 'd like 8 Turn 9 Go 10 Cross

9 water, soup, green salad, tea

Tapescript ⏯**1.33**
Conversation 1
Waiter: Good evening. My name's Mario and
             I'm your waiter.
Customer: Hello.
Waiter: Would you like the wine menu?
Customer: Yes, please. And we'd like some water,
             please.
Waiter: Certainly.

Conversation 2
Customer: Excuse me, we'd like to order now.
Waiter: Sure.
Customer: I'd like some soup and he'd like a green
             salad.
Waiter: Certainly. Would you like some wine?
Customer: No, thanks. But I'd like a cup of tea, please.

Unit 26

1 1 faster 2 older 3 cheaper 4 less expensive 5 hotter
6 better 7 happier 8 more beautiful 9 safer

2 1 A motorbike is faster than a bicycle.
2 She is taller than him.
3 The red bike is less expensive than the blue bike.
4 Her book is more interesting than his book.

3 1 Karen's younger than Tom. Tom's older than Karen.
2 The Mississippi River is shorter than the Amazon River. The Amazon River is longer than the Mississippi River.
3 My flat is smaller than your house. Your house is bigger than my flat.
4 Today, it's hotter in Rome than in London. Today, it's colder in London than in Rome. / Today, Rome is hotter than London. Today, London is colder than Rome.

Unit 27

1 1 tallest 2 shortest 3 biggest 4 most dangerous
5 longest 6 oldest 7 safest 8 most expensive
9 highest 10 heaviest

2 1 A snake is slower than a cheetah.
The tortoise is the slowest animal.
2 Italy is hotter than Norway.
Ethiopia is the hottest country.
3 The Indian Ocean is bigger than the Mediterranean Sea.
The Pacific Ocean is the biggest ocean.
4 India is smaller than Russia.
Switzerland is the smallest country.
5 A car is faster than a bicycle.
The aeroplane is the fastest transport.

3 1 I'm the worst at English in my class.
2 I think Brazil is the best football team in the world.
3 Snakes are the most dangerous animals in my country.
4 I don't think he's a better actor than De Niro.
5 Your bags are heavy but my bag is the heaviest.

Unit 28

1 1 beautifully 2 loudly 3 quietly 4 quickly 5 slowly
6 well 7 fast 8 happily 9 badly 10 late 11 hard
12 early

2 1 badly 2 beautiful 3 loudly 4 quietly 5 quickly
6 slow 7 happy 8 loud 9 well 10 happily 11 quiet
12 slowly

3 1 fast 2 beautifully 3 early 4 quietly 5 well
6 happily

4 Students' own answers.

Unit 29

1 1 later 2 earlier 3 better 4 faster 5 more slowly / slower 6 harder 7 better 8 more quietly 9 louder

2 1 You get up later than me.
2 I get up earlier than you.
3 Michael runs slower than Martin.
4 Martin runs faster / quicker / more quickly than Michael.
5 Victoria plays the piano better than Julia.
6 Julia plays the piano worse than Victoria.

3 a Can you speak more slowly?
b Can you speak more loudly?
c our meeting starts earlier
d He starts work later on Tuesdays.

4 1 b 2 d 3 c 4 a

Unit 30

1 1 faster 2 less expensive 3 best 4 harder 5 well
6 hot 7 quiet

2 1 Can you play golf better than your dad?
2 The weather today is hotter than yesterday.
3 Blue whales are the biggest animals in the world.
4 He's the happiest student in my class.
5 I can run faster than you.
6 Is he worse at English than me?
7 A tortoise goes more slowly than a snake.
8 This ice cream is the best in the world.
9 This café is more expensive than that café.
10 This TV show is funnier than the other one.

3 1 younger 2 heaviest 3 quietly 4 loudly 5 later
6 badly 7 early 8 quickly

4 1 London is bigger than Edinburgh.
2 This film isn't longer than the other one.
3 They study very hard for exams.

5 1 <u>Whales</u> are <u>bigger</u> than <u>elephants</u>.
2 <u>Mike's</u> <u>bigger</u> than <u>Martin</u>.
3 <u>English</u> is <u>easier</u> than <u>Maths</u>.
4 <u>Your</u> <u>car</u> <u>isn't</u> <u>faster</u> than <u>mine</u>.
5 <u>Tom</u> is <u>taller</u> than his <u>brother</u>.
6 <u>This</u> is the <u>most</u> <u>expensive</u> car.

6 1 blue whale 2 supermarket 3 library 4 office
5 loudly 6 slowly 7 early

7 **Across**
3 good 6 short 7 interesting 9 slow 10 loud

Down
1 hot 2 young 4 dangerous 5 cheap 8 small

8 **Across**
3 bad – worse – worst, good – better – best
6 long – longer – longest, short – shorter – shortest
7 boring – more boring – most boring, interesting –
more interesting – most interesting
9 fast – faster – fastest, slow – slower – slowest
10 quiet – quieter – quietest, loud – louder – loudest

Down
1 cold – colder – coldest, hot – hotter – hottest
2 old – older – oldest, young – younger – youngest
4 safe – safer – safest, dangerous – more dangerous
– most dangerous
5 expensive – more expensive – most expensive,
cheap – cheaper – cheapest
8 big – bigger – biggest, small – smaller – smallest

9 1 Pierre 2 earlier 3 2

Tapescript 🔊 1.38
A: Good morning. Can I help you?
B: Hello. Can I speak to Pierre?
A: Sorry, I can't hear you. Can you speak more loudly?
B: I'd like to speak to Pierre, please.
A: Sorry, he isn't here. He starts work later on
Tuesdays. Can I take a message?
B: Yes, please. My name is Agathe. Can you tell him
our meeting starts earlier tomorrow?
A: Sorry. Can you speak more slowly?
B: Sure. Our meeting starts at twelve o'clock, not
two o'clock tomorrow.
A: OK. Thanks.

Unit 31

1 1 Sam isn't cooking. He's having a shower.
2 Catherine and Ali are watching television. They
aren't reading.
3 Antonio and Julia aren't cooking. They're playing
chess.
4 Lucia's reading a book. She isn't playing chess.
5 Julia isn't watching television. She's sleeping.
6 Mike and Tom aren't reading. They're cooking.

2 1 No, she isn't. 2 No, they aren't. 3 Yes, she is.
4 Yes, they are. 5 No, they aren't. 6 Yes, he is.

3 Lewis: 5, 3, 9, 1, 7
Marie: 6, 2, 4, 10, 8

Unit 32

1 1 works 2 isn't working, 's reading 3 cycles
4 isn't cycling, 's raining, 's driving

2 1 live 2 drive, 'm taking 3 's raining 4 don't smoke
5 Do you like, do 6 are you doing, 'm writing
7 's boiling 8 freezes 9 always go 10 rains
11 speak 12 'm watching 13 have 14 's doing
15 's watching 16 Do you want

3 1 'm having 2 'm learning 3 starts 4 study 5 have
6 are 7 'm having 8 'm sitting 9 'm eating
10 'm doing 11 are 12 'm making

Unit 33

1 Order: 5, 2, 3, 1, 4

2 1 I'm seeing Anne on Monday morning.
2 I'm going to the cinema on Tuesday evening.
3 Louise isn't having lunch with Rita on Sunday.
4 Max is going to the beach on Friday morning.
5 Where are you having dinner on Wednesday
evening?
6 Who are they meeting on Monday morning?

3 1 g 2 f 3 d 4 i 5 j 6 b 7 c 8 a 9 e 10 h

4 1 are you doing on
2 are you having dinner with on
3 are you playing football
4 are you doing on Saturday
5 are you going on
6 are you going shopping

Unit 34

1
1 He's going to travel around the USA.
2 She's going to work in a laboratory.
3 They're going to have a holiday in Spain.
4 She's going to learn to drive.

2
1 Yes, he is. 2 Yes, they are. 3 No, he isn't.
4 Yes, she is. 5 No, they aren't.

3
1 Are we going to book   4 's going to meet
2 is going to drive   5 s' going to take
3 isn't going to know

4
1 are you going to do   4 're going to work
2 are going to teach   5 are you going to do
3 are you going to stay   6 'm going to travel

5
1 What are you going to do in the summer?
2 I'm not going to have a holiday.
3 I'm going to work in a laboratory.
4 What are you going to study?
5 I'm going to study Physics.
6 What are you going to do after university?

6
1 I'm going to buy a new jacket.
2 We're going to leave at three o'clock.
3 Maggie is going to get a job in the college.
4 They're going to go home after school.
5 Is he going to meet us there?
6 When are you going to have lunch?
7 I think it is going to snow tonight.
8 Are Jemima and Hugo going to work in an office?

Unit 35

1
1 He's playing tennis.
2 They're cooking.
3 She's reading a book.
4 He's sleeping.
5 He's watching television.
6 They're playing chess.

2
1 He isn't playing tennis.
2 They aren't cooking.
3 She isn't reading a book.
4 He isn't sleeping.
5 He isn't watching television.
6 They aren't playing chess.

3
1 On Monday I'm playing tennis with Jules.
2 On Tuesday I'm going to the cinema with Mazda.
3 On Wednesday I'm going to the beach with my mum.
4 On Thursday I'm going to the library with Sarah.
5 On Friday I'm having dinner with Joe.
6 On Saturday I'm shopping with Nicky.
7 On Sunday I'm having lunch with my family.

4
1 are you doing on Monday
2 are you playing tennis with
3 are you doing on Wednesday
4 are you going with Sarah / on Thursday
5 are you seeing Joe
6 are you shopping with on Saturday
7 are you doing on Sunday

5
1 I'm going to read my emails.
2 I'm going to phone my mum.
3 He's going to have a piano lesson.
4 She's going to study in the library.
5 We're going to play tennis.
6 They're going to go shopping.

6   1 3 2 4 3 5 4 5 5 6 6 6

Tapescript 🎧 **1.43**
1 I'm having dinner.
2 Are they watching television?
3 He's going to buy it.
4 What are you doing later?
5 She isn't going to be late.
6 Who are you seeing at eight?

7   1 play 2 play 3 have 4 have 5 play 6 have 7 play
8 play 9 have

8
1 Are you free on Saturday evening?
2 Is it any good?
3 It's excellent.
4 Can I call you back?

9   1 c 2 f 3 e 4 a 5 b 6 d

10   1 are you doing on 2 'm not doing 3 're going to the
4 film are you 5 starts at eight

Tapescript 🎧 **1.44**
A: What are you doing on Friday?
B: I'm not doing anything. Why?
A: We're going to the cinema. Would you like to come?
B: Yes, please. What film are you seeing?
A: *On the Beach* 2. It starts at eight o'clock.

Answer key (and tapescript)

Unit 36

1 1 was 2 was 3 were 4 was 5 was 6 Were

2 1 T 2 F 3 T 4 F 5 T 6 F 7 T 8 F

3 1 was 2 were 3 was 4 Was 5 wasn't 6 was 7 was
8 were 9 weren't 10 was 11 Was 12 weren't

Unit 37

1 1 There was 2 There were 3 There wasn't
4 There wasn't 5 there were 6 there weren't

2 1 Yes, there was.
2 No, there wasn't. There were cars.
3 No, there wasn't. There was a cinema.
4 Yes, there were.
5 No, there weren't. There was one restaurant.
6 No, there wasn't.
7 No, there wasn't. There was an Italian restaurant.

3 1 b 2 e 3 f 4 d 5 a 6 h 7 g 8 c

Unit 38

1 1 couldn't 2 could 3 couldn't 4 could 5 couldn't
6 could 7 could 8 couldn't 9 couldn't 10 could

2 1 Could you speak Chinese
2 Could your father speak Chinese?
3 How well could you play the piano
4 What could he play?
5 How far could you run?
6 I couldn't play tennis.

Unit 39

1 1 Could 2 Would 3 Could 4 Could 5 Could
6 Would 7 Could 8 Would 9 could 10 Would
11 Could 12 could 13 Could 14 Could 15 Would

2 1 Could I leave a message?
2 Would you like to buy something, madam?
3 Could you give me your number again, please?
I can't find it.
4 Harry is out. Would you like him to call you later?
5 I'd like some soup and she'd like a salad. And
could we see the wine menu, please?
6 You can borrow the films but could I have them
back by the weekend?

3 1 Would you like me to help you?
2 Could I leave a message?
3 Could you lend me a DVD?
4 Would you like to speak to Marc?
5 Could I borrow a pen?
6 Could you spell your name?
7 Would you like something to drink?
8 Would you like to borrow the/my car?
9 Could you lend me your mobile phone?
10 Would you like to see the menu?

Unit 40

1 1 was 2 could 3 were 4 couldn't 5 wasn't 6 weren't

2 Students' own answers.

3 Order: 5, 3, 1, 6, 4, 7, 2

4 1 They weren't at the party.
2 Sorry, I couldn't come yesterday.
3 I was born in Brazil.
4 There were houses on the left.
5 Would you like to sit here?
6 Could I order some ice cream?
7 Were they born in Italy?
8 Could you tell him I called?
9 Could I borrow your car?

5 1 /wɒz/ 2 /wəz/ 3 /wɒznt/ 4 /wɒz/ 5 /wəz/

Tapescript 🔊 1.48
1 Yes, he was.
2 The weekend was great!
3 The film wasn't very interesting.
4 I'm sure it was.
5 Was she at Oxford University?

6 1 bus station 2 supermarket 3 bank 4 train station
5 cinema 6 café 7 post office

7 1 boxer 2 car 3 singer 4 bridge 5 today

8 1 order 2 leave 3 have 4 spell 5 lend 6 speak
7 run 8 buy

9 1 T 2 F 3 T 4 F 5 F 6 F

Unit 41

1 1 F 2 T 3 F 4 T 5 T 6 T

2 1 studied 2 ✓ 3 visited 4 ✓ 5 ✓ 6 stopped 7 travelled 8 qualified

3 1 started 2 finished 3 graduated 4 visited 5 worked 6 travelled 7 walked 8 stopped 9 lived 10 studied

4 1 finished 2 started 3 graduated 4 travelled 5 studied 6 qualified 7 joined

Unit 42

1 1 eat – ate 2 sit – sat 3 do – did 4 swim – swam 5 get – got 6 go – went 7 have – had 8 make – made 9 buy – bought 10 take – took 11 give – gave 12 see – saw

2 1 ate 2 went 3 bought 4 had 5 did 6 swam 7 took 8 made 9 got 10 sat 11 gave 12 saw

3 1 got up 2 swam 3 ate 4 had 5 took 6 sat 7 went 8 did 9 bought

4 1 made 2 ✓ 3 ✓ 4 went 5 ✓ 6 bought 7 ✓ 8 ate 9 sat 10 swam 11 had 12 ✓ 13 ✓ 14 joined 15 tried 16 ✓ 17 ✓ 18 gave

Unit 43

1 1 She left school in 1995.
   2 She didn't go to university.
   3 She started work in an office.
   4 She got married in 1998.
   5 She didn't have any children.
   6 She got divorced.
   7 She met a new partner.
   8 She didn't get married again.

2 1 Did, didn't 2 Did, did 3 Did 4 Did, didn't

3 1 Did you get married?
   2 Did you meet Bill at university?
   3 Did you have any children?
   4 Did you do your homework last night?
   5 Did you take the bus to the airport?
   6 Did you go to Spain on holiday?
   7 Did you get up late this morning?

Unit 44

1 1 Where did you stay?
   2 Who stayed there?
   3 What did you do yesterday?
   4 Who made your sandwich?
   5 How many people went to the party?
   6 What changed your plans?
   7 What time did the TV programme start?

2 1 e 2 b 3 d 4 g 5 f 6 a 7 c

3 1 O 2 S 3 O 4 S 5 S 6 S 7 O

4 1 When did she leave home?
   2 What did they study at university?
   3 Who studied Biology at university?
   4 When did you start your job?
   5 What changed your plans?
   6 Where did you meet Sheila?
   7 Why did you leave your job?
   8 Who lived in this house?
   9 How long did you travel in Patagonia?

Unit 45

1 1 I ate breakfast at seven o'clock.
   2 They went on Tuesday.
   3 We didn't have time for lunch.
   4 Who lived here?
   5 Did you know her?

6 Why did you walk to work?

7 Sorry, I wasn't at home.

8 How far did you swim?

2 **1** Did you like Spain?

2 When did you live there?

3 Who wrote that book?

4 I studied in Bologna for a year.

5 We didn't go to the cinema last night.

6 Why did you leave university early?

7 Did you visit the Eiffel Tower?

8 She made a delicious pasta dish.

9 When did you get divorced?

3 **1** this morning **2** yesterday **3** last week
4 two weeks ago **5** last month **6** last year **7** in 1990

4 **1** did **2** left **3** got **4** celebrated **5** went **6** took
7 made **8** graduated **9** stopped **10** travelled

5 **1** went **2** left **3** celebrated **4** did **5** travelled
6 stopped **7** graduated **8** took **9** got **10** made

6 **1** g **2** h **3** f **4** b **5** e **6** c **7** a **8** d

7 **1** 2 **2** 2 **3** 2 **4** 1 **5** 3 **6** 1 **7** 1 **8** 1 **9** 2 **10** 1
11 1 **12** 4

8 **1** a **2** b **3** a **4** a **5** b **6** c **7** b **8** c

Tapescript 🎧 **1.55**

Matt: How was your holiday?

Anna: Great! We got up late every day and swam in
the hotel pool before breakfast.

Matt: How was the food at the hotel?

Anna: Not bad, but we usually ate in one of the local
restaurants. We had some delicious fish dishes.

Matt: So, were you near the coast?

Anna: Yes, we were. We took the hotel bus down to
the sea and sat on the beach in the afternoon.

Matt: Were there many places to visit?

Anna: Mark went sightseeing but I wasn't interested.
I did some shopping on the last day. Look! I
bought this beautiful bracelet at a local market.

Unit 46

1 **1** parents **2** doctor/parents **3** boss **4** doctor
5 police officer **6** parents **7** parents **8** boss

2 **1** You mustn't use your mobile here.

2 You must eat more fruit.

3 You mustn't drink the water here.

4 You must park on the left.

5 You must visit your grandparents.

6 You mustn't take photographs here.

7 You mustn't talk in class.

8 You must turn your mobile off.

9 You must phone me when you arrive.

10 You mustn't phone after ten o'clock.

3 **1** must **2** mustn't **3** must **4** mustn't **5** must
6 mustn't **7** must **8** mustn't **9** mustn't **10** must
11 mustn't **12** must **13** must

4 **1** Rachel must leave at six.

2 You mustn't do that.

3 We must drive on the left in the UK.

4 She mustn't be late for her interview.

5 I must get up at six every day.

6 They must ask their parents.

Unit 47

1 **1** must **2** don't have to **3** must **4** have to **5** mustn't
6 have to **7** don't have to **8** have to

2 **1** have to **2** mustn't **3** Do **4** have to **5** do **6** do
7 have to **8** have to **9** have to **10** Does **11** have to
12 does **13** has to **14** mustn't **15** has to
Conversation 1: waiter
Conversation 2: shop assistant

3 **1** Paulo has to cook the food.
Macy doesn't have to cook the food.

2 Paulo and Macy mustn't smoke.

3 Paulo doesn't have to clear the tables.
Macy has to clear the tables.

4 Paulo and Macy have to wear a uniform.

5 Paulo and Macy mustn't be late.

6 Paulo doesn't have to serve the customers.
Macy has to serve the customers.

Unit 48

1 **1** That's not true. You shouldn't smoke.

2 That's true.

3 That's true.

4 That's not true. You shouldn't drink a lot of coffee.

5 That's not true. You shouldn't work twelve hours a
day.

6 That's not true. You should go on holiday.

2 1 You should buy it.
  2 You shouldn't buy them.
  3 You should buy them.
  4 You shouldn't buy it.
  5 You should buy it.
  6 You shouldn't buy them.

3 1 should 2 should 3 shouldn't 4 should 5 should
  6 should

4 1 I think you should buy those shoes.
  2 They shouldn't pay that much money.
  3 Rita should ask me first.
  4 Should we leave now or later?
  5 Gerald should do more exercise.
  6 What should he do about the problem?

Unit 49

1 1 They had to study Maths.
  2 Lisa didn't have to study French.
  3 Tony had to study French.
  4 They didn't have to study Geography.
  5 They had to study Science.

2 1 e 2 c 3 b 4 a 5 d 6 f

3 1 Did 2 have to 3 did 4 had to 5 had to 6 Did
  7 have to 8 didn't 9 had to 10 Did 11 have to
  12 did 13 had to 14 had to

4 1 Did he have to do that?
  2 Did Mike and Lelia have to stay late?
  3 What time did you have to get up?
  4 Did you have to clean the house today?
  5 Why did we have to pay for the ticket?
  6 Did she have to study French at school?

Unit 50

1 1 You mustn't smoke.
  2 You mustn't eat or drink.
  3 You mustn't take photographs.
  4 You mustn't walk.
  5 You mustn't park.
  6 You mustn't use your mobile.

2 1 I have to start work at eight o'clock.
  2 I mustn't park in the boss's parking space.
  3 I mustn't be late.
  4 I must learn the rules.
  5 I don't have to wear a uniform.
  6 I must wear a jacket and tie.

  7 I don't have to call my boss 'sir'.
  8 I don't have to make coffee.

3 1 I shouldn't drink coffee.
  2 I should drink water.
  3 I shouldn't eat doughnuts.
  4 I should do exercise.
  5 I should eat vegetables.
  6 I shouldn't drink wine.

4 1 had to 2 had to 3 Did 4 have to 5 didn't 6 had
  to 7 had to 8 didn't 9 have to

5 1 mustn't 2 should 3 don't 4 could 5 shouldn't
  6 mustn't

6 1 awful 2 boss 3 homework 4 great 5 job

7

8 Order: 5, 3, 4, 1, 7, 2, 6

Tapescript 🔊 **1.61**

Joe:	You work too hard. You should work less.
Mark:	Yes, but …
Joe:	You should go on holiday.
Mark:	Yes, but …
Joe:	And you shouldn't drink all that coffee.
Mark:	Yes, but …
Joe:	And you smoke? You should stop now.
Mark:	Yes, but …
Joe:	And you look terrible! You should take more exercise.
Mark:	Yes, but …
Joe:	And doughnuts! You should eat healthier food.
Mark:	Yes, but …
Joe:	Yes, but what?
Mark:	Oh, nothing.

Answer key (and tapescript)

Unit 51

1
1 Mark's combed his hair.
2 Rick hasn't combed his hair.
3 Mark's ironed his shirt.
4 Rick hasn't ironed his shirt.
5 Mark's cleaned his shoes.
6 Rick hasn't cleaned his shoes.

2
1 've cleaned
2 's left
3 haven't finished
4 've had
5 haven't done
6 's tidied
7 've bought
8 's made

3
1 I've lost my credit card.
2 Julia's borrowed my dictionary.
3 Christina's bought a new top.
4 The car has stopped.
5 I've broken my phone.

4
1 Have you cleaned
2 Have you had
3 Have you combed
4 Have you cleaned

Unit 52

1
1 They've just moved house.
2 She's just had a baby.
3 They've just got married.
4 He's just graduated from university.

2
1 Have you done the washing up yet?
2 Has he made his bed yet?
3 Have they cleaned the bathroom yet?
4 Has she tidied the living room yet?
5 Have you made dinner yet?
6 Has he done the shopping yet?

3 1 yet 2 yet 3 already 4 already 5 yet 6 already

4 1 ✓ 2 at two o'clock 3 this afternoon 4 ✓ 5 ✓

5 I haven't phoned Angelina yet. I'm going to do that at four o'clock. I've already phoned Tom and I've already talked to Kevin. I haven't emailed Sharon yet. I'm going to do that this afternoon. I haven't talked to Martin yet. I'm going to do that after lunch.

Unit 53

1 1 since 2 since 3 for 4 since 5 since 6 since 7 for 8 for

2 1 28 2 seven years 3 six years 4 25 5 three years 6 18

3
1 have you lived
2 've been
3 for
4 have you had
5 Since
6 've been
7 since
8 've had
9 since
10 've been
11 for
12 've known
13 since

4 Students' own answers.

Unit 54

1
1 Have you ever been to Australia?
2 Have you ever ridden a motorbike?
3 Have you ever drunk Red Bull?
4 Have you ever played basketball?
5 Have you ever eaten Greek yoghurt?
6 Have you ever seen a James Bond film?

2 1 d 2 c 3 a 4 b 5 f 6 e

3
1 I've been to Canada but I've never been to the USA.
2 I've drunk Coca-Cola but I've never drunk Pepsi-Cola.
3 I've played table tennis but I've never played tennis.
4 I've ridden a bicycle but I've never ridden a motorbike.
5 I've spoken/studied French but I've never spoken/studied Spanish.
6 I've played the piano but I've never played the guitar.
7 I've eaten sushi but I've never eaten curry.
8 I've seen a dolphin but I've never seen a blue whale.

4
1 A: Have you ever been to Canada?
   B: Yes, I have. I went to Montreal last year.
2 A: Have you ever played rugby?
   B: Yes, I have, I played rugby when I was at school.
3 A: Have you ever eaten curry?
   B: Yes, I have. I ate curry in London last summer.
4 A: Have you ever seen *Romeo and Juliet*?
   B: Yes, I have. I saw Romeo and Juliet at the Globe Theatre in May.

Unit 55

1 1 haven't 2 's 3 hasn't 4 hasn't 5 haven't 6 've 7 's 8 've

2 1 already 2 yet 3 already 4 yet 5 just

3
1 He's been a dentist for fifteen years.
2 He's lived in Edinburgh for five years.
3 He's supported Arsenal FC since he was five.
4 He's had a BMW since he was eighteen.
5 He's known his wife/Meg for eight years.
6 They've been married since January.
7 Rosey's had her own business since 2005.

4
1 Have you ever been to Canada?
2 Have you ever drunk Greek wine?
3 Have you ever played golf?
4 Have you ever read *Hamlet*?
5 Have you ever eaten caviar?

5 1 e 2 c 3 a 4 b 5 d

6 1 've 2 have 3 have 4 haven't 5 have not 6 's
7 has 8 hasn't

Tapescript 2.06
1 We've read your book.
2 Yes, they have.
3 Have you ever been to Spain?
4 No, I haven't.
5 No, I have not had lunch.
6 He's lived here for three years.
7 She has been there.
8 It hasn't finished yet.

7 1 b 2 e 3 f 4 a 5 d 6 c

8 1 clean 2 have 3 iron 4 do 5 make 6 comb
7 tidy 8 ride

9
1 No, he hasn't.   5 No, he hasn't.
2 At four o'clock.   6 This afternoon.
3 Yes, he has.   7 No, he hasn't.
4 Yes, he has.   8 After lunch.

Tapescript 2.07
I haven't phoned Angelina yet. I'm going to do that at four o'clock. I've already phoned Tom and I've already talked to Kevin. I haven't emailed Sharon yet. I'm going to do that this afternoon. I haven't talked to Martin yet. I'm going to do that after lunch.

Unit 56

1
1 The snow was falling and the children were playing in it.
2 The telephone was ringing but Mike was working in the garden.

3 The students weren't doing their work when the teacher came in.
4 The baby was crying because a dog was barking.
5 It wasn't raining so we ate outside.
6 I wasn't planning to go out but my friend was bored.

2 1 No, it wasn't. 2 Yes, it was. 3 Yes, they were.
4 No, it wasn't. 5 No, they weren't.

3
1 were you living   4 were they living
2 were you studying   5 wasn't talking
3 were studying   6 were living

Unit 57

1 1 rang 2 was watching 3 were barking 4 found
5 saw 6 was having 7 stopped 8 arrived

2 1 were, doing 2 was driving 3 stopped
4 were waiting 5 was raining 6 was barking
7 opened 8 Did, enter 9 was walking 10 saw
11 did, do

3
1 I met an old friend while I was waiting at the bus station.
2 They weren't working when we arrived.
3 When she called, I was having a bath.
4 Everyone was looking at the sky. Suddenly, they saw the aliens!
5 While we were eating breakfast, my taxi arrived.
6 I was reading my book when the lights went out.
7 While we were watching TV, Molly told us her news.
8 My parents were living in Italy when I was born.

Unit 58

1 1 After 2 because 3 and 4 or 5 Before 6 When
7 so 8 While 9 but

2 1 and 2 while 3 after 4 but 5 so 6 or 7 because
8 when

3
1 We went to London and Paris.
2 We didn't have time to visit the palace or the park.
3 We booked tickets before we went to the theatre.
4 We had dinner after we went to the theatre.
5 She liked the theatre but she didn't enjoy the opera.
6 While I was waiting for a taxi, my friend arrived with his car.
7 When the art gallery closed, I went for a drink.
8 We didn't go to the palace because we were hungry.
9 The museum was closed so he went shopping.

Answer key (and tapescript)

Unit 59

1
1 I used to work in a shop.
2 correct
3 correct
4 Television didn't use to be in colour.
5 I used to love chocolate!
6 Did you use to live here?

2
1 use 2 used 3 use 4 used 5 use 6 use 7 used

3
1 She didn't use to wear a lot of make up.
2 He used to wear this suit.
3 He used to act in the theatre.
4 They didn't use to argue (a lot).

4 Students' own answers.

Unit 60

1
1 was running   4 were having
2 were, talking   5 Was, studying
3 wasn't working   6 wasn't looking

2
1 was sleeping   5 was cycling
2 woke up   6 drove
3 looked   7 weren't looking
4 was barking   8 said

3
1 after 2 and 3 because 4 Before 5 but 6 or 7 so
8 when 9 while

4
1 I used to live in Beijing when I was a child.
2 What did you use to do when you worked there?
3 He didn't use to like carrots before he left home.
4 They used to have long hair in 1975.
5 She didn't use to drive before last year.
6 As a student, when did you use to go to bed?

5
1 /z/ 2 /s/ 3 /s/ 4 /z/ 5 /s/ 6 /z/

6
1 bedroom 2 dining room 3 kitchen 4 library
5 living room 6 study

7
1 palace 2 gallery 3 park 4 monument 5 beach

8
1 when I was sixteen
2 while I was taking
3 after Australia
4 but I only travelled
5 so I didn't have time
6 Australia or New Zealand
7 because we had problems
8 When we were leaving

Unit 61

1
1 None 2 Some 3 most 4 Most 5 Some 6 None
7 None 8 All

2
1 Ø 2 of 3 Ø 4 of 5 Ø 6 of 7 of 8 of

3 Order: 5, 3, 6, 2, 4, 1

Unit 62

1
1 Everybody, nothing 2 nobody, Everybody
3 anything, anybody 4 somebody, anybody
5 nobody, everything

2
1 anybody, anywhere 2 something, somebody
3 anything, nothing 4 everywhere, anywhere
5 somewhere, nowhere

3
1 There isn't anybody in the house.
2 There's nothing to do.
3 There isn't anywhere to go.
4 There isn't anything on TV.
5 There's no one I want to phone.
6 There's nowhere worse than here.

4
1 something 2 everything 3 anything 4 nothing
5 anything 6 someone/somebody
7 no one / nobody 8 everywhere 9 anything
10 anywhere

Unit 63

1
1 Both 2 Both 3 Neither 4 Both 5 Neither
6 Both 7 Both 8 Neither 9 Neither 10 Both
11 Both 12 Neither

2
1 I don't like either type of music.
I like neither type of music.
2 I haven't been to either country.
I've been to neither country.
3 I can't speak either language.
I can speak neither language.
4 I don't play either sport.
I play neither sport.

3
1 both 2 Neither 3 either 4 Both 5 Either
6 Neither

Unit 64

1
1 U 2 U 3 C 4 C 5 U 6 U 7 U 8 U 9 U 10 U
11 U 12 C 13 C 14 C 15 C 16 U

2 1 much 2 many 3 many 4 much 5 much 6 much
7 much 8 much 9 much 10 many 11 much
12 many 13 many 14 many

3 1 correct
2 We don't have much salt.
3 How much milk do you need?
4 correct
5 correct
6 How many rooms do you need?
7 correct
8 How much rice do you want?
9 correct
10 There isn't much milk in the fridge.
11 Are there many people at the party?
12 A lot of people are vegetarians these days.

Unit 65

1 1 All 2 Some 3 Most 4 None 5 All 6 Most
7 Most 8 Some 9 None

2 1 Everybody 2 anybody 3 somebody 4 Nobody
5 Everybody 6 Nobody 7 anybody

3 1 anywhere 2 everywhere 3 nowhere 4 anywhere
5 somewhere 6 nowhere 7 somewhere

4 1 something 2 anything 3 something 4 nothing
5 Everything 6 anything 7 nothing

5 1 Both 2 Neither 3 Neither 4 either 5 both
6 either 7 neither 8 Either

6 1 much, is 2 much, is 3 many, are 4 many, are
5 much, is 6 much, is 7 many, are 8 many, are

8 1 speaking 2 listening 3 vocabulary 4 grammar
5 literature 6 writing

9 1 About an hour.
2 About twenty.
3 Not much.
4 No, there wasn't.
5 No, there weren't.
6 About five hundred.
7 About a thousand.
8 About two hundred.

Unit 66

1 1 an 2 Ø 3 a 4 Ø 5 Ø 6 an 7 an 8 Ø 9 a
10 Ø 11 an 12 a

2 1 a 2 a 3 an 4 an 5 a 6 a 7 a 8 a 9 an 10 a

3 1 He lives in a small apartment.
2 Maria was a Maths teacher for three years.
3 They've got tickets for the match.
4 My uncle is an engineer.
5 That's a beautiful bracelet.
6 Would you like a table for two?
7 Robert De Niro is an American actor.
8 Have you seen an umbrella anywhere?
9 I'm going to be a chef when I'm older.
10 Is there a bank near here?

4 Why do we love celebrities? Perhaps it's because our favourite star is <u>a</u> singer or <u>an</u> actor. But what about celebrities who are famous because they are 'famous'? For example, Paris Hilton grew up in <u>a</u> rich family. Then, as <u>an</u> adult, she was always in <u>a</u> magazine. She spent all her time at parties with other famous people. She has had many different jobs. She was <u>a</u> model for a while. She made <u>an</u> album, worked as <u>an</u> actress in some TV commercials and films and has also written <u>a</u> book. But her most successful job is as <u>a</u> celebrity – whatever that is!

Unit 67

1 1 This is Anouk. She's from <u>the</u> Netherlands.
2 Sri Lanka is in <u>the</u> Indian Ocean.
3 Cheetahs are <u>the</u> fastest animals on land.
4 Harald V is <u>the</u> King of Norway.
5 <u>The</u> Earth is 384,000 km from <u>the</u> moon.
6 My mother cooks <u>the</u> best cakes in <u>the</u> world!
7 Can you play <u>the</u> piano?
8 Paris is famous for <u>the</u> Eiffel Tower.
9 That was <u>the</u> worst film I've ever seen!
10 <u>The</u> Black Sea used to be part of <u>the</u> Atlantic Ocean.
11 There are twenty-seven countries in <u>the</u> European Union.
12 I love to listen to <u>the</u> violin.

2 1 Tortoises live the longest.
2 Yuri Gagarin was the first man in space.
3 The Atomium monument is in Brussels.
4 The North Pole is in the Arctic.
5 The Suez canal connects the Mediterranean Sea to the Red Sea.
6 Ferdinand Magellan went round the world in 1519.

Unit 68

1 1 a 2 the 3 a 4 the 5 the 6 an 7 the 8 the 9 the 10 a

2 1 c 2 h 3 j 4 i 5 b 6 e 7 a 8 f 9 d 10 g

3 1 a 2 the 3 a 4 the 5 a 6 an 7 The 8 the 9 the 10 a 11 an 12 the 13 the 14 a 15 a 16 the 17 The 18 a 19 the 20 the 21 a 22 the 23 the

4 Students' own answers.

Unit 69

1 1 Italian food 2 The people 3 the sandwiches 4 the girl 5 rock music 6 time 7 elephants 8 Life 9 foot 10 Chinese

2 1 correct
2 Have you ever been to ~~the~~ Disneyland?
3 I go to ~~the~~ school at eight o'clock.
4 My father works at ~~the~~ home.
5 She goes to work by ~~the~~ bicycle.
6 I would love to see ~~the~~ Mount Everest.
7 I hate ~~the~~ golf. I never play it.
8 We study ~~the~~ Urdu at school. It's a great language.
9 ~~The~~ Spanish people are very friendly.
10 correct
11 My grandmother lives in ~~the~~ Berlin.
12 I eat a lot of ~~the~~ apples.

3 1 c 2 c 3 b 4 c 5 a 6 c

4 1 Ø 2 a 3 Ø 4 The 5 Ø 6 Ø 7 Ø 8 a 9 an 10 the 11 Ø 12 Ø 13 the

Unit 70

1 1 The 2 Ø 3 a 4 the 5 Ø 6 the 7 a 8 the 9 the 10 a 11 the 12 Ø 13 Ø 14 the

2 1 the largest 2 the United States 3 a football 4 a small town 5 the oldest 6 a Spanish 7 a coffee 8 a headache 9 the most popular actress 10 The History 11 a flat 12 is in the 13 a dish 14 a song

3 1 /ðiː/ 2 /ðə/ 3 /ðə/ 4 /ðiː/ 5 /ðə/ 6 /ðiː/ 7 /ðə/ 8 /ðə/ 9 /ðiː/ 10 /ðə/

4 **Across**
1 destination 5 by 6 arrive 7 taxi 8 tour

Down
2 subway 3 tourist 4 on

5 1 composer 2 pop star 3 chef 4 celebrity 5 engineer 6 teacher

6 1 the Indian Ocean   4 the North Pole
2 the United Kingdom   5 the White House
3 the European Union   6 the Statue of Liberty

7 1 tortoises 2 Yuri Gagarin 3 Brussels 4 the Arctic 5 the Suez Canal 6 Ferdinand Magellan

Unit 71

1 1 Tomorrow <u>will</u> be a beautiful day.
2 One day I'<u>ll</u> be famous.
3 We'<u>ll</u> be in Rome tomorrow so meet us there.
4 <u>Will</u> your new girlfriend be at the party?
5 I think John <u>will</u> pass all his exams.
6 When <u>will</u> you be eighteen?
7 Who <u>will</u> win: Real Madrid or AC Milan?
8 Don't worry: I'm sure you'<u>ll</u> get better.
9 Next week it'<u>ll</u> be the summer holidays!
10 Do you think it <u>will</u> rain tomorrow?
11 Nobody <u>will</u> be in the office tomorrow so don't call.
12 <u>Will</u> we ever find a cure for cancer?

2 1 P 2 P 3 F 4 F 5 P 6 F 7 P 8 P 9 F 10 P
11 F 12 P

3 1 China will become the richest country in the world.
2 People will buy everything on the internet.
3 The world will get hotter.
4 Everybody will speak English.
5 Humans will reach Mars in 2020.
6 Everybody will live for a hundred years.

4 1 Will 2 will 3 'll 4 Will 5 will 6 won't 7 will 8 'll

5 1 will you be 2 I'll be 3 Will you be 4 I won't
5 I'll be 6 will you be 7 I'll be 8 I'll be

Unit 72

1 1 Don't worry. I'<u>ll</u> help you.
2 No, but I'<u>ll</u> make one.
3 I'<u>ll</u> carry it for you.
4 I'<u>ll</u> read you one, I promise.
5 I don't know yet. <u>Will</u> you pick me up?
6 I'<u>ll</u> lend you mine.
7 I'<u>ll</u> help you if you like.
8 Don't worry. I'<u>ll</u> remember.
9 That's OK. We'<u>ll</u> change it.
10 <u>Will</u> you send the books by post?

2 1 I'll make you a cup of tea.
2 I'll make you a sandwich.
3 I'll pick you up.
4 I'll wait for you.
5 I'll lend you some.
6 I'll get you a glass of water.

3 1 I'll always 2 I'll never 3 I'll always 4 I'll never
5 I'll never 6 I'll always 7 I'll never

4 1 Will you lend me your car?
2 Will you drive me to the party?
3 Will you pay for a taxi?
4 Will you give me some money for a bus ticket?

Unit 73

1 1 I think I'll have the tomato soup.
2 I think I'll have a pizza.
3 I think I'll have a chicken sandwich.
4 I think I'll have the steak with salad.

2 1 I think I'll have some pasta.
2 I think I'll turn on the heating.
3 I think I'll have a glass of water.
4 I think I'll go to bed.
5 I think I'll turn on the air conditioning.
6 I think I'll go for a walk.
7 I think I'll go home.

3 1 I'm going to 2 I think I'll 3 I'm going to
4 I think I'll 5 I'm going to

4 Order: 2, 4, 1, 3, 5

5 1 I'll pay for it.
2 I'm going to have a holiday in Florida.
3 I'll help you.
4 I'm going to be a doctor like my father.
5 I'll get it.
6 I'm going to have a dinner party tonight.

Unit 74

1 1 e 2 a 3 b 4 d 5 c

2 1 Rita and I are playing tennis on Tuesday.
2 It's OK. I'll pay for lunch.
3 This year I'm going to learn to play the piano.

3 1 I'm having 2 will get 3 Will it snow
4 are you getting 5 are you going 6 Will I like

4 1 are having 2 'm going to 3 's going to see
4 both 5 are you going to tell 6 both

Answer key (and tapescript)

5 Students' own answers.

Unit 75

1 1 're 2 aren't 3 are 4 'll 5 will 6 's 7 's 8 Will
9 won't

2 1 What ~~do~~ are you doing tonight?
2 I'm ~~to~~ celebrating at the Irish Pub.
3 Please ~~will~~ come.
4 I'll be ~~being~~ there at eight o'clock.
5 Also my dad is ~~are~~ going to pay for a holiday
6 I think I'll ~~going~~ travel to somewhere like Spain or Greece.
7 Anyway, I'll ~~am~~ see you tonight I hope.

3 1 Will you be 2 won't 3 'll be 4 are you doing
5 're going 6 see 7 'm going 8 going to snow

4 Students' own answers.

5 1 a 2 b 3 a 4 b 5 a 6 b 7 b 8 a

> **Tapescript** ⓑ **2.31**
> 1 The plane leaves at five.
> 2 Pills'll replace food.
> 3 I have tea in the morning.
> 4 We'll pick you up from the airport.
> 5 Prices go up before Christmas.
> 6 They'll learn the piano.
> 7 Don't worry. I'll open it.
> 8 We always have lunch together.

6 1 thirsty 2 difficult 3 cold 4 hungry 5 tired
6 hot 7 bored

7 1 pizza 2 chicken 3 salad 4 steak 5 fish 6 pasta
7 tomato 8 soup

8 Order: 9, 1, 4, 8, 6, 3, 7, 5, 2, 10

> **Tapescript** ⓑ **2.32**
> A: Cassia? This is Bernardo. Can you talk?
> C: Yes, of course.
> A: When will you be in Amsterdam?
> C: I'll be in Amsterdam on 1 August.
> A: Will you be alone?
> C: No, I won't. I'll be with Henri.
> A: Which hotel will you be in?
> C: I'll be in the Four Seasons.
> A: Be careful.
> C: Don't worry. I'll be very, very careful.

Unit 76

1 in: 1999, the evenings, August, summer, the middle
of winter, the 1990s, the early morning
on: New year's Day, 29th February, the third Friday
of the month, Sundays, weekdays
at: half past ten, midday, night, 5 p.m., the same
time, the weekend

2 1 on 29th February
2 in the middle of winter
3 at half past ten
4 in the early morning
5 on Sundays
6 on the third Friday of the month
7 at the same time
8 in the 1990s

3 1 b 2 d 3 f 4 e 5 c 6 a

4 1 on 2 In 3 At 4 In 5 at 6 On 7 at 8 at 9 at
10 at 11 In

5 Students' own answers.

Unit 77

1 1 a 2 b 3 c 4 h 5 d 6 e 7 f 8 g

2 1 at 2 at 3 on 4 on 5 in 6 on 7 in

3 1 in the middle 2 on the left 3 next to 4 on the right
5 Behind 6 in front of 7 Under 8 in the corner

Unit 78

1 1 d 2 g 3 a 4 h 5 f 6 c 7 b 8 e

2 1 which 2 who 3 who 4 which 5 who 6 which
7 which 8 who

3 1 which 2 which 3 which 4 who 5 who 6 who
7 which 8 which 9 who 10 which

4 1 correct
2 I don't like food <u>which</u>/<u>that</u> has a lot of salt in it.
3 A biologist is a person <u>who</u> works in a laboratory.
4 He bought a new bike <u>which</u>/<u>that</u> cost him over
two thousand euros.
5 correct
6 I've always liked people <u>who</u> laugh really loudly.
7 We stayed in a hotel <u>which</u>/<u>that</u> was over 200 years
old.
8 correct
9 This is a machine <u>which</u>/<u>that</u> translates words into
English.

Unit 79

1 1 which 2 who 3 who 4 which 5 which

2 1 This is my new car which my parents gave me.
2 This is my friend who helped me with my exam.
3 This is the book which I was reading last week.
4 This is the film which I went to see last night.
5 These are the CDs which I bought online.
6 This is the song which they sang at our wedding.

3 1 Would you like to see the photos ~~that~~ I took on my holiday?
3 And this is the couple ~~that~~ we met on the plane. They were great fun.
5 This is one of the hotels ~~that~~ we stayed at. It was really nice.
6 And this is the swimming pool ~~that~~ they had on the roof.
Sentences 2, 4 and 7 cannot omit the relative pronoun.

Unit 80

1 1 on 2 at 3 at 4 in 5 in

2 1 on 2 to 3 on 4 in 5 in 6 behind 7 in
8 between 9 at 10 At 11 in 12 of

3 1 a person who follows a particular team or sport
2 correct
3 a person who works in a school
4 a thing which you use to light a fire
5 correct
6 a person who looks after plants
7 correct
8 correct
9 a machine which prints things from your computer
Sentences 4 and 7 can omit the relative pronoun.

4 1 I loved the film we saw last night.
2 My favourite actor was the woman who stole the car.
3 These are the photos I took at the party.
4 This is the photo which won an award.
5 Do you like the CD my brother gave to me?
6 I like the singer who sings in Spanish.

5 1 correct
2 She's the woman <u>who</u> sings that song.
3 correct
4 correct
5 Put her CD in the player.
6 I think they're arriving <u>at</u> eight.
7 Are you the person <u>who</u> has the big black dog?
8 correct
9 Take the lift and his office is <u>at</u> the top of the building.
10 Sit ~~on~~ between Mike and me and tell us what happened.

6 1 top 2 corner 3 middle 4 left 5 next 6 front

8 1 swimming pool 2 changing rooms 3 sauna
4 dance studio 5 tennis courts 6 aerobics classes
7 solarium 8 yoga

9 1 supporter 2 player 3 teacher 4 lighter 5 writer
6 gardener 7 hairdryer 8 cleaner 9 printer

10 1 on 15th March 2 in 1988 3 around 11 p.m.
4 at about 7.30 a.m. 5 at 11.30 p.m.

Tapescript ⑤2.38
Conversation 1
A: When's your birthday?
B: It's on 15th March.
A: When were you born?
B: In 1988.
A: What time were you born?
B: I'm not sure. At around eleven, I think.
A: In the morning?
B: No, at night.

Conversation 2
A: When do you usually get up?
B: On weekdays, I get up at about seven thirty, but at the weekend I get up at any time. Whenever I wake up, really.
A: When do you usually go to bed?
B: It depends. During the week I usually go to bed at eleven thirty. In winter I go to bed a bit earlier.

Unit 81

1 1 When you heat ice, it melts.
2 If you go into space, you float.
3 When you press this button, the computer starts.
4 If you have a headache, an aspirin helps.
5 When you sneeze, you always close your eyes.
6 If you add two and two, you get four.

2 1 e 2 c 3 d 4 a 5 b

Answer key (and tapescript)

3 1 don't sleep 2 get 3 have 4 don't ask 5 'm not

Unit 82

1 1 close it 2 turn it off 3 put it back 4 mend it
5 tidy it up 6 don't use it

2 Order: 3, 1, 6, 2, 4, 5

3 1 If you need help, ring this bell.
2 If the light is red, don't cross the road.
3 If you'd like to apply for a job, complete this form.
4 If you don't have a security badge, do not enter.
5 If you want a drink, put some money in the slot.
6 If you don't feel better tomorrow, phone a/the doctor.

4 1 Unless you hear from me, don't wait.
2 Don't call the police unless it's an emergency.
3 Unless it's important, don't spend time on it.
4 Meet at five unless Rachel changes the time again!

Unit 83

1 1 leave, 'll call 2 don't give, 'll tell 3 'll pay, help
4 phones, 'll say 5 won't pass, don't work
6 go, 'll catch 7 arrive, 'll ask 8 Will they visit, have
9 will Jane do, doesn't hear

2 1 If you work hard at school, you'll go to university.
2 You'll catch the bus if you run.
3 If you don't get a job, you won't have any money.
4 The police will stop you if you drive too fast.
5 If you don't tell me the answer, I won't be your best friend.
6 If you give me your email address, I'll send you the attachment.

3 1 If you turn left, you<u>'ll</u> see the house on the left.
2 But it's a one-way street. If I turn left, the police <u>will</u> stop me.
3 If my plane lands at three, <u>will</u> you pick me up?
4 Sure, but if it's delayed, <u>will</u> you call?
5 I<u>'ll</u> send you to your bed if you hit your brother again!
6 I<u>'ll</u> stop if he stops hitting me!
7 If you ignore him, he<u>'ll</u> leave you alone.
8 If I tell you a secret, <u>will</u> you keep it?
9 Sure. It<u>'ll</u> be between you and me.

4 1 when 2 If 3 If 4 when 5 If 6 when 7 if 8 If
9 when 10 If

Unit 84

1 1 check out before 10 a.m. 2 use / pay with Visa or Mastercard 3 enter 4 use the stairs 5 press 0

2 1 have to 2 must 3 might 4 can 5 don't have to
6 might 7 Should 8 have to 9 'll

3 1 If you're late, you should call me.
2 He can come later if you want.
3 If you have to stay another day, that's fine.
4 She can learn French if she uses this computer program.
5 We'll take a break now if you like.
6 The taxi can pick you up if you want.
7 We must meet up for dinner when you come to England.
8 You can stay with Lars if you visit Stockholm.

4 1 c 2 f 3 b 4 e 5 d 6 a

5 Students' own answers.

Unit 85

1 1 go 2 dream 3 rains 4 'll call 5 'll stay 6 Don't
7 will give 8 do 9 is 10 don't 11 do 12 will

2 1 g 2 h 3 a 4 d 5 c 6 e 7 f 8 b

3 1 If 2 When 3 unless 4 When 5 when 6 if
7 unless 8 if

4
1 starts	5 'll have
2 tell	6 won't be
3 comes	7 'll pick
4 don't tidy	8 wants

6 1 around 2 off 3 back 4 up 5 back 6 up

7 1 can't answer 2 it's 3 it isn't 4 leave 5 I'll call
6 call 7 if you like 8 could email

Tapescript 🔊 **2.44**
Hello, this is Braxton. Sorry, but I can't answer the phone at the moment. If it's between nine and five, I'm at work. Call me there on 020 7998 1234. If it isn't urgent, leave your name and number and I'll call you back. Or call me on my mobile if you like. That's 0770 879 3345. Or you could email me at braxton51@hotmail.com. Bye!

Unit 86

1 1 interested 2 exciting 3 surprised 4 boring
5 tired 6 annoying

2 1 interested 2 tired 3 excited 4 frightened
5 embarrassed 6 surprised 7 bored 8 worried
9 annoyed 10 relaxed

3 1 worrying 2 boring 3 exciting 4 annoying
5 frightening 6 tiring 7 surprising 8 interesting
9 relaxing 10 embarrassing

4 Students' own answers.

Unit 87

1 1 feel smoother 2 Look younger 3 smell fresh
4 Sound fluent 5 taste delicious

2 1 cool 2 rough 3 awful 4 delicious (or lovely)
5 lovely 6 sad 7 polluted 8 relaxing 9 sweet
10 old

3 1 feel 2 look 3 sounds 4 smells 5 taste 6 looks
7 smells 8 tastes 9 sounds 10 feel

Unit 88

1 1 large, white, metal   4 ancient, tall, Japanese
2 practical, square, plastic 5 stylish, brown, wooden
3 two, comfortable, red   6 long, yellow, cotton

2 1 a new cotton   5 an eighteenth-century French
2 a very fast Korean 6 a huge modern
3 a lovely Russian   7 green plastic
4 old black   8 cool Italian

3 Suggested answers:
1 elegant Australian
2 enormous eighteenth-century
3 beautiful diamond

4 Students' own answers.

Unit 89

1 1 at 2 on 3 of 4 with 5 at 6 with 7 about 8 of

2 1 with 2 by 3 of 4 about 5 with 6 at 7 of
8 from 9 to 10 in 11 at 12 about

3 1 excited about 2 worried about 3 married to
4 different from 5 good at 6 interested in

4 1 I'm really frightened of flying.
2 I'm interested in History.
3 Everyone was surprised by your news.
4 The kids are bored with this TV show.
5 Why are you worried about your new job?
6 Peter is annoyed with Saffron.

5 Students' own answers.

Unit 90

1 1 bored 2 great 3 annoying 4 tiring 5 frightening
6 worried 7 exciting 8 beautiful 9 married
10 fluent 11 polluted 12 awful 13 interesting
14 delicious 15 surprised

2 1 sounds 2 looks 3 smells 4 feel

3 1 correct
2 I have a <u>new white</u> fridge for sale.
3 They're keen <u>on</u> golf.
4 correct
5 Emily is really excited <u>about</u> her birthday.
6 Who does that frightening <u>big brown</u> dog belong to?
7 I'm really bad <u>at</u> Maths. Can you help me?
8 correct
9 He looks <u>intelligent</u>.
10 correct
11 correct
12 I was surprised <u>by</u> his new haircut.
13 This is a really <u>annoying romantic</u> film.
14 correct
15 Why are you worried <u>about</u> your results?

4 1 <u>interesting</u>, 3 2 <u>interested</u>, 3 3 <u>boring</u>, 2
4 <u>bored</u>, 1 5 ex<u>ci</u>ting, 3 6 ex<u>ci</u>ted, 3 7 <u>worrying</u>, 3
8 <u>worried</u>, 2 9 <u>tiring</u>, 2 10 tired, 1 11 an<u>noy</u>ing, 3
12 an<u>noyed</u>, 2 13 <u>frightening</u>, 3 14 <u>fright</u>ened, 2
15 sur<u>prising</u>, 3 16 sur<u>prised</u>, 2

5 size/shape: large, round, small, square
age: ancient, modern, old, young
colour: brown, orange, red, yellow
material: cotton, metal, plastic, wooden
opinion: beautiful, boring, cool, elegant

6 1 cooker, c 2 armchair, d 3 table, b 4 vase, e
5 desk, f 6 lamp, a

7 Lisa
Age: 41
Interests: art and painting, nature and the countryside
Dislikes: spiders

Prescott
Age: 56
Marital status: divorced
Likes: fast food
Dislikes: (being alone), sport

Pam
Age: 28
Concerns: global warming, pollution

Tapescript 2.49

Name: Lisa
Age: 41
I'm good at art and very keen on painting. I love nature and the countryside but I'm frightened of spiders. I need a man to protect me.

Name: Prescott
Age: 56
I'm divorced and bored with being alone. I love fast food and I'm bad at sport but I'm loving and caring.

Name: Pam
Age: 28
Are you annoyed with the world? I'm really worried about global warming and tired of pollution. I want to meet someone with similar beliefs. Let's change the world together!

Unit 91

1 1 b 2 a 3 f 4 c 5 e 6 d

2 1 I'm hoping to run the New York marathon.
2 I've decided to study Economics at university.
3 I'm not planning to work immediately after my degree.
4 She refused to talk to me.
5 We agreed not to tell the police.
6 I don't want to work in an office.

3 1 to meet at nine
2 to wear her red dress
3 to study medicine
4 to leave early
5 to take a taxi

6 to have her own TV show one day
7 to come with us tonight

4 1 We're planning <u>to</u> go to Greece for our holidays.
2 She's agreed not <u>to</u> tell David.
3 I hope <u>to</u> move house in September.
4 I've agreed <u>to</u> work late on Tuesday.
5 The bank refused <u>to</u> lend me the money.
6 Carrie's decided not <u>to</u> go to university.
7 Would you like <u>to</u> borrow my dictionary?
8 I plan <u>to</u> go on a diet.
9 We invited them but they refused <u>to</u> come.
10 We decided not <u>to</u> go to the cinema.

5 Students' own answers.

Unit 92

1 1 She doesn't like skiing.
2 He likes sunbathing.
3 We don't like camping.
4 She likes surfing.
5 He doesn't like doing homework.
6 They like eating out.

2 1 Smoking 2 Swimming 3 Watching 4 Stealing
5 Being 6 Eating 7 Parking 8 Cleaning
9 Learning 10 Skiing

3 1 learning languages 2 buying a guitar
3 going on a diet 4 getting old 5 flying
6 not phoning

4 1 I don't mind helping you.
2 Do you enjoy playing sports?
3 Swimming is good exercise.
4 They worry about driving at night.
5 Are you good at skiing?
6 They like playing computer games.
7 Sunbathing is bad for your skin.

5 Students' own answers.

Unit 93

1 1 living 2 both 3 to move 4 to go 5 applying
6 both 7 to give 8 playing 9 to have 10 both
11 eating 12 to help

2 1 to sit 2 to drink / drinking 3 trying 4 bringing

3 1 playing / to play tennis
  2 to go tonight
  3 to call her back
  4 painting your picture
  5 listening to that new CD
  6 watching / to watch horror films (to comedy films)

Unit 94

1 1 to eat 2 writing 3 playing 4 smoking 5 to buy
  6 eating 7 to have 8 to smoke 9 buying 10 having

2 1 Stop smoking 2 Stop eating 3 stop driving
  4 stop taking 5 Stop to spend 6 Stop watching
  7 stop to relax

3 1 to pick 2 working 3 to watch 4 smoking
  5 doing 6 eating 7 watching

Unit 95

1 1 going 2 Snowboarding 3 to try 4 trying
  5 doing 6 coming 7 to help 8 help 9 fixing
  10 agree 11 to be 12 to meet 13 cooking
  14 to change 15 to say 16 to take

2 1 to call 2 find 3 to have 4 meeting 5 preparing
  6 to get 7 to spend

3 1 a 2 both 3 b 4 both 5 b 6 a 7 both

4 1 not to go 2 to talk to 3 to photocopy this
  4 stop smoking 5 to talk 6 at making things
  7 to travel around Europe 8 a lot of coffee

6 1 I'd like to /w/ ask for a pay rise.
  2 He promised to /w/ answer my call.
  3 Do we need to /w/ employ anyone else?
  4 Would you like to /w/ order now?
  5 When do they want to /w/ interview you?

7 1 camping 2 eating out 3 sunbathing 4 skiing
  5 surfing 6 swimming

8 1 stop smoking 2 lose, weight 3 break, leg
  4 take, exercise 5 have, headache 6 feel, sick
  7 get better

9 1 travel 2 work 3 help children 4 marry
  5 have children 6 be happy

Tapescript ⏏2.56

First, I want to travel around the world. Then, I hope to work for Save the Children. If possible, I'd like to help children in the developing world. One day, I hope to get married. I'd like to have two children. But basically, I just want to be happy.

Unit 96

1 1 Tell him to phone me.
  2 Ask her to come to my office.
  3 Tell them to be here at six.
  4 Ask him to send me a copy.
  5 Tell them to give you the money.
  6 Tell her to come and see me.
  7 Ask Michelle to photocopy this.
  8 Tell the driver to stop at the station.

2 1 He, her 2 We, them 3 I, him, us
  4 They, me, them 5 She, us, her 6 He, me, them
  7 you, me 8 she, him

3 There are a few things I need you to do.
  First of all, Jack Greer from our New York office is going to visit you in September. He'd like you to book him a room in the Park Plaza for the night of the 27th.
  Also, he wants you to organise meetings with all the people in your team for him.
  Secondly, Marta Castro needs you to send her copies of the January reports.
  Lastly, Paul McCann doesn't answer my emails or answer my phone calls. Can you ask him to call me as soon as possible. Tell him to use my mobile (8796 543 643).

4 1 I'd like you to photocopy this report.
  2 The boss wants Mike to send a copy of the letter to him.
  3 Please ask your secretary to book the hotel room now.
  4 Tell Jerry to meet us at the café on the corner.
  5 I'd like you to bring me another steak.

Unit 97

1 1 b 2 a 3 f 4 e 5 g 6 c 7 h 8 d

2 Isn't it time for a break? Join us on a cruise of the Mediterranean sea <u>to</u> visit some of the most famous sites in the world.

DAY ONE: Fly to Venice <u>to</u> meet the cruise liner *The Golden Angel*.

DAY TWO: Before we leave you'll have a few hours <u>to</u> buy souvenirs from one of Italy's most famous cities. Then at midday, we leave for Athens. In the evening you can sit on the deck <u>to</u> enjoy the sunset and the live entertainment.

DAY THREE: We arrive at the port of Piraeus <u>to</u> take a tour of the city. We'll walk into town <u>to</u> see the Acropolis and try some wonderful Greek food.

3 1 She's cycling to get to school.
2 He's at the market to buy some fish.
3 He's waiting to catch a bus.
4 You press this button to take a photograph.
5 They went to the zoo to see the elephant.
6 They flew into space in 1969 to land on the moon.

4 Students' own answers.

Unit 98

1 1 are 2 are 3 is 4 are 5 is 6 are

2 1 are grown 2 is picked 3 is taken 4 are dried
5 isn't drunk 6 is used

3 1 What is this machine used for?
2 How is this computer switched on?
3 What is made with flour?
4 How often are these rooms cleaned?
5 Where are coffee beans grown?
6 When is the post delivered?
7 How is this word pronounced?
8 How much is known about dinosaurs?

Unit 99

1 1 was discovered 2 grew 3 was eaten 4 arrived
5 was grown 6 became

2 1 was written 2 wasn't published 3 was chosen
4 wrote 5 used 6 were changed 7 said 8 changed
9 was bought

3 1 was, written 2 was, invented 3 was, paid
4 were, spoken 5 was, climbed 6 was, discovered
7 was, flown 8 were, held 9 were, used
10 was, invented

4 1 b 2 b 3 a 4 a 5 a

Unit 100

1 1 wants 2 Tell 3 to 4 need 5 go 6 something
7 To 8 you

2 1 are burnt 2 is, celebrated 3 is served
4 was called 5 was born 6 was joined 7 is spoken

3 Students' own answers.

4 1 The Eiffel Tower was built in 1889.
2 Pasta is made with flour and eggs.
3 How is cotton grown?
4 A message was left on your desk.
5 When was the letter sent?
6 Spanish isn't spoken by Brazilians.
7 I am paid £500 a week.
8 Packages are delivered all over the world.
9 The weather was bad but our plane wasn't delayed.

5 1 Tell <u>her</u> to give me a call.
2 We're going to the theatre to watch a play.
3 I need you to copy this report.
4 Do you want him to send <u>me</u> an email?
5 <u>They</u> would like to meet us at the station.
6 How many of these do you want <u>to</u> buy from us?
7 Is Angie there? Tell <u>her</u> to come and see me straight away.
8 Water <u>is</u> heated to 100 degrees.
9 How many different languages are <u>taught</u> in your school?
10 This building <u>was</u> designed by a famous architect in 1999.
11 A famous architect designed this city.
12 No one knows when the wheel was <u>invented</u>.

6 /əʊ/ no: grown, told, drove
/e/ met: read, left, said
/eɪ/ say: paid, made
/ɔː/ or: brought, worn, taught
/ɪ/ it: lit, built

7 1 photocopy 2 send 3 book 4 meet 5 take

8 1 1957 2 *Time* magazine 3 three weeks 4 his life
5 $2.4 million

Tapescript 🔊 2.62

On the Road was written in 1951 but it wasn't published until 1957. In 2005, it was chosen by *Time* magazine as one of the best 100 English-language novels of the last century.

Jack Kerouac wrote the book in only three weeks but he used notes and diaries from seven years of travel across the USA. Often the names of real people and places were changed. Many poets, writers and musicians said the book was important to them. Bob Dylan said: 'It changed my life.'

In 2001, the original text was bought for $2.4 million.

Progress test 1

1 a 2 c 3 b 4 c 5 b 6 a 7 c 8 b 9 a 10 c 11 b 12 b
13 c 14 b 15 c 16 a 17 b 18 b 19 b 20 a 21 a 22 c
23 c 24 b 25 c 26 c 27 a 28 b 29 c 30 b 31 c 32 b
33 b 34 c 35 b 36 b 37 b 38 c 39 b 40 a 41 a 42 c
43 b 44 c 45 c 46 a 47 a 48 b 49 b 50 a

Progress test 2

1 b 2 a 3 b 4 c 5 a 6 c 7 a 8 c 9 b 10 c 11 a 12 b
13 a 14 a 15 a 16 a 17 c 18 a 19 a 20 c 21 c 22 c
23 a 24 b 25 c 26 a 27 c 28 b 29 a 30 b 31 b 32 b
33 b 34 c 35 a 36 b 37 a 38 a 39 b 40 c 41 a 42 c
43 a 44 a 45 b 46 c 47 b 48 b 49 b 50 a

Progress test 3

1 b 2 a 3 a 4 b 5 a 6 c 7 c 8 b 9 b 10 a 11 b 12 a
13 a 14 b 15 c 16 a 17 b 18 b 19 b 20 a 21 b 22 a
23 b 24 c 25 b 26 c 27 c 28 c 29 b 30 a 31 b 32 b
33 c 34 b 35 b 36 c 37 a 38 c 39 c 40 a 41 b 42 a
43 b 44 c 45 b 46 c 47 b 48 b 49 b 50 c

Progress test 4

1 a 2 c 3 a 4 c 5 b 6 b 7 c 8 c 9 a 10 b 11 a 12 b
13 a 14 a 15 b 16 c 17 c 18 a 19 a 20 b 21 b 22 a
23 b 24 c 25 a 26 a 27 b 28 b 29 a 30 b 31 b 32 b
33 c 34 b 35 b 36 c 37 a 38 b 39 a 40 a 41 a 42 b
43 b 44 b 45 c 46 c 47 b 48 b 49 a 50 b

Progress test 5

1 a 2 b 3 c 4 b 5 a 6 a 7 a 8 c 9 b 10 c 11 c 12 a
13 c 14 b 15 a 16 b 17 b 18 a 19 c 20 c 21 b 22 b
23 c 24 c 25 a 26 a 27 b 28 a 29 b 30 b 31 b 32 a
33 a 34 b 35 b 36 a 37 b 38 b 39 a 40 b 41 a 42 c
43 c 44 a 45 c 46 c 47 b 48 c 49 a 50 b

Progress test 6

1 a 2 c 3 a 4 a 5 c 6 c 7 b 8 c 9 b 10 a 11 a 12 b
13 a 14 c 15 b 16 b 17 b 18 a 19 b 20 a 21 c 22 c
23 c 24 c 25 b 26 a 27 c 28 a 29 a 30 b 31 a 32 b
33 b 34 b 35 a 36 a 37 b 38 c 39 c 40 a 41 c 42 c
43 b 44 a 45 b 46 c 47 b 48 a 49 a 50 c

Progress test 7

1 c 2 a 3 c 4 b 5 c 6 a 7 b 8 b 9 a 10 a 11 a 12 c
13 c 14 a 15 c 16 c 17 b 18 a 19 c 20 b 21 b 22 c
23 a 24 b 25 c 26 a 27 b 28 b 29 c 30 c 31 c 32 c
33 a 34 c 35 a 36 c 37 a 38 c 39 a 40 c 41 b 42 b
43 b 44 a 45 a 46 c 47 c 48 a 49 b 50 b

Progress test 8

1 a 2 c 3 c 4 b 5 a 6 a 7 b 8 b 9 b 10 a 11 c 12 c
13 c 14 a 15 b 16 a 17 a 18 b 19 c 20 c 21 b 22 a
23 c 24 a 25 c 26 a 27 a 28 b 29 a 30 a 31 c 32 b
33 a 34 c 35 b 36 b 37 b 38 c 39 a 40 b 41 b 42 a
43 a 44 b 45 a 46 b 47 c 48 b 49 b 50 a

Progress test 9

1 a 2 b 3 a 4 a 5 b 6 a 7 c 8 c 9 b 10 a 11 b 12 b
13 a 14 a 15 c 16 a 17 c 18 a 19 b 20 c 21 b 22 a
23 c 24 b 25 a 26 a 27 b 28 b 29 b 30 b 31 a 32 a
33 a 34 b 35 b 36 c 37 b 38 c 39 a 40 a 41 c 42 a
43 c 44 c 45 b 46 a 47 a 48 c 49 c 50 c

Progress test 10

1 b 2 b 3 a 4 b 5 c 6 c 7 c 8 b 9 b 10 c 11 c 12 c
13 c 14 b 15 c 16 b 17 b 18 c 19 b 20 c 21 c 22 a
23 b 24 a 25 b 26 b 27 c 28 b 29 a 30 b 31 c 32 a
33 b 34 a 35 a 36 b 37 b 38 b 39 a 40 a 41 a 42 a
43 b 44 c 45 a 46 c 47 b 48 a 49 b 50 a

Appendix 2

1 1 cats 2 addresses 3 cars 4 potatoes 5 apples
6 dresses 7 babies 8 people

2 1 goes 2 drives 3 buys 4 tries 5 pushes
6 marries 7 teaches 8 plays

3 1 stopped 2 hotter 3 happiest 4 moving
5 swimming 6 danced 7 biggest 8 planning

Appendix 4

1 1 travels 2 work 3 don't open 4 're doing 5 isn't
eating 6 is singing 7 are they living 8 has gone
9 haven't been 10 've finished 11 played 12 won
13 did you move 14 was watching 15 were you

2 1 won't 2 can 3 'd 4 should 5 mustn't 6 Would
7 shouldn't 8 could

Index

Note: The numbers in this index are page numbers. Key vocabulary is in *italic*.

Index

Index

Photo credits

The publishers would like to thank the following sources for permission to reproduce their copyright protected photographs:

Cover image: Shutterstock Inc.

pp 12a (Shutterstock Inc.), 12b (Shutterstock Inc.), 12c-g (Shutterstock Inc.), 15a (Shutterstock Inc.), 15b (Shutterstock Inc.), 15c (Shutterstock Inc.), 15d (Shutterstock Inc.), 15e (Debra James/ Shutterstock Inc.), 18 (Shutterstock Inc.), 32 (Daniel Rodriguez / iStockphoto.com), 33t (Getty Images), 33b (Stephane Reix/For Picture/Corbis), 34 (Najlah Feanny/ Corbis), 38 (Shutterstock Inc.), 39a (iStockphoto.com), 39b (iStockphoto. com), 39c (Matteo De Stefano / iStockphoto.com), 39d (iStockphoto.com), 39e (iStockphoto.com), 39f (iStockphoto.com), 39g (Sándor Kelemen/ iStockphoto.com), 39h (iStockphoto.com), 39i (iStockphoto.com), 42 (Tom Merton/ Getty Images), 43 (Bob Daemmrich/ PhotoEdit Inc.), 49a (Jan Will/ iStockphoto.com), 49b (David Ciemny/ iStockphoto.com), 49c (Chiya Li/ iStockphoto.com), 49d (Shutterstock Inc.), 50l (Angelika Schwarz/ iStockphoto.com), 50r (Franck Camhi/ iStockphoto.com), 59b (Shutterstock Inc.), 59c (Shutterstock Inc.), 59d (Shutterstock Inc.), 59e (Wendy Kaveney Photography/Shutterstock Inc.), 59f (Corstiaan Elzelingen, Van/ iStockphoto.com), 59g (Shutterstock Inc.), 64l (Paul Banton/ iStockphoto.com), 64c (Bruce Block/ iStockphoto.com), 64r (Mike Johnson/ Marine Natural History Photography/ earthwindow. com), 70a (Mark Evans/ iStockphoto.com), 70b (iStockphoto.com), 70c (Jacob Wackerhausen/ iStockphoto.com), 70d (Jure Porenta/ iStockphoto. com), 74l (Shutterstock Inc.), 74r (Shutterstock Inc.), 76l (MonkeyBusiness Images/ Shutterstock Inc.), 76c (DaSilva/ Shutterstock Inc.), 76r (iStockphoto.com), 77 (iStockphoto.com), 83l (Jordan Chesbrough/ iStockphoto.com), 83r (Shutterstock Inc.), 86t (iStockphoto.com), 86r (Hulton Archive/Getty Images), 86b (Time & Life Pictures/Getty Images), 87t (Landov/ DPA), 87c (Hulton Archive/ Getty Images), 87b (Michael Ochs Archives/ Getty Images), 88l (Amanda Rohde/ iStockphoto.com), 88r (Ned Frisk/ Corbis), 90tl (Bettmann/ Corbis), 90cl (Lebrecht Music and Arts Photo Library / Alamy), 90bl (WireImages/ Getty Images), 90tr (Time & Life Pictures/Getty Images), 90cr (Hulton Archive/Getty Images), 90br (Mary Evans Picture Library/ Alamy), 92 (iStockphoto.com), 93 (Shutterstock Inc.), 94 (Shutterstock Inc.), 95 (W H Chow/ Shutterstock Inc.), 96l (Shutterstock Inc.), 96r (Geoffrey Hammond/ iStockphoto), 98t (iStockphoto.com), 98b (Andy Green/ iStockphoto.com), 101 (W H Chow/ Shutterstock Inc.), 106l (Andrew Johnson/ iStockphoto. com), 106c (iStockphoto.com), 106r (Matjaz Boncina/ iStockphoto.com), 107a(Jacom Stephens/ iStockphoto.com), 107b (Andrey Armyagov/ iStockphoto.com), 107c (iStockphoto.com), 107d (iStockphoto.com), 107e (Kateryna Govorushchenko/ iStockphoto.com), 107f Daniel Kourey/ iStockphoto.com), 115t (Shutterstock Inc.), 115b (Deborah Cheramie/ iStockphoto.com), 116 (iStockphoto.com), 117l (Shutterstock Inc.), 117r (Shutterstock Inc.), 118l (Shutterstock Inc.), 118c (Jon Helgason/ iStockphoto.com), 118r (Spencer Rowell/ Taxi/ Getty Images), 119tl (Neale Cousland/ Shutterstock Inc.), 119tr (Vibrant Image Studio/ Shutterstock Inc.), 119cl (Ruaridh Stewart/ZUMA/ Corbis), 119cr (Olga Mirenska/ iStockphoto.com), 119bl (Ashley Cooper / Alamy), 119br (MGM/UNITED ARTISTS/SONY / THE KOBAL COLLECTION), 121 (Deborah Cheramie/ iStockphoto.com), 123b (Lori Martin/ Texasescapes. com), 126 (iStockphoto.com), 131l (Shutterstock Inc.), 131r (Shutterstock Inc.), 136c (Valery Potapova/ Shutterstock Inc.), 136d (Liv frisis-larsen/ Shutterstock Inc.), 137t (Shutterstock Inc.), 137b (Shutterstock Inc.), 138a (GettyImages), 138b (iStockphoto.com), 138c (iStockphoto.com), 138d (iStockphoto.com), 143 (Wire images/ GettyImages), 144a (Christian Miller/ iStockphoto.com), 144b (S. Greg Panosian/ iStockphoto.com), 144c (Hiroya Minakuchi/ Minden Pictures/FLPA), 145a (Eric Isselée/ iStockphoto.com), 145b (Popperfoto/Getty Images), 145c (Anderm/ Shutterstock Inc.), 145d (Peter Guttman/ Corbis), 145e (Adrian Beesley/ iStockphoto.com), 145f (Bettmann/ Corbis), 148a (Shutterstock Inc.), 148b (Shutterstock Inc.), 148c (Shutterstock Inc.), 149t (Shutterstock Inc.), 149b (Shutterstock Inc.), 150t (The Stocktrek Corp/Brand X/ Corbis), 150b (Sergei Ilnitsky/EPA/Corbis), 155 (Ben Blankenburg/ iStockphoto), 161a (Illustrations/ Shutterstock Inc.), 161b (Illustrations/ Shutterstock Inc.), 161c (Illustrations/ Shutterstock Inc.), 161d (Illustrations/ Shutterstock Inc.), 161e (Illustrations/ Shutterstock Inc.), 161f (Illustrations/ Shutterstock Inc.), 161g (Illustrations/ Shutterstock Inc.), 161h (Illustrations/ Shutterstock Inc.), 169t (Guillermo Lobo/ iStockphoto. com), 169b (Patricia Hofmeester/ iStockphoto.com), 180 (Kelly Cline/ iStockphoto.com), 181 (iStockphoto.com), 182l (iStockphoto.com), 182c (iStockphoto.com), 182r (iStockphoto.com), 184d (iStockphoto.com), 184e (Ekaterina Solovieva/ iStockphoto.com), 184f (Dmitriy Melnikov/ iStockphoto.com), 184g (Jeremy Edwards/ iStockphoto.com), 184h (Elena Elisseeva/ iStockphoto.com), 185a (Shutterstock Inc.), 185b (iStockphoto. com), 185c (Shutterstock Inc.), 185d (Izabela Habur/ iStockphoto.com), 185e (George Manga/ iStockphoto.com), 185f (Pang Chee Seng Philip/ Shutterstock Inc.), 185g (Shutterstock Inc.), 185h (Shutterstock Inc.), 185i (Monkey Business Images/ iStockphoto.com), 185j (iStockphoto. com), 186a (R. Gino Santa Maria/ Shutterstock Inc.), 186b (Balaikin/ Shutterstock Inc.), 186c (Tyler Boyes/ Shutterstock Inc.), 186d (Brett Mulcahy/ Shutterstock Inc.), 187t (Shutterstock Inc.), 187c (Shutterstock Inc.), 187b (Shutterstock Inc.), 188a (iStockphoto.com), 188b (iStockphoto. com), 188c (iStockphoto.com), 188d (iStockphoto.com), 188e (iStockphoto. com), 191g (iStockphoto.com), 191h (iStockphoto.com), 191i (iStockphoto. com), 192 (Stephanie Sinclair/ Corbis), 193 (Steve Broer/ Shutterstock), 194a (iStockphoto.com), 205 (Shutterstock Inc.), 209 (Permission granted by Penguin UK), 211 (Permission granted by Penguin UK)

Illustrations by artists at KJA-artists.com:
Adrian@KJA-artists.com: pp 13, 26tr, 26tl, 27tl, 27c, 30, 57, 91, 114a, 114b, 114c, 139, 153, 157, 161i, 164a, 175, 194, 204; Andrew@KJA-artists.com: pp 16, 19f, 37a-f, 46, 48, 52, 66, 72, 73, 112, 129, 134, 146, 155, 166a, 166b, 166c, 200; Debbie@KJA-artists.com: pp 44; Inge-Marie@KJA-artists.com: pp 97, 140; Kath@KJA-artists.com: pp 14, 22a, 40, 41, 102t, 102b, 107g, 111, 113, 114d, 14e, 114f, 114g, 156, 158, 168, 176, 190, 196, 197; Peter@ KJA-artists.com: pp 25br, 28tl, 29t, 29b, 36a, 36b, 54, 68, 78, 110, 136a, 136b, 152, 154, 198, 199; Sean@KJA-artists.com: pp 19a-e, 24tr, 25cl, 25cr, 35, 36i-m, 37g-i, 56, 62, 80, 109, 122, 124, 128, 142, 162, 165, 183, 184, 202, 206

Illustrations by Kathrin Jacobsen: pp 20, 22b-f, 23, 24b, 26c, 31, 36c-h, 47, 53, 59a, 63, 75, 81, 84, 85, 108, 123c, 127, 130t, 130b, 159, 164b, 164c, 164d, 164e, 164f, 164g, 164h, 164i, 164j, 164k, 164l, 164m, 164n, 164o, 164p, 164q, 166d, 166e, 166f, 166g, 166h, 166i, 166j, 166k, 178, 191a, 191b, 191c, 191d, 191e, 191f, 205, 207

Designs by Mark Slader, Echelon Design: pp 7, 11, 39, 49, 58, 64, 70, 77, 78, 82, 86, 87, 92, 104, 106, 107, 108, 122, 124, 132, 133, 138, 144, 145, 152, 162, 174, 178, 180, 182, 184d-h, 186, 188, 192, 199, 206, 208

CD track list

CD 1

Unit and Exercise	Track	Unit and Exercise	Track	Unit and Exercise	Track
Unit 1, Ex 4	1.02	Unit 17, Ex 5	1.22	Unit 34, Ex 4	1.42
Unit 3, Ex 4	1.03	Unit 18, Ex 4	1.23	Unit 35, Review, Ex 6	1.43
Unit 4, Ex 2	1.04	Unit 19, Ex 4	1.24	Unit 35, Review, Ex 10	1.44
Unit 5, Review, Ex 6	1.05	Unit 20, Review, Ex 7	1.25	Unit 36, Ex 3	1.45
Unit 5, Review, Ex 10	1.06	Unit 20, Review, Ex 11	1.26	Unit 38, Ex 2	1.46
Unit 6, Ex 3	1.07	Unit 21, Ex 4	1.27	Unit 39, Ex 1	1.47
Unit 7, Ex 3	1.08	Unit 22, Ex 2	1.28	Unit 40, Review, Ex 5	1.48
Unit 8, Ex 3	1.09	Unit 23, Ex 1	1.29	Unit 40, Review, Ex 9	1.49
Unit 9, Ex 1	1.10	Unit 23, Ex 3	1.30	Unit 41, Ex 4	1.50
Unit 10, Review, Ex 5	1.11	Unit 24, Ex 1	1.31	Unit 42, Ex 3	1.51
Unit 10, Review, Ex 9	1.12	Unit 25, Review, Ex 6	1.32	Unit 43, Ex 3	1.52
Unit 11, Ex 3	1.13	Unit 25, Review, Ex 9	1.33	Unit 44, Ex 4	1.53
Unit 11, Ex 5	1.14	Unit 27, Ex 2	1.34	Unit 45, Review, Ex 7	1.54
Unit 12, Ex 3	1.15	Unit 28, Ex 2	1.35	Unit 45, Review, Ex 8	1.55
Unit 13, Ex 4	1.16	Unit 29, Ex 4	1.36	Unit 46, Ex 3	1.56
Unit 14, Ex 1	1.17	Unit 30, Review, Ex 5	1.37	Unit 47, Ex 2	1.57
Unit 15, Review, Ex 6	1.18	Unit 30, Review, Ex 9	1.38	Unit 48, Ex 3	1.58
Unit 15, Review, Ex 10	1.19	Unit 31, Ex 3	1.39	Unit 49, Ex 3	1.59
Unit 16, Ex 3	1.20	Unit 32, Ex 3	1.40	Unit 50, Review, Ex 5	1.60
Unit 17, Ex 3	1.21	Unit 33, Ex 1	1.41	Unit 50, Review, Ex 8	1.61

CD 2

Unit and Exercise	Track	Unit and Exercise	Track	Unit and Exercise	Track
Unit 51, Ex 4	2.02	Unit 69, Ex 4	2.23	Unit 85, Review, Ex 7	2.44
Unit 52, Ex 5	2.03	Unit 70, Review, Ex 3	2.24	Unit 86, Ex 1	2.45
Unit 53, Ex 3	2.04	Unit 70, Review, Ex 7	2.25	Unit 87, Ex 3	2.46
Unit 54, Ex 4	2.05	Unit 71, Ex 4	2.26	Unit 89, Ex 1	2.47
Unit 55, Review, Ex 6	2.06	Unit 71, Ex 5	2.27	Unit 90, Review, Ex 4	2.48
Unit 55, Review, Ex 9	2.07	Unit 72, Ex 4	2.28	Unit 90, Review, Ex 7	2.49
Unit 56, Ex 3	2.08	Unit 73, Ex 4	2.29	Unit 91, Ex 1	2.50
Unit 57, Ex 2	2.09	Unit 74, Ex 2	2.30	Unit 92, Ex 3	2.51
Unit 58, Ex 2	2.10	Unit 75, Review, Ex 5	2.31	Unit 93, Ex 2	2.52
Unit 59, Ex 2	2.11	Unit 75, Review, Ex 8	2.32	Unit 94, Ex 3	2.53
Unit 60, Review, Ex 5	2.12	Unit 76, Ex 4	2.33	Unit 95, Review, Ex 5	2.54
Unit 60, Review, Ex 8	2.13	Unit 77, Ex 3	2.34	Unit 95, Review, Ex 6	2.55
Unit 61, Ex 3	2.14	Unit 78, Ex 3	2.35	Unit 95, Review, Ex 9	2.56
Unit 62, Ex 4	2.15	Unit 80, Review, Ex 6	2.36	Unit 96, Ex 4	2.57
Unit 63, Ex 3	2.16	Unit 80, Review, Ex 7	2.37	Unit 97, Ex 1	2.58
Unit 64, Ex 2	2.17	Unit 80, Review, Ex 10	2.38	Unit 98, Ex 2	2.59
Unit 65, Review, Ex 7	2.18	Unit 81, Ex 3	2.39	Unit 99, Ex 2	2.60
Unit 65, Review, Ex 9	2.19	Unit 82, Ex 2	2.40	Unit 100, Ex 6	2.61
Unit 66, Ex 2	2.20	Unit 83, Ex 3	2.41	Unit 100, Ex 8	2.62
Unit 67, Ex 2	2.21	Unit 84, Ex 4	2.42		
Unit 68, Ex 3	2.22	Unit 85, Review, Ex 5	2.43		